Robert Mangaliso Sobukwe

New Reflections

By the same author

War of Words: Memoir of a South African Journalist

Nelson Mandela

Drawing Fire: Investigating the Accusations of Apartheid in Israel

Shared Histories: A Palestinian-Israeli Dialogue (co-editor)

*Southern African Muckraking: 300 Years of Investigative Journalism
that has Shaped the Region* (part-author)

1938: Why We Must Pay Close Attention Today (part-author)

Hope whoever reads this book
enjoys the read :-)

Love,
Ohra Sotolive (granddaughter)

Robert Mangaliso Sobukwe

New Reflections

Edited by Benjamin Pogrund

Jonathan Ball Publishers
Johannesburg & Cape Town

Published in South Africa in 2019 by
JONATHAN BALL PUBLISHERS
A division of Media24 (Pty) Ltd
PO Box 33977
Jeppestown
2043

ISBN 978-1-77619-004-1
ebook ISBN 978-1-77619-005-8

Every effort has been made to trace the copyright holders and to obtain their
permission for the use of copyright material. The publishers apologise for any errors
or omissions and would be grateful to be notified of any corrections that should be
incorporated in future editions of this book.

Twitter: www.twitter.com/JonathanBallPub
Facebook: www.facebook.com/JonathanBallPublishers
Blog: http://jonathanball.bookslive.co.za/

Cover by Michiel Botha
Cover photo by africamediaonline
Design and typesetting by Catherine Coetzer
Set in Bembo

Printed by **novus print**, a division of Novus Holdings

In memory of two friends and soulmates,
Bob Sobukwe and Ernie Wentzel

Contents

About this book   ix

The man whose sacrifice and suffering changed
South Africa
Benjamin Pogrund   1

A voice that could not be silenced
N Barney Pityana   18

The truth of who I am will set me free
Claudelle von Eck   40

Radical politics, yes, but with civility and humanity
Adam Habib and Alexandra Leisegang   56

Rise like an eagle: Reinterpreting Sobukwe
Thandeka Gqubule-Mbeki and Duma Gqubule   70

The road map that still helps to guide us
Barney Mthombothi   84

Making our way through expectations, demands,
fears and hurts
Paul Verryn   100

Sobukwe as an inspiring metaphor for business
Bonang Mohale   117

The 'political spirituality' of Sobukwe's leadership
Kwandiwe Kondlo   124

Why is freedom such a bitter fruit?
Anele Nzimande   139

The lonely prisoner was a man of letters
　　Derek Hook 　　　　　　　　　　　　　　　143

Blacks and whites in building a just South Africa
　　Bobby Godsell 　　　　　　　　　　　　　　165

In his grave, still paying a price for his integrity
　　Joel Mbhele 　　　　　　　　　　　　　　　181

Farmers: Common ground is needed for land reform
　　Willem Pretorius 　　　　　　　　　　　　　191

Shallow non-racialism destroys our people
　　Ishmael Mkhabela 　　　　　　　　　　　　204

The indomitable spirit of Sobukwe is testament to
our African agenda
　　Nkosazana Dlamini-Zuma 　　　　　　　　　223

'Speaking as one African to another': The letters of two
men in unfriendly times
　　EF Daitz 　　　　　　　　　　　　　　　　228

Getting to know his true grace
　　Andrew Walker 　　　　　　　　　　　　　236

Sharing my grandfather's pains and hopes
　　Otua Sobukwe 　　　　　　　　　　　　　243

Notes 　　　　　　　　　　　　　　　　　　255
Sources 　　　　　　　　　　　　　　　　　263
Index 　　　　　　　　　　　　　　　　　　267

About this book

THE LETTER OF INVITATION that I sent to the contributors explains the purpose of this book:

> It will be a collection of viewpoints from significant and interesting people about Robert Mangaliso Sobukwe:
>
> (a) His life and work, and/or
>
> (b) His current, and possible future, relevance.
>
> Views can be supportive and/or critical. We want frank assessments and insights. The book is of course set within the South African context – past, present and future. But because of Sobukwe's pan-Africanism, with his vision of a United States of Africa, writers can if they wish extend into the continent.

The responses were enthusiastic, and I thank all the writers who agreed to take part. They lead busy lives and many are prominent public figures. They gave time and energy to write a chapter and were helpful and courteous in dealing with my questions.

This book does not seek to present a cross-section of South African views. Instead, a mixture of logic and quirkiness went into deciding whom to invite: a particular person had expertise in regard to current events or pan-Africanism, or I thought he or she might have an unusual perspective. In the process I have renewed friendships from the past and have made new friends.

Jeremy Boraine, publishing director of Jonathan Ball Publishers, backed the idea for this book from the start, and generously left it to me to decide who would write. My thanks, too, to Alfred LeMaitre: the text has greatly benefited from his sensitive and professional editing. And thank you to the imaginative Michiel Botha, who designed the cover.

Author Peter Storey, and Gill Moodie of Tafelberg Publishers, kindly gave permission to publish an extract from *I Beg to Differ*.

I am grateful to my wife, Anne, for comments about the texts; to my son, Gideon, for suggesting possible contributors; and to Miliswa Sobukwe and Derek Hook for their support.

Benjamin Pogrund
October 2019

The man whose sacrifice and suffering changed South Africa

Benjamin Pogrund

Benjamin Pogrund was deputy editor of the Rand Daily Mail *in Johannesburg and pioneered the reporting of black politics and existence in the mainstream South African press. He was also the southern African correspondent of the* Sunday Times *and* The Boston Globe. *He was a close friend of Robert Sobukwe and wrote his biography. His other books include* Nelson Mandela, War of Words: Memoir of a South African Journalist, Drawing Fire: Investigating the Accusations of Apartheid in Israel, *and* Shared Histories: A Palestinian-Israeli Dialogue. *He lives in Jerusalem.*

ROBERT MANGALISO SOBUKWE'S defiance of apartheid on Monday, 21 March 1960 dramatically changed South Africa and ignited inter-national campaigning to end white rule. On that day, as leader of the Pan Africanist Congress (PAC, later the Pan Africanist Congress of Azania), he urged blacks to leave their passes at home and offer themselves for arrest at the nearest police station. The pass was the booklet used for apartheid control, recording the details where blacks could live and work; men and women had to carry it at all times or face immediate arrest. The anti-pass protest led to the police opening fire on unarmed demonstrators at Sharpeville, killing 69 people.[1]

Sobukwe called for 'Service, Sacrifice, Suffering' and said that he would not ask anyone to do what he would not do himself. He was the first to offer himself up for arrest and was sent to prison. Feared by the government, he was never allowed to be free again until his death 18 years later.

Sharpeville was so fundamental a turning point in the country's history that today's democratic South Africa observes 21 March every year as Human Rights Day. Reflecting its world impact, UNESCO marks this date as the International Day for the Elimination of Racial Discrimination.

Yet, despite Sobukwe's significance in the struggle for freedom, he is unknown to the world and is ignored by many, perhaps most, South Africans. On the other hand, those who know of Sobukwe revere him as a shining exemplar of integrity for a country which, a quarter century after the end of apartheid, is beset by deep corruption and gross social and economic inequalities.

Sobukwe was born in a ramshackle black 'location', as the ghetto areas were known, outside the small town of Graaff-Reinet, where it was said that 'even the dogs bark in Afrikaans'. His father, Hubert, a labourer, had been to school; his mother, Angelina, was a domestic worker and illiterate. They pushed their children to study: his father brought home discarded books from the local library (for whites only); his mother, books from white families for whom she worked. Sobukwe became not only a political leader but also an outstanding intellectual, and was nicknamed 'Prof'. His elder brother, Ernest, was one of the first black bishops in the Anglican Church.

Sobukwe learnt his politics while studying at the blacks-only University College of Fort Hare (now the University of Fort Hare) in the late 1940s. He embraced African nationalism as the new thinking in fighting white rule. He put his views into practice as a leader in the Youth League of the African National Congress (ANC): in 1949, at the ANC's annual conference, he helped secure a radical change in policy through the adoption of the

Programme of Action. The essence of the Programme of Action was non-collaboration with the oppressor, a refusal to cooperate in implementing the growing tyranny of apartheid laws. It led the ANC to launch the Defiance Campaign in 1952, with some 10 000 people of all races breaking the law and being prosecuted for using racially 'wrong' entrances to post offices and railway stations, or sitting on segregated park benches. But the ANC halted the campaign after the government enacted harsh new penalties and longer prison sentences, and with lashes for repeat offences.

Sobukwe and his supporters, calling themselves 'Africanists', accused the ANC of betraying the Programme of Action by failing to mount any more radical campaigns. They blamed communists, especially minority whites and Asians, who had been secretly influencing the ANC since the banning of the Communist Party in 1950. Amid angry internal conflict, the Africanists broke away from the ANC and in April 1959 created the PAC, with Sobukwe unanimously elected president.

He set out the main aim of the PAC: white supremacy must be destroyed. African people could be organised to do this only under the banner of African nationalism in an all-African organisation to 'decide on the methods of struggle without interference from either so-called left-wing or right-wing groups of the minorities who arrogantly appropriate to themselves the right to plan and think for Africans'.[2] Sobukwe rejected the 'multiracialism' of the ANC, which allowed only blacks as its members but worked with separate racial organisations for whites, coloureds and Asians in the Congress Alliance. He spoke instead of the 'Human Race' and sought 'the government of the Africans, by the Africans, with everyone who owes his only loyalty to Africa and who is prepared to accept the democratic rule of an African majority being regarded as [...] African. [The PAC] guarantees no minority rights because [it] think[s] in terms of individuals, not groups.'[3] And, new to the black struggle within South Africa, Sobukwe looked northward to the wave of new states obtaining their independence from European colonial powers and proclaimed the vision of a United States of Africa.

It was a powerful message, and he was hailed for revitalising and developing African nationalism. But his call for 'Africa for Africans' drew accusations of anti-whiteism from the mainstream press, uniformly white-owned and staffed overwhelmingly by journalists entirely ignorant of the forces at work among blacks. The negative racist image projected at this time was to persist down the years and, although entirely untrue about Sobukwe, would later be reinforced by the actions of other PAC members.

Within less than a year of the founding of the PAC, Sobukwe launched the first major campaign, aimed at the hated pass, the 'distinctive badge of slavery and humiliation', as he described it. But he first had to wrestle with himself: he was on the faculty of the University of the Witwatersrand (Wits University) in Johannesburg – a rare status for a black person – albeit as a 'language assistant' because he was denied the rank of lecturer. Although his parents were Sotho and Xhosa, he was a fluent linguist and was teaching Zulu to white students. It was at this time that the (white) Rhodes University, in what is now the Eastern Cape, offered him even greater status, as a full-time lecturer; he and his family would enjoy security and live well. He agonised and decided to turn it down, believing that his life's mission was to commit himself to gaining freedom for his people, whatever the consequences.

He wrote to the commissioner of police about the coming launch of the anti-pass campaign. He said it would be non-violent and warned against any provocation by the police (political protests by blacks often ended with police shooting and deaths). At sunrise on the fateful Monday of 21 March, he and a small group of men – no women took part – walked to the Orlando police station in the vast black township of Soweto and demanded that they be arrested. Sobukwe was supremely confident that blacks would respond in huge numbers to his personal example: they would do so, he believed, because of their loathing of the pass system and due to the passion of his African nationalist call. He miscalculated. He also had to contend with the government's massive intimidation of blacks. Countrywide, only small numbers of people responded – except notably in Sharpeville township, nearly 60 kilometres from Johannesburg, where up to 20 000 people gathered outside the police station, and in Cape Town, where thousands protested.

The Sharpeville killings, in which scores of protesters were shot in the back as they fled, set off national and international outrage. The Afrikaner nationalist policy of apartheid – racial separateness to ensure control and privilege for the country's white minority – had begun in 1948. Such brazen official racism, only three years after the end of Nazism and the Holocaust in Europe, had created much outrage in the world. The killings at Sharpeville and the turbulent and oppressive events that followed catapulted apartheid onto the world's front pages. Condemnation of apartheid soared, in international forums and in popular protests and boycotts. South Africa became the polecat of the world and remained a target of attack for more than thirty years until non-racial democracy was finally achieved in 1994.

In South Africa, blacks turned to mass strikes and riots. By 25 March, the government was so rattled by the unprecedented scale of the unrest that it announced the suspension of pass arrests, giving the PAC an exceptional victory. The ANC had rejected Sobukwe's appeal to join the anti-pass action but, responding to the public rage, on 28 March its leaders publicly burned their passes and declared a national day of mourning. Sobukwe, locked up in prison, criticised them as unprincipled opportunists. In Cape Town on 30 March, a PAC leader emerged – a young university student named Philip Kgosana – who led 30 000 blacks in a march to the city centre, stopping them four blocks from the whites-only Parliament. The marchers scrupulously obeyed Sobukwe's instruction to be peaceful. But the government was terrified that they might tear the city centre apart and promised Kgosana a meeting with a cabinet minister if he marched the crowd back to the townships. He did so. But he was a victim of cynical crookery: when he returned for the meeting later in the day, he was seized by the police, detained and kept without trial for four months. Armed police and soldiers surrounded and moved into the townships in strength and, going from door to door, brutally suppressed protest.

The government could do what it wanted because on that day it declared a state of emergency. In mass raids by the security police, about 1 800 people of all races with any history of opposing apartheid were detained without trial, as well as another 18 000 blacks deemed to be 'vagrants'. On 8 April, the PAC and the ANC were declared illegal. On 9 April, in the fevered climate of the time, a white farmer shot the prime minister, Dr HF Verwoerd; he survived, and the farmer was said to be insane. On 10 April, pass arrests resumed. The government was again in control. But the country, shaken to its roots, was changed forever.

The defects of the PAC's campaign against the pass system now became evident. The entire National Executive, except for two members, had willingly gone to prison with the slogan, 'No bail, no defence, no fine'. It was brave, noble and inspirational. It was also politically naive because the organisation was so new that there was no second level of leadership to take over. For the next two years, the effective president was a shy and inarticulate man who had been doing some typing in the PAC's office.

In Johannesburg, Sobukwe and his colleagues were charged with and found guilty of 'incitement'. He was sentenced to three years' imprisonment with hard labour. Breaking the campaign promise, the PAC men lodged an appeal, but lost. There was no early parole. As the date of Sobukwe's release – 3 May 1963 – approached, the government rushed a special law through Parliament specifying that a security prisoner could continue to be kept in jail without trial for a year at a time, renewable indefinitely. Dubbed the 'Sobukwe Clause', it was only ever applied to Sobukwe himself. He was taken to Robben Island, off the Cape Town coast, the new maximum-security prison for the rising number of political prisoners after Sharpeville. All the warders were white.

Sobukwe was kept on his own in two sparsely furnished rooms inside a barbed-wire stockade, guarded day and night. He could wear his own clothes, his food was provided from the warders' kitchen, he could work on his university studies and he could write and receive a restricted number of letters (but was never told whenever warders seized these). He could have occasional visitors, and later his wife, Veronica Zodwa, and their four children were allowed to spend a week locked up with him, but he had to pay for their meals. There was no contact with the rest of the prisoners on the island, except sometimes a distant view when they were taken to work.

———

Bishop Peter Storey was a young Methodist priest when he was assigned to minister to the prisoners on Robben Island. In his book *I Beg to Differ* (Tafelberg, 2018), he gives a moving account of his encounters with Sobukwe:

Sobukwe had been a Methodist lay preacher, so I asked to see him. I was refused at first, but some persistence revealed that the authorities were legally obliged to give me access. For every visit, however, I had first to get written authority from the Chief Magistrate of Cape Town.

By the time I visited him, Robert Sobukwe had already earned the grudging respect of his gaolers. My driver, a tough non-commissioned officer in his fifties, remarked that none of the baiting by bored young guards around the perimeter had succeeded in evoking a reaction from him. 'Every morning, this man comes out of his house dressed as if he is going off to work,' he said. 'He is very dignified.'

As we approached the weathered hut, I wondered what kind of welcome I would receive. The SABC and the press had portrayed Sobukwe as a dangerous black nationalist with a hatred of whites. Would he want to see me – a young white minister?

Sobukwe met me on the steps of his bungalow. I was immediately struck by his handsomely chiselled features and patrician bearing. Tall and wiry and dressed in neat slacks and a white shirt and tie, he offered me a guarded but polite welcome, inviting me inside as if this was his own home and I was a guest coming for tea. The room we entered served as both bedroom and living space, with a neatly made bed, a simple bedside cabinet, a table and chair, and a small bookcase. It was spartan but adequate. Sobukwe gestured to the only chair and sat on the edge of the bed. Conversation was desultory at first. I knew he was sizing me up and didn't blame him. I said that many Methodists would be excited to know that one of our ministers had got to see him. We swopped names of mutual acquaintances and stories of Healdtown, the Methodist college both he and Nelson Mandela had attended. It was the year that Reverend Seth Mokitimi was about to be elected the first black President of MCS (Methodist Church of South Africa) and he spoke admiringly of Mokitimi's influence as a chaplain and housemaster at Healdtown.

Our conversation soon warmed, and after that, each time I came to the island we were able to have about thirty minutes together. He had a consistent aura of calm about him, sucking contentedly on his pipe while we talked. He chose his words carefully, spoke quietly, and had a gentle sense of humour. Our discussions were perforce circumscribed, always in the presence of the guard, who stood near the door, pretending to be uninterested. Even so, it was possible to engage something of the depth and breadth of his thinking. His Christian faith was informed by wide reading and it was quite clear that he saw his political activism as an extension of his spirituality. He was excited by Alan Walker's 1963 preaching campaign in our country, and the furore around Walker's challenge to the apartheid state. This was the kind of witness he expected of his own church leaders, only to be frequently disappointed. He was impressed when I told him I was hoping to go and work under Walker for a year. I was later permitted to bring him a few theological books, and included all of Walker's writings. Both of us being pipe-smokers, I could also bring his favourite tobacco and we used to chuckle that both this Methodist minister and lay preacher had a taste for Three Nuns blend.

Robert Sobukwe impacted me very powerfully. For all my contact with black South Africans, here, for the first time, I was engaging with somebody risking all for the liberation of his people. The calibre of this man, the cruel waste of his gifts, and the silence of most South African Christians around his incarceration, touched me to anger. On his part, he always expressed genuine appreciation of our times together, but even though I was the only person, apart from his captors, ever permitted to see him, I sensed that he would never put too much trust in these visits. Why should he place faith in this white man, any more than any other? I always came away angered and ashamed. Once, when leaving him, I expressed my shame that I could depart the island so freely, leaving him a prisoner. His response was quick. Gesturing toward Cape Town, with its Houses of Parliament occupied by his tormentors, he said, 'I'm not the prisoner, Peter – they are.'

Every visit made it more evident to me why the apartheid government feared Robert Sobukwe so much.

———

Sobukwe's isolation and never knowing when he might be released went on for six years. He was allowed occasional visitors, and he told one of them that he was forgetting how to speak. The strain finally began to tell and he was hurriedly removed from the island and banished to Kimberley, 480 kilometres west of Johannesburg. He was dumped among strangers in a large house with little furniture in Galeshewe township. Veronica Zodwa (who later also used the name Zondeni) joined him. He was subjected to severe restrictions: house arrest from sunset to sunrise and over weekends. He could not be with more than one person at a time. Nothing he said or wrote could be quoted. He was not allowed to leave the township and could not enter schools or factories without permission. Despite the obstacles, he qualified as an attorney and opened a practice. He was called the 'social-welfare lawyer' because he charged clients little or nothing.

After nine years, he was diagnosed with lung cancer. The restrictions on his freedom of movement delayed getting treatment that might have saved his life. A doctor who met him then spoke of his 'grace and dignity'. A former Methodist minister quoted the dying Sobukwe as praying: 'Father, forgive them ... Take away all bitterness from us and help us to work for a country where we will all love each other, and not hate each other because hate will destroy us all.' He died in February 1978 and was buried in Graaff-Reinet.

The reason for the extreme restrictions was simple: the government feared Sobukwe. It feared his personal strength and courage, his commitment to fighting for freedom, his eloquence, his quiet charisma and his enunciation of African nationalism. He was closely watched during his initial three years in jail, and the security authorities concluded that this was an enemy too dangerous to be let loose. The same happened on Robben Island, this time to the extent that within the first year the government in effect threw away the key and decided to let him rot in virtual solitary confinement. Only the deterioration in his health led to his banishment to Kimberley, where he was always under surveillance and his visitors followed.[4] The police were not always successful: the next crop of political leaders in the Black Consciousness Movement (BCM) regularly slipped in to seek his views.

Keeping Sobukwe out of public sight for so many years, and the pitiless treatment that was meted out to him, inevitably gave rise to rumours. Three in particular have spread, although none have any basis in fact. The first is that on Robben Island his food was laced with broken glass with the intention of harming or killing him. This did indeed happen on one occasion, but there is no reason to believe that it was an official action; indeed, the prison authorities were highly alarmed by it. Second is the allegation that his death was caused by poisoning. But the facts are that he had tuberculosis as a young man, he was a smoker for much of his life and he was a victim of lung cancer.

The conspiracy stories persist, and with time grow even more lurid. Thus, 'he was fed glass'.[5] And, even more absurdly, the 'authorities allegedly continually mixed his food with the glass of a finely crushed bottle to covertly kill him through a slow and painful death, medically diagnosed as cancer'.[6] In a wholesale collection of fabrications, he was said to have been 'poisoned on Robben Island'; he was 'systematically assassinated … by the collaboration of the racist apartheid state with the medical establishment'; at Cape Town's Groote Schuur Hospital he was operated on for 'an alleged cancer tumour' by Dr Chris Barnard (the heart-transplant surgeon) 'without the knowledge of his family'; he 'did not die a natural death'.[7] (For the record: it was cancer, Dr Barnard was not the surgeon, and the family was fully informed.)

The third spurious claim has to do with the fact that no TV footage of Sobukwe exists, nor has any recording of his voice been found. This has spawned allegations that his voice has been deliberately obliterated by unnamed enemies in order to wipe him out of history. However, the explanation is straightforward: when he was a free man, TV and audio recordings were unusual in

11

South Africa; then he was locked in prison out of sight and sound for nine years; and when he was banished to Kimberley, he was under banning orders that made it illegal for anything he said to be recorded or reported. The security police were watching him: they could have intercepted anyone making a recording – and Sobukwe would have faced serious criminal charges for breaking his banning order. So, no recordings of his voice were made. It would have been too dangerous.

Does it matter that these falsehoods and distortions are being peddled? Robert Sobukwe lived a life of personal honesty and integrity. His legacy demands that his life story be told untainted by untruths circulated by people who either don't know or are playing to some political agenda of their own. He suffered so terribly under apartheid that there is no need to invent or exaggerate what happened to him. Sticking to the truth is enough and is what he deserves.

———

Post-Sharpeville, with the PAC and ANC proscribed and driven underground, many blacks despaired of whites ever peaceably yielding power. Unknown to Sobukwe, a movement dedicated to the mass murder of whites emerged inside the PAC: called Poqo (Our Own), it carried out several attacks until the police learnt of its existence, only days before countywide violence was due to start. More than 3 200 men were arrested; their trials went on for months, and led to the imposition of the death penalty or lengthy prison sentences on Robben Island.

The PAC's general secretary, Potlako Leballo, after two years in prison, left the country to lead Poqo, and then the PAC, in exile. As a speaker, Leballo could bring a crowd to its feet within minutes with a screaming, incoherent rant against whites. The PAC enjoyed support in newly independent countries because of its Africanism, but Leballo squandered this goodwill. The PAC fell into internal murders and theft of funds. Out of Poqo came the Azanian People's Liberation Army (Apla), which, right until to the coming of democracy in 1994, was killing white civilians under its slogan of 'One settler, one bullet'. In the general elections that year, the PAC won 1.2 per cent of the votes; later this slumped to 0.7 per cent. Today's PAC can hardly be compared with the organisation led by Sobukwe. Still riven by dissent, its president, Narius Moloto, claims that the PAC has 100 000 members.[8]

The ANC, on the other hand, maintained its dominance. Together with the Communist Party, it formed Umkhonto we Sizwe (Spear of the Nation) in 1961 to mount armed resistance against apartheid. It decided to attack property, not people, and this policy was largely adhered to in the years that followed. The ANC opened its membership to people of all races in 1969. It won overwhelmingly in the democratic elections of 1994, under the leadership of Nelson Rolihlahla Mandela, who earned national and international admiration for his humanity and lack of bitterness towards the whites who had kept him imprisoned for 27 years. He and Sobukwe had been colleagues in the ANC, but the PAC's breakaway made them political rivals. They were brought together at one time in Pretoria Prison, sitting side by side on the concrete floor repairing canvas mailbags and discussing who was the world's best English-language author.

The ANC has retained political power, though its popular support has been slipping. It honours the leaders of its struggle against apartheid, with Mandela deservedly the icon, but brushes rivals aside, Sobukwe more than anyone else. His name is even usually excluded, along with that of the PAC, from references to the turning-point Sharpeville massacre. It is as though he had nothing to do with it. Denied national recognition, Sobukwe has been written out of history.

However, Mandela himself, while president, did not forget Sobukwe. A simple ceremony in December 1997 to present Sobukwe documents to Wits University's Africana Library was transformed into a special event because Mandela heard of it and came 'to pay homage' to Sobukwe.[9]

————

South Africans have freedom. And millions are better off in their daily lives. Yet the dreams and hopes of millions have not been realised: they lack clean water, they cannot get work, they live in iron and cardboard shanties, their children get low-quality schooling and healthcare is poor. HIV/Aids is widespread. They suffer robbery, murder and rape. Their plight, caused by government failure and incompetence, grew more acute during the nine years that Jacob Zuma was president: the cost of so-called state capture – corruption by private individuals and corporations in league with the highest levels of officials – cost the country many billions of rands. Zuma was deposed in February 2018 and replaced by Cyril Ramaphosa, who has a long way to go to repair the damage.

Starting only a few years ago, Sobukwe's name began to circulate as an example of what a leader should be: one with honesty, integrity and commitment, who would not have tolerated the harsh social inequalities of today. And with pressure mounting for redistribution of land, to make reparation for the land historically stolen by whites from blacks, there is renewed interest in Sobukwe's African nationalism (although his qualification that 'Africa for Africans' is colour-blind is not always appreciated).

As a sign of changing attitudes, in September 2017, Wits University named the central building at the heart of its campus the Robert Sobukwe Block – with a bit of rewriting of history by saying Sobukwe had been a 'lecturer'. Criticism of the lack of recognition of Sobukwe has become a repeated, often angry theme. Early in 2018, a newspaper headline read: 'Conspiracy of silence circles Sobukwe'.[10] Another headline was, 'The nation needs a Sobukwe Day', noting that he 'deserves to be honoured more substantially by the national government in recognition of his leadership and sacrifice'.[11] In a letter to *The Star*, a reader complained: 'Sobukwe's ideas and teachings remain suppressed, and I am also a victim of that unjust act. For 12 full years of my life in a government school I have never heard of his name, or even his organisation …'[12]

Great plans to lionise the memory of Sobukwe as an 'intellectual and leader' referred to plans by the Vaal University of Technology to establish an African cultural museum.[13] A review of *The Black Consciousness Reader*[14] said: 'Forgotten heroes deliver a timely lesson on struggle: New book places young lions like Mangaliso Sobukwe at the front of the fight against apartheid and colonialism'.[15] Getting to the nub of it was an article by Panashe Chigumadzi titled 'ANC version of history overshadows the real story of resistance',[16] while a letter to the *Sunday Times* was topped by the headline: 'History belongs to the victors'.[17]

In 2019, Wits University Press published Sobukwe's Robben Island correspondence. Titled *Lie on Your Wounds: The Prison Correspondence of Robert Mangaliso Sobukwe*, the book was edited by Dr Derek Hook of Duquesne University, Pittsburgh. The psychologist and educationist Professor N Chabani Mangani said the letters 'represent the height of human decency in the face of unmitigated racist apartheid white tyranny'.

———

Veronica Zodwa Zondeni lived for 40 years after her husband's death. She had been steadfast and she went on enduring, with immense dignity. Shy and reticent, Veronica avoided publicity but fought unremittingly for her husband and family. The government ignored her until very late in her life when she – aged 90 – was given a national honour in April 2018; she was too ill to attend the ceremony in Pretoria. One writer said of the belated recognition that it was 'a shameful indictment on the conscience of a government that is structurally biased and selective in whose contributions and legacies it celebrates and whose memories it remembers'.[18] Veronica passed away on 15 August 2018. President Cyril Ramaphosa ordered flags to be flown at half-mast and for her to have a 'Category 2' state funeral. Unfortunately, the ANC showed arrogance and insensitivity in running the funeral, starting with the cabinet minister in charge giving the '*Amandla!*' ('Power!') salute – the hallmark of the ANC – rather than the Africanist '*Izwe Lethu*' ('It is Ours') salute. . A group in the divided PAC took over and ordered the government leaders to leave. The funeral was chaotic and did not do Veronica justice.

Among the countrywide outpouring of tributes to her was this Facebook post on 18 August 2018 by Modise Moiloanyane:

Mama Sobukwe! May your soul rest in peace! Please convey our warm greetings to Prof! You have run your race, you were a revolutionary and played a gallant role amongst our Women warriors. Many don't know your struggles, many don't even know you. Many suppressed who you are and your contribution to our beautiful land. Many and most of them in power are and were afraid to tell us about you and Prof Mangaliso Sobukwe because they know that your contributions to our free land will dwarf their claim to victory. We love you and may you rest in peace amongst our gallant martyrs!

———

That Sobukwe's memory and example are at last coming to the fore was projected in a large headline in *The Star* in July 2018: 'The indomitable spirit of Sobukwe is testament to our African agenda.'[19] It wasn't only the words and the thought but also the writer who made this so striking, even startling: she was Dr Nkosazana Dlamini-Zuma, who is in the top ranks of the ANC leadership, came close to winning the presidential contest against Ramaphosa in 2017, serves as a minister in the Presidency, and is a former chairperson of the African Union.

At a personal level, there is Johnson Mlambo. At the age of 23, Mlambo was sentenced to 20 years' imprisonment for his involvement with Poqo. He served his sentence in full. He was tortured by sadistic warders on Robben Island. Once, warders buried him up to his neck in the ground and urinated on his face. He still suffers back pain from the blows and kicks. After his release, he escaped from the country and led the PAC in exile. He now lives quietly outside Johannesburg with his wife, Nomsa, who he met after his prison term. He never met Sobukwe but saw him at a distance on the island. Mlambo explains Sobukwe's profound effect on his life:[20]

To inspire us to leave our passes at home and surrender ourselves was a very big task. The police couldn't believe that these people who were always running away were able to come and say they wouldn't carry passes any more. Sobukwe lived up to his commitments. I was saying to myself as a young man, if this man who is the best of all of us, could sacrifice his very high position at the university, could sacrifice his own peace and welfare, why can't I emulate him?

A voice that could not be silenced

N Barney Pityana

Nyameko Barney Pityana was a founding member of the Black Consciousness Movement (BCM). Banned by the government, he went to study theology at King's College London, and was ordained as an Anglican Church minister. He was Vice Chancellor of the University of South Africa (Unisa) and is Professor Emeritus of Law. He is Visiting Professor at the Allan Gray Centre for Leadership Ethics (AGCLE) at Rhodes University, and a Fellow at the Stellenbosch Institute for Advanced Study (STIAS), Stellenbosch University. He holds the Order of the Grand Counsellor of the Baobab (Silver).

ROBERT MANGALISO SOBUKWE, popularly known as 'Prof', was at the prime of his life when he passed away on 27 February 1978, at the age of 53. However, he had packed so much into a young and brief candle of a life that his example is of enduring significance and meaning for South Africa. After all, he was 35 when he led a demonstration by the Pan Africanist Congress of Azania (PAC) against the pass laws, confronting a system of injustice with the moral power of defiance. For that he paid dearly. He was jailed for three years, after which, by a device that came to be known as the Sobukwe Clause of the General Law Amendment Act, he was kept in solitary confinement on Robben Island and then banned and banished to Kimberley. He died without ever having tasted freedom since 1960.

The PAC held its founding congress on 6 April 1959, with

Sobukwe as its inaugural president. The PAC was a faction of pan-Africanists who had left the African National Congress (ANC) out of disillusionment with the adoption of the Freedom Charter in 1955. At the time, the PAC promised to bring vigour and a radical posture to resistance against apartheid. More importantly, the PAC redefined its ideological position as both pan-Africanist and unapologetically radical in the urgency and methods of struggle. For that, the PAC attracted a great deal of attention in its early life and drew into its ranks many younger African activists who were eager for a phase of struggle defined by an uncompromising impatience for freedom.

One must remember that the PAC operated for barely one year before the 1960 campaign against the pass laws that resulted in the Sharpeville massacre, and the demonstration that led to Sobukwe and many leaders of the PAC being arrested and incarcerated for long periods. This meant that this young political organisation might not have been firmly established enough before the events that shook it to the core in 1960 crippled its capacity to function effectively. Yet, remarkably, the PAC did make its mark in the politics of liberation of South Africa and competed as equals with the ANC, the much older and more traditional political organisation of the mass of the oppressed people of South Africa. Even more so, as the ANC and the PAC were banned organisations under the most repressive security laws of the apartheid regime, the PAC was never able to develop a strong culture of leadership and to become as deeply established in the minds of the masses as was the case with the ANC.

The span of lawful operation of the PAC was exceedingly short – less than one year! But the PAC never died. Strategies and tactics changed even though many of its leaders were in jail, but more importantly, the PAC adopted armed struggle and established the Azanian People's Liberation Army (Apla). The assessment of the effectiveness of the PAC as a liberation organisation alongside the ANC is not the subject of this chapter. What it seeks to do is to assess the legacy of Robert Mangaliso Sobukwe, his ideas and their influence on subsequent developments in South Africa's political and constitutional landscape.

———

The funeral of Zondeni Veronica Sobukwe, Robert Sobukwe's widow, who died aged 90, was held at his birthplace, Graaff-Reinet, on 25 August 2018. President Cyril Ramaphosa declared it a special official funeral in honour of Mrs Sobukwe, and no doubt of her pre-deceased husband. As it turned out, the funeral became a spectacle on the sad state of affairs in Sobukwe's beloved PAC. Factions of the PAC denounced the party's leadership and appeared to pledge allegiance to a former president who had been expelled from the party but who remained its sole representative in Parliament in defiance of the party.

More dramatically, the confusion not only pained the Sobukwe family, who were in mourning, but also undermined the family's efforts at conciliation by seeking to negotiate with all the factions of the PAC to ensure a funeral that would be worthy of the honour justly deserved by Mrs Sobukwe.

Finally, the histrionics of the day were directed against the very idea of a 'state funeral'. Significantly, the protesting faction rejected the role undertaken by cabinet ministers deployed for the occasion, including the deputy president, who was to deliver a eulogy on behalf of the government. There was contestation about the role of the South African National Defence Force (SANDF), and the Chaplain-General, and most explosively, against the use of the South African flag that had draped the coffin of the departed.

I attended the funeral as a speaker from the National Foundations

Dialogue Initiative (NFDI), a collection of foundations established to champion the legacies of former leaders in the liberation struggle, and which continue to seek to advance a vision of South Africa established under the constitutional democracy model of the new dispensation since 1994. As the Robert Sobukwe Trust is an affiliate member of the NFDI, it was correct for the NFDI to attend and to honour such a stalwart of our struggle as Mrs Sobukwe. In the event, I found myself occupying a front row in the dispute that unfolded.

There were moments when I became confused about what exactly the dispute was about. Was it about the struggle for ascendancy and relevance within the PAC, or was it a more fundamental dispute about the nature of the South African state? It may well be the case that the two questions are interrelated and suggest that, in the minds of at least some within the PAC, the struggle was not resolved in 1994, and that the factional struggles within the PAC have, in part at least, to do with the ideological questions about South Africa and its future.

I remembered that the PAC had chosen to remain outside the Convention for a Democratic South Africa (Codesa) process from 1990 that led to the constitutional democracy on which we now pride ourselves. The party did not seem to have a common negotiating position about how to resolve the question of apartheid. It must be recorded that even up to 1993, acts of violence attributable to Apla were staged in places such as Cape Town and elsewhere. When the PAC eventually decided to agree to contest the 1994 general elections, it had neither the resources nor the organisational power, nor a coherent message to offer to the electorate. No wonder, then, that it received less than one per cent of the popular vote.

What the events at Graaff-Reinet demonstrated, not for the first time, and not only within the PAC, is that so many of our symbols of state are under contestation. These include the national anthem and the flag. The PAC is not in isolation in questioning the legitimacy of these symbols. Above all, however, elements of the PAC were contesting the authority of the president and the legitimacy of the government and the SANDF. I make these observations with some hesitation because they have never been articulated as clearly as I would prefer.

What exactly is at issue? Is it that the electoral system does not adequately reflect the popular will? That can hardly be the case. It is more likely that the Constitution of the Republic of South Africa was never subjected to a referendum or a plebiscite, except, at best, by means of the 1994 vote. That may be true. Even then, the vote was held using the party-list system, with proportional representation. Such a system allows political parties to become dominant, and the view of the electorate then occupies a subordinate position. In any event, was it likely that these matters under contestation now would have yielded different results if the electoral system had been the more traditional Westminster system? It is hard to tell. Most likely, though, at least for some of the PAC diehards, the new South African democratic state was illegitimate not least because it is not Azania, but also because it does not resolve the question of land ownership by the indigenous people of South Africa. But one thing is certain: some of these fundamental matters continue to be subject to contestation, and they undermine the task of building national unity and social cohesion. Yes, what they also do is to isolate the PAC into a minority of abstruse debaters and not nation-builders.

When Sobukwe was buried at Graaff-Reinet in March 1978, there were some ugly scenes there as well, which would have been most distressing to the family and which divided the PAC. First, the difference was that at the time the PAC was a banned organisation and as such was not operating legally in South Africa.

Second, the violent scenes were about evicting those who were perceived either to be operating within the Bantustan system, such as Dr Mangosuthu Buthelezi, now a Member of Parliament (MP) and leader of the Inkatha Freedom Party (IFP), or were known or suspected to be informers. I was then in prison in Grahamstown (as it was then known) together with a number of Black Consciousness (BC) activists arrested under preventive-detention laws when reports came of the upheavals in Graaff-Reinet. In those days, there was universal acceptance that those who collaborated with the system were not deserving of sympathy or acceptance among those who bore the brunt of the struggle.

In 1978, those who sought to defend Sobukwe's honour were activists under the influence of Black Consciousness. They too may not have had the experience of Sobukwe as a leader of the PAC on account of their age, and they would definitely not have read any of his writings because these would have been banned, except for various accounts of the controversies regarding his unjust incarceration without trial on Robben Island for a period double the original sentence, and the brutal treatment he received upon his release from prison and throughout the period of his illness.

Many, however, who were active in BC would have understood that the PAC was an important strain of the politics of liberation. They would also have understood that BC, while not making choices between the ANC and the PAC, sought to recognise all parties of liberation and to honour the leaders of all organisations of liberation that preceded the Black Consciousness formations.

The year 1978, however, also marked the birth of another wave of militancy among young South Africans to accelerate the pace of revolution. It is fair to say that the 1980s were the years when the struggle within South Africa was at its most intense, and the backlash from the apartheid system was at its most vicious in a bid to stem the tide of liberation unleashed since Graaff-Reinet in 1978.

But 2018 suggested vastly different circumstances. The PAC, though now a legal political party in a democratic South Africa, had just one MP in the National Assembly. The party was seriously riven by dissent and conflict, so much so that its electoral support was waning and its political performance was lacklustre. Even its sole MP was not making a great impression in Parliament, as his few interventions did not fire up the popular mood on the issues that he raised. It is fair to observe that the PAC (such as it is) was in the news for all the wrong reasons – leadership squabbles, almost always fighting about who was to occupy the sole seat in Parliament. The PAC in recent years has also seen a spate of breakaway parties. None of this would have commended the party to the voting public in South Africa.

Besides that, the protesters at the funeral of Mrs Sobukwe were youngsters who gave the impression that they had been rented from the streets and bused in for the event. They wore brand-new PAC T-shirts that looked as if they had been for the occasion. Besides, one could not detect any ideological expression suggestive of seasoned political activists. In 2018, by all accounts, the protesters on behalf of the PAC just did not seem schooled in PAC ideology or discipline. They did not recognise any of the leaders of the PAC who appealed for order in the name of the party. Even if one was to concede any of this, the PAC leaders who did speak seemed incapable of presenting the assembled PAC and Sobukwe loyalists any revolutionary or alternative vision for South Africa, nor any template or hope for a future role for the PAC.

———————

Drawing from the *Speeches of Robert Mangaliso Sobukwe, 1949–1959*, published in exile by the PAC,[1] and from the biography by Benjamin Pogrund,[2] who was a close friend and confidant of

Sobukwe, one can sketch three elements that account for Sobukwe's endurance. That is, despite many years of silence and absence, his name has powerful resonance, especially for those active in various aspects of the struggle. For the reasons explained above, Sobukwe's name, I suspect to his disapproval, is more popular than the PAC. I wonder what it would do to the fortunes of the PAC if they were to rename it the Sobukwe Party? I do not know if the publicity machinery of the PAC has ever thought about that. What, then, accounts for the popularity of Sobukwe?

Leadership and personality

I cannot explain how it is that I never met Prof in person. At the time of his release from prison, I was among the group of students who were shaping the thinking and activism about Black Consciousness at black campuses in South Africa. We took responsibility for visiting as many members of the then banned liberation organisations to dialogue about our vision and determination, and to explain what we were about. As a young person, my uncle was an avid disciple of Sobukwe and the PAC, for which he served years on Robben Island and, upon his release, was banished to Dimbaza. This is merely to say that, while I was growing up, Sobukwe was a household name!

The persons we interacted with came from all political persuasions. Some had been imprisoned for their political activities, others were under banning orders or were banished to some remote parts of the country. I was aware from our comrades from Kimberley that Prof was in Galeshewe, but our journeys never took us to that part of the country. One understood from those who came across him, and many BC activists from Kimberley definitely did, that he was a highly learned and articulate man who was regarded as a symbol of the struggle. Those who could meet with him valued their interaction with him. He was a man of quiet persuasion, a teacher and someone held in high regard in the township into which he had been banished.

Those who interacted with him were not only activists, but also clients and, amazingly, church people in Kimberley who recognised his presence among them. To many, what was most outstanding was his humility and, if you like, his ordinariness. Sobukwe did not flaunt his political credentials, although this was made so obvious by the security police who watched his every move. He did not display his learning. A teacher by profession, who was employed by Wits University in the Department of African Languages, misleadingly as a 'language assistant' instead of as a lecturer, he was known for his care of the students under him, and was diligent in his work. In a manner that must have seemed rather abrupt, he resigned from Wits in March 1960, ostensibly in preparation for the PAC campaign against the pass laws that he was to lead. He expressed sensitivity about getting Wits embroiled in his political activities and thought it best rather to officially resign his post.

On 2 March 1997, the then Anglican Archbishop of Cape Town, Njongo Ndungane (himself a young activist in the PAC in 1960 as a university student, and who was jailed on Robben Island for PAC activities), organised a Pilgrimage of Hope to Robben Island. His idea was that the island had much of the pain and history of the liberation struggles spanning over a hundred years embedded in it: from the Xhosa and Khoisan chiefs from the Eastern Cape who resisted British imperialism, to Makhanda, who perished in the waters between Cape Town and the island in a bid to escape unjust imprisonment in 1819, to the modern-day Sobukwe and Nelson Mandela, Robben Island was the symbol of white colonial and imperial oppression and of resistance by generations of the oppressed people. If the walls and the soil of Robben Island could speak (especially the quarry where the Mandela generations spent years in useless hard labour), they could reveal the many stories that were told, prayers that were made, cruelty that was endured, pain that was suffered and joys of freedom that were experienced. During the Pilgrimage of Hope, I was assigned the responsibility of doing a meditation at Sobukwe House. The walls were adorned, so many years later, with the correspondence between Sobukwe and Veronica, showing his sense of dignity and feelings of love, as well as the stark basic surroundings that he endured for so long. It was enough to produce feelings of anger and revulsion. Much of the spirit of Sobukwe is preserved in the house – letters and photographs, a desk and bed. It was not difficult to evoke the spirit of Sobukwe in prison, alone and lonely in his own thoughts, studying and learning with no one to speak to.

The archbishop wished to test the idea of the island becoming a place of pilgrimage for the healing of South Africa. There is an Anglican church on the island, previously a leper colony and a place of care and healing for leprosy sufferers. This could have been the base for the prayers of the nation, thought Ndungane. It was in that spirit that I undertook the meditation at Sobukwe House. In his solitary life, Sobukwe was loving and caring of his family in total loneliness, though there were occasional visits by his beloved Veronica and the children. At times and in places like those, during spells of utter desolation, a wrestling with God becomes a spiritual duty – God as presence and absence, and a sense of abandonment. In solitary confinement, God becomes one's debating partner, an interlocutor, the one on whom to pin one's hopes of salvation and the one from whom one seeks answers to life's intractable problems. Out of the years of loneliness, and the pain and hurt of injustice, Sobukwe emerged in some respects spiritually unscathed, but his body was broken such that he was never the same again.

A lifelong member of the Methodist Church, Sobukwe had an intelligent engagement with matters of faith. He was often angry with the church that he loved so much, critical of the role of Christianity in colonialism, and dismissive of those who used theology and the church to perpetuate oppression. At the same time, he had no time for glib expressions of faith, and he wrestled with the challenges that faith confronted him with, including the cruelty of man to man. He also read theological works intelligently and argued with the most modern of theological developments of his time. After all, this was the time of Bertrand Russell's *Why I Am Not a Christian*, Bishop JAT Robinson's *Honest to God* and Dietrich Bonhoeffer's *Letters and Papers from Prison*. On world affairs, he read biographies of statesmen and followed world events. He was educated in the true sense of the word, rather than merely learned. His formal education spanned studies in African languages, African studies, economics and law. But, more than that, he delved into political philosophy and creative writing, including his own poetry in isiXhosa, and short stories. As an educated person, Sobukwe was a rounded intellectual.

As a leader, his personality was people-oriented, and his leadership style inclusive. He believed that a leader should set the example but that a leader never makes decisions alone. Once the PAC had made a decision to confront the system of apartheid pass laws, he was there to lead the way. If the plan was to instigate mass arrests in March 1960, he was there to be the first to be arrested without a pass. He led by example.

As a leader, Sobukwe was confident about what he believed. He expressed it in language that the people understood. After all, he was a linguist, comfortable in many South African languages. Besides his mother tongue, isiXhosa, he was proficient in English and Afrikaans. In Kimberley, in the Methodist Church and at funerals, he often acted as an interpreter. The bedrock of his life was his devotion to his family, especially Veronica, as she was then popularly known, and his unshakeable faith. As a family man, he was devoted to his children and played an active role in their upbringing. His children attest to the fact that, as a father, he was strict but loving, and consistent in family practices and values such as prayer and respect towards others. He himself showed that respect in his dealings with others, however humble.

In the preface to the *Speeches of Robert Mangaliso Sobukwe, 1949–1959*, the unnamed writer says that Sobukwe was a 'leader of men … distinguished by [his] devotion, dedication and determination'. As a leader, and one who led the way, his living testament was 'revolutionary optimism [is] the secret of […] life'. What this means is best expressed by journalist Patrick Laurence, who said that the 'bedrock of [Sobukwe's] strength is faith – belief in the slow but inexorable advance of African nationalism'. In other words, his Christian faith translated into his political activism. It was important that as a leader he remained steadfast. Years later, he wondered whether the PAC had been ready for the revolutionary steps that were taken so early in its life. In truth, however, in the execution of the revolution, there can be no moment better than the present.

Education and ideology

As an educated person and a teacher by profession, Sobukwe could not but be expected to value learning and to impart education in his leadership. He became popularly known as 'Prof' not because he earned that elevated academic title but rather because he was recognised among the rank and file of the PAC not only due to his position as a lecturer at Wits University, but also by the fact that he was undoubtedly a man of learning and erudition. In a well-rehearsed speech to the Completers' Social at the University College of Fort Hare on 12 October 1949, he said that 'education to us means service to Africa'. In other words, to him education was important to the extent that it equipped one for service to the people of Africa. Africa was to be the locus of the endeavours of the people of the continent. His speeches were peppered with the invocation to 'Remember Africa!' and to never forget the duty and responsibility that Africans owe to Africa. Africa had to be the subject of memory even as Africans lived Africa, imagined the Africa of their dreams, and shaped the Africa they wanted. 'Remember Africa!' was not a mere invocation to abstract thought but a call to arms.

Education, therefore, was not only formal but it also meant that all who were pan-Africanists had to have knowledge of Africa, its people and their aspirations. They must be imbued with the duty to serve Africa and not themselves, to be in step with the aspirations of the leaders of Africa and to overcome all forms of bondage. For Sobukwe, 'we can never do enough for Africa; nor can we love her enough'. The inclusive and integrated expression of Sobukwe's pan-Africanism is stated in his injunction:

> We have a mission –
> A nation to build we have
> A God to glorify, a contribution
> Clear to make towards the blessing of mankind.
> We must be the embodiment of our people's aspirations.

He had a vision of Africa that he often expressed in poetic language:

> Let me plead with you, lovers of my Africa, to carry with you into the world the vision of a new Africa, an Africa reborn, an Africa rejuvenated, an Africa re-created, young Africa. We are the first glimmering of a new dawn.

The fact is often lost sight of that the PAC ideology worked with an expansive definition of 'an African'. Sobukwe preached against the doctrine of hate and racism. He said:

We aim, politically, at government of the Africans, by Africans, for Africans, with everybody who owes his only loyalty to Africa and who is prepared to accept the democratic rule of an African majority being regarded as [...] African. We guarantee no minority rights because we think in terms of individuals, not groups.

In this, Sobukwe asserts the conviction that 'Africa and humanity are inseparable'. Curiously, Sobukwe defined pan-Africanism as focused on individuals and not the collective. That was his way of rebutting the narrative of minorities and majoritarianism. One doubts that this was a statement against communalism as Mwalimu Julius Nyerere would have had it at the time, or of socialism. The PAC has always wrestled with its ideological posturing as an anti-communist organisation. Elsewhere in his inaugural speech at the founding congress of the PAC in 1959, Sobukwe made the statement that later became the mantra of the PAC: 'Africa for Africans, the African for humanity and humanity for God ...' In South African terms, therefore, it is historically correct to say that Sobukwe was the father of pan-Africanism.

Intersections: pan-Africanism and Black Consciousness

Many commentators have sought to draw parallels between the ANC, PAC and BCM. This was inevitable because in many respects all these organisations draw inspiration from the same sources of struggle. In many respects, the exponents of these organisations were educated in the same mould, and historically they all represented stages in the march of history.

The first point to make emphatically is that the PAC is a product of the ANC. It broke away from the ANC in 1959 not because the ANC had ditched its nationalist credentials but rather to emphasise the centrality of pan-Africanism that, it was believed, the Freedom

Charter of 1955 had watered down. In a very real sense, the ANC itself was constantly reviewing its African nationalist credentials until Thabo Mbeki, who became president of the ANC in 1997 and president of the Republic of South Africa in 1999, made his elegiac speech, 'I am an African', in the National Assembly on the occasion of the adoption of the Constitution in 1996, extolling an African nationalism not much different from that of Sobukwe's in its inclusiveness and in its evocation of the history, heroism and aspirations of the people of Africa. When Mbeki became president, he framed his policy, both domestic and international, on the African Renaissance and the priority of development and self-determination for Africa. Mbeki's idea of an inclusive Africanism led him to invite leaders from the BCM and other parties, such as the IFP's Mangosuthu Buthelezi, to join the government.[3]

In his presentation of what could be termed the manifesto of the PAC at its founding congress, Sobukwe raised matters that were pertinent to, and later at the heart of, BC philosophy. The clarion call of the PAC, he said, was that pan-Africanism had to be matched by a mental revolution. This was to restore the people's revolutionary confidence in their own agency, banish fear and inferiority and result in the refusal to accept any form of indignity. In a 'campaign to free the mind of the African', Sobukwe touched on some of the pillars of BC philosophy: 'They must *think* of themselves as men and women before they can demand to be treated as such' (author's emphasis).

Black Consciousness and the writings of Steve Biko are replete with expressions that address the mental state of the oppressed: to banish fear and overcome a culture of suffering in silence. Indeed, the PAC never had enough occasion to spell out these philosophical standpoints. Many PAC activists today may not be aware of how close the PAC was to the BCM. In his essay 'The Black Consciousness Movement in South Africa: A Product of the

Entire Black World', Unisa historian Mgwebi Snail discloses that, in the years after he was released from prison, Sobukwe acknowledged that the BCM's explanation of pan-Africanism was much easier to understand and more cogent than the pan-Africanism that the PAC championed in 1959.[4]

———

Forty years after the death of Robert Mangaliso Sobukwe, and nearly sixty years after the founding of the PAC, South Africa is in the throes of a debate on matters that were raised in the PAC manifesto of 1959, and in Sobukwe's inaugural PAC presidential address. These are the matters of race and racism, and the economy, within which land is perhaps most divisive.

On race, the debate within the ANC and in the public discourse raises questions about the ANC's historic declarations on the national question, in particular the affirmation in the Freedom Charter that South Africa 'belongs to all who live in it'. That declaration has since found its way into the Preamble of the Constitution: 'South Africa belongs to all who live in it, united in our diversity …' The Constitution also defines South Africa as a democratic and constitutional state founded on, among others, the 'value' of 'non-racialism'.[5]

That constitutional undertaking has been somewhat unravelling of late. In part, this has to do with the prominence of incidents of racism and racial abuse and violence that have found their way into the media and the courts. There are elements within the white community who persist in making pejorative racist statements about fellow South Africans of different race groups, and in practising blatant discrimination. Indeed, statements by some political leaders have been racist and the courts have declared them as such. From what one can observe, especially during the time of President Jacob

Zuma, the ANC has abandoned any aspirations to a non-racial society. By and large, these matters have gone before the courts. Out of it all it is fair to surmise that race and racism remains the soft underbelly and the fault line in the South African social system.

The position of the PAC is different. The party spells out that there shall be no minorities and speaks to a common African identity. Understandably, the PAC manifesto has not addressed the manner in which such a common African identity was to be expressed in national life, especially where politics, geography and every aspect of life have been defined in racial terms. To dismantle the structures of racial determinism in South Africa will take generations. Notwithstanding what the manifesto says, in practice the PAC has presented itself as a party with a bias towards what it calls 'indigenous Africans', a phrase nowhere to be found in the original documents of the PAC. The PAC has also redefined itself with a narrower view of African nationalism. Racism is a scourge of South Africa, but racial intolerance is not just a problem among a certain class of white society: it is also to be found in the utterances of prominent politicians. It cuts across and intersects the multifold identities that South Africa is fortunate to embrace. More than 25 years since the dawn of democracy, the race question remains an unresolved issue in the country's social and political environment.

Sobukwe spoke about an Africanist social democracy. One pre-sumes that this was a reference to an economic policy for Africa based on African values. The vision expressed in his inaugural presidential address was that the PAC aspired to the establishment of 'a genuine democracy in which all will be citizens of a common state and will live and be governed *as individuals and not as distinctive sectional groups*' (author's emphasis). Granted, this is not a statement of economic policy, but it does ignore the class character of the South African democracy. As a result, the social-democratic ideals of the PAC needed to be better spelt out. There is no doubt that in the PAC's statement there is an invitation to all race groups in the country, as individuals, to recognise the primary claims of the African population and their aspirations to the leadership of society. 'Here is a tree rooted in African soil,' says Sobukwe, 'nourished with waters from the rivers of Africa. Come and sit under its shade and become, with us, leaves of the same branch and branches of the same tree.' Steve Biko expresses the same idea but uses the idiom of a dinner table decked out in true African style to which all are invited to sit as equals.[6]

On the land question, it must be acknowledged that the PAC has been consistent in decrying the extent to which the 'African people', narrowly perceived, have not enjoyed land restitution under the new dispensation in South Africa. There is a view within the PAC that suggests that the ANC, having been the main negotiator with the National Party regime at Codesa, had gone soft on the matter of land. The PAC called for the scrapping of section 25 of the Constitution because it allowed the 'willing buyer, willing seller' policy, which meant that land redistribution would become unaffordable and slow down the effective restitution of land. The PAC has been consistent on the land question. Of course, it is debatable whether the slow pace of land restitution is attributable solely to the constitutional provision thus stated, or is, as with so much else, a victim of the corruption and inefficiency that has characterised episodes of the new South Africa.

Other political parties, including the ANC, have now climbed onto the bandwagon and expressed a need for urgency in bringing resolution to the land question. At its conference in December 2017, the ANC passed such a resolution authorising that 'land expropriation without compensation' would become policy. To that effect, Parliament undertook an extensive consultative exercise about amending of section 25 of the Constitution. The committee charged with the task has resolved to recommend the amendment of the Constitution to remove the constitutional obligation to provide compensation for expropriated land, as provided for in section 25(2)(b). The government has pronounced that expropriation of land without compensation will be done according to law, and in such a manner as to promote equality, food security and strengthen the agricultural sector.

Arguably, the loudest proponents of this change of policy as well as the obligation to amend the Constitution, are one of the minority parties in Parliament, the Economic Freedom Fighters (EFF). The constitutionality of such a move is yet to be tested. However, even more important than the constitutionality of the intended amendment is whether such a move could undermine the guarantees in the Bill of Rights, or affect efforts at social cohesion, and indeed whether it would enhance economic democracy, as is hoped.

In a 2016 manifesto on land, the PAC states that:

> The PAC believes that the African land, inclusive of its mineral resources, its air and its oceans, is the inheritance and property of the indigenous African people. That it belongs to the past generation, the current and the future generation. That the current generation rightfully become the custodians of the land and that they will pass it onto the generation yet unborn.

By the introduction of the phrase, 'African indigenous people', the PAC means to redefine the national question in a manner that was not envisaged in 1959. However it is expressed, the statement does not assist the policy debate on land. To what extent is it being suggested, and how can it be done, while adhering to the principles of the Constitution, especially to ensure that non-discrimination, avoidance of arbitrary application of law and the general application of the law are honoured?

It is regrettable that the majority of political parties in Parliament appear to have focused on populist rhetoric and not on sound policy formulation. It is doubtful that the concerns of South Africans, however legitimate, are likely to be addressed in the manner in which this matter is being handled. In reality, this is hardly a constitutional matter and more a public-policy question. What the country urgently needs is an expropriation law that spells out mechanisms for land redistribution in the public interest and for the advancement of economic equality. In a memorandum on the land debate, former president Thabo Mbeki rightly expressed concerns about the danger that the ANC might proceed in a manner that undermines its historic political and ideological positions on the national question, and, more seriously, that the ANC could surrender its historic role as the leader of society. Frankly, in the prevailing debate, there is evidence of more policy incoherence and obfuscation, not less. As we can see, and as far as the legacy of Sobukwe is concerned, there are more questions to be resolved than answers.

––––––––

In conclusion, Robert Mangaliso Sobukwe offered South Africa the possibility of an authentic, brave and principled leadership that the country was robbed of for far too long. For one thing, a strong PAC could have served South Africa better as an alternative to the one-party state that we have effectively become. Sobukwe would have matched Nelson Mandela in providing an alternative vision for South Africa. It is submitted that by reason of the short span of life of the PAC before it was crippled in 1960, it was not able to build the depth of leadership required to sustain it into the future. Since Sobukwe, the PAC leadership has been marked by a litany of disasters right up to the present day.

Perhaps a visionary leadership would have recognised the

opportunity that the emergence of the BCM in the 1970s could have provided as a lifeline for the PAC – in much the same way that it did for the ANC. I am not aware that there were any talks between the PAC and BCM formations about a common approach towards a more stable and diverse politics for South Africa. On the other hand, the wisdom of the late Oliver R Tambo, president of the ANC, who actively reached out to like-minded elements within the BCM and thus gave new blood to the ANC, was commendable.

More fundamentally, the demise of Sobukwe meant that South Africa faltered in the articulation of its pan-African ideology. South Africa's role in Africa could have been intellectually grounded by Sobukwe's vision as events in Africa developed. Thabo Mbeki's leadership of South Africa (1999–2008) helped the country stand tall in Africa and the world. Sobukwe's heart and feeling about Africa might have gone a long way towards strengthening the emotional ties to Africa and establishing among South Africans a higher degree of pride in Africa, a commitment to Africa's well-being and a desire to join others in the transformation of the continent.

Sobukwe endured nine years of solitary imprisonment, having served a sentence for protesting against the unjust system of pass laws under apartheid. Although much is made of the fact that when he came out of prison he was not bitter, I cannot help but sense that the years of isolation affected him psychologically. Indeed, there is evidence to believe that he was released in a panic by the government because it was feared that his mental state had been broken. Even upon his release, he was subjected to restrictions. The intention was to break his spirit, undermine his intelligence and silence his voice. This chapter has shown that, in all respects, the apartheid system failed. The publication of Sobukwe's papers and his writings, both poetry and fiction, is long overdue. Moves in this regard are to be welcomed. We have heard much about Sobukwe. South Africa needs to get to appreciate his full humanity. Reverend John Knox Bokwe's anthem, 'A Plea for Africa', has become popular today. Sobukwe is reported to have found inspiration in the words of Bokwe: 'Give a thought to Africa.'

The truth of who I am
will set me free

Claudelle von Eck

Claudelle von Eck holds a DPhil in leadership and, although not an auditor, is the former CEO of the Institute of Internal Auditors South Africa (IIA SA), and is acting CEO of its Leadership Academy for Guardians of Governance. Internationally, she is on the IIA SA's Global Executive Leadership Team. She serves on supervisory business and accounting boards at Pretoria University and Unisa. She is an executive member of the Public Sector Audit Committee Forum, and chairs the Anti-Intimidation and Ethical Practices Forum.

I AM A GEN-XER. My generation falls somewhere between the baby boomers who fought for the liberation of our country and the millennials, dubbed the 'born-frees'. We are often referred to as the 'lost generation'. It is an awkward space to be in, lost in-between: too young to have been a freedom fighter, and to be celebrated for it, and too old to have been born free.

I am a South African, intrinsically bound to the country where I first opened my eyes and took my first steps as a child, walking on the soil before I knew that this was a country, with borders determined by the others from the north. I was born with a free mind ... until the system did its work.

My first recollection of something not being right with the world can be traced back to when I was about six years old. Less than two years before we lost Robert Sobukwe. The mid-1970s in South Africa was a turbulent time and a scary place for little people living in townships. They forgot about us, the little people who were watching. I have this vivid memory of a six-year-old version of myself standing at the edge of the school grounds, fearfully watching the older kids in the nearby school with placards, protesting, while police Casspirs[1] were rolling in. I had no idea what was really going on. All I knew in that moment was that I was captivated, afraid, and sensed that something was not right with the world. Then there was the necklacing.[2] Those images would fundamentally shape a whole generation.

Through the sacrifices of so many who came before us, we have since gained political freedom, with all its complexities. Well, at least to a certain degree. Strings are still being pulled in the corridors of power and particular interests served at the expense of the people. I was in my early twenties when we stood in long queues, waiting to cast our first vote as members of the new 'rainbow nation'. We stood for hours, patiently. What were a few hours compared to waiting for generations? That was just the first step.

Today there is a battle being waged for the economic freedom of our people, while the inequality gap only grows wider by the day. Many are shouting that we cannot be free until we are economically free. The wealth of the country remains in the hands of the few. Fat cats growing fatter. The more things change, the more they remain the same. A World Bank report based on a study published in 2016 claims that South Africa is the most unequal society in the world, with wealth inequality being much higher than income inequality. The report states that the high wealth inequality and low intergenerational mobility inherited from apartheid has resulted in these disparities being passed down from generation to gen-eration. The report, which covers the period 2006–2015, gives some sobering statistics, such as that 40 per cent of South Africans were living below the poverty line in 2015, up from 36.4 per cent in 2011, with at least 78 per cent of South Africans having slipped into poverty at least once in that period.[3] The signs point to matters worsening. Thus, a battle for the economic freedom of those who suffered under apartheid is a noble and justified cause. And then there is the land question. The soil under our feet. Who does it belong to?

Will economic freedom make us a free people?

I watch and I worry. Why are we not talking about the third battle to be fought? Are we completely blind to the existence of the chains that must be broken before we can declare ourselves completely free? To become the great nation we are meant to be, we need to unshackle our minds and reimagine our collective future. Freedom of the mind.

We all look at the psyche of South Africa from different vantage points. Most fit into a broad spectrum, with two opposite extremes – superiority and inferiority – linked to the racial complexities in the country. The unfortunate reality is that many, if not the vast majority of, South Africans suffer from one of the two complexes, some to a greater degree than others. I very specifically say 'suffer' because both an inferiority and a superiority complex are harmful conditions of the mind that have health consequences for the sufferer. So, much healing has to take place. You cannot find healing if you are unable to recognise that there is a wound.

I was already in my mid-forties when I realised how deep my wounds were cut. Much closer to the bone than I had realised. There were of course earlier signs, but these hadn't sunk in. I would later discover why. I was marching along obliviously with the masses of walking wounded. How was I to know?

How was I to know that the little girl in me was still hurting? That her wings were bound and she had forgotten how high her wings could take her? As a child, I used to daydream about having wings and I could see, feel myself flying, soaring, floating in space. Funny how strong our imaginations are when society has not yet completed its job of cementing us into the matrix. The sameness of thought. You must conform. I am like the group I belong to. They look like me, talk like me. We are a group because we are not like them.

As a species, what puts us in a class of our own is our imagination. Free when untouched by society. The glue that confines us as a collective. We can collectively imagine a system into being and make it our reality. Our collective imagination can achieve wonderful things. It has bound societies together and taken humans to the moon. It can also conjure up demons that creep into the actions of individuals and groups. If we can imagine that a certain group is inferior or superior to us, then it becomes so, irrespective of whether the belief is based on fact or not, with prejudice and racism being consequences thereof.

Many tend to conflate prejudice and racism, or use them interchangeably, although the two concepts are not the same. Prejudice is exercised at an individual level, based on a person's belief system. Although often drawn from a broader context, prejudice does not necessarily constitute racism. Racism is when one group systematically exerts power over another group, with the 'other' being differentiated on the basis of race. This is when individual prejudice becomes common practice in society. It is only in modern times that racism as we know it has been promoted and institutionalised. Sadly, among those entrusted with the souls of individuals, for example spiritual leaders and psychologists, there were many avid proponents of racism who contributed to a belief system that favoured some and miserably failed others. European imperialism, slavery and colonial rule created the perfect breeding ground for a belief system based on a Darwinian evolutionary hierarchy, with Europeans at the top.

The irony is that biological race is a myth. Scientists agree that racial categories are a weak proxy for genetic differences.[4] I can't help but wonder whether Sobukwe understood the science behind it when he said that he was fighting for a non-racial society, a unified human race. Race is a social construct deeply rooted in the darkest crevices of our collective imagination, a myth fervently adopted even by those considered educated. If race is a myth, then a natural conclusion would be that racism is a nonsensical concept. Thus, in this chapter I use race as a descriptor in the socio-economic and political contexts only, because that is where the real distinctions lie.

It took me a while to discover that many people do not consider me as eligible to be at the top of the human hierarchy. It never occurred to me as a child. I was just me. Later, it never really oc-curred to me that people saw a coloured or black woman when they looked at me, as well as all the prejudices and biases that would go with that association. I simply thought people saw me, the soul, the personality. This naturally led to many an occasion when I simply did not 'know my place', occasions when I incurred the wrath of those who believed I should have bowed down (whether they themselves understood where that prejudice came from or not). Yet, at the same time, I did not realise that I had absorbed some of that imaginary hierarchy into my own imagination. The dissonance. Knowing yourself and not knowing the being society says you are.

'Stop trying to catch up, you caught up a long time ago.' My mind battled to assimilate those words with what my conscious mind thought it knew. In grade 10, I was transferred from a town-ship school to the German school in Pretoria. My parents couldn't afford it, so I was there by the good graces of the Germans. This is the point where the tricks that had been played on my imagination started to manifest themselves. Back then, different schooling systems existed for the different racial groups, with white children afforded access to a superior system. Black children were not supposed to go beyond servanthood.

The subliminal messages society planted in the vulnerable mind of a child. You are inferior. I had never consciously thought that. But 'they' had told me that white people were superior. I already 'knew' that the boys weren't necessarily smarter than I was. The evidence was in my marks. Here I was, having gone from being the top student in my grade to a student struggling somewhere in the middle. The top student at the new school was a white male, and light years ahead of me (or that is what it felt like when I compared our marks). So, maybe they were smarter. I was far too underdeveloped in my understanding of the way of the world to comprehend at that time that he had an advantage. To realise that is to realise how privilege manifests itself. He had grown up in a superior education system and had access to resources. And his mind had not been tricked into questioning his own abilities. Where would I have been if I had had the same access, the same freedom of mind? But, then, I am a woman, and one with a darker hue. Intellect with an inability to understand the hierarchy. After my shock tumble to the struggling middle, I had to run to catch up. At some point, I ran past the catch-up goalpost and did not notice it was there. Nobody told me where it was. I don't know if anybody really knows where it is. 'Stop trying to catch up,' my coach,[5] a white man, would say.

Feminine intelligence. Is there such a thing? What on earth happened to my wings? You can only walk among others as a true equal when you are healed. When your wings are unbound.

Who told you white people are superior? What a question. I don't know. This question comes from my coach. Is he patronising me? But, yes, who told me that? The subliminal messages. For one, they said God was a white male. Who said that? Nobody said it directly. So, why did you conjure up images of God as a white male? He. Hmmm ... yes, He was always portrayed as an old white man in all the pictures of God. Sounds so absurd now. Who could ever capture God in a picture? Books, posters, journals, paintings. Everywhere. The poor little girl. How did it damage my mind? He – yes, He – did not look like me. The day I realised that this construct was the imagining of others, and had become part of my imagination, was the day that many other things unravelled. How could I be so gullible in the first place?

Babies enter the world with no opinion of, God, race, gender, hierarchies, etc. Then we get fed ideas and we are assimilated into the collective imagination. Don't blame yourself, little girl. The odds were against you. They were all standing ready to teach you, like good adults should. You were completely dependent on them for your survival, and you trusted them. They were the all-knowing adults who could never be wrong. As they were taught by those before them. Handing the sins down from one generation to the other. The way of the world. Know your place. You're a girl. One with chocolate skin. A delicious colour, but it does not make you beautiful.

Why, then, when the truth peeks around your corner, is it so difficult to unlearn the deception? Why is it so difficult to deconstruct and reconstruct our intrinsic beliefs? Neuroscience says it was hard-wired into my brain when I was a vulnerable child.

The wound inflicted. You are inferior in cognitive intelligence. But, I never consciously believed that, did I? No, but it caused you pain. What pain? I don't feel pain. Ah, but pain does not always announce itself in its true colours. There are so many signs. Remember how rattled you were the first time you stood in front of an all-white audience? What could I possibly teach them? Flashback to the time I first communed with them and I struggled somewhere in the middle.

The wound inflicted. You are inferior in emotional strength. But, I never believed that. Did I? How could I? I watched too many men go into hiding when the going got tough. You are the weaker vessel,[6] they said. The man must lead because he is stronger. How could I not believe the man of God endowed with God's wisdom? Weaker vessel. What does that even mean? Why was I created weaker? Why me? What did I do to God to deserve that? What a painful thought. A deliberate thought in the creation – make her weaker. Whose God? The One created in the image of man?

The wound inflicted. You are inferior in appearance. It took the help of an Israeli woman to pull the veil off this wound for me.[7] Why don't you see yourself as beautiful? I don't know. It was never important to me. Really? A little girl growing up in a society where a woman is often judged based on her looks? It was never important? Was it not important because making it unimportant was easier than facing the pain of not meeting the standard of beauty? Whose standard? What beauty? Well, as beauty was portrayed in the magazines. I did not look like them. If that is beauty and I don't look like them, then logic dictates that I am not beautiful. But, why is it important? Why are we having this conversation? If you concluded that you are not beautiful based on 'their' standard, then you are wounded. You bought into the imagination of others and assimilated it into yours. Oh, goodness. An awakening. The wound is deep and the pain intense.

And then the anger comes.

Anger is only an expression of pain. See how angry we are. We throw stones, we burn things. It is the pain speaking; perhaps we know it, perhaps we don't. They say we are irrational. Is *Homo sapiens* not always irrational when we act out of emotion, pain?

The trauma of being dismantled as a human being to one less than human. Cast as the inferior character on the stage of life. Rooted in that trauma are elements of insecurity, feelings of low self-confidence, vulnerability, outbursts and the use of a veneer of arrogance as a means of defence. Apartheid was institutionalised with a sociologist at the helm.[8] The psychological effects of the system on the oppressed would not have been lost on him. Create an inferiority complex in the masses and the masses will do some of your work for you. Signs of an inferiority complex (perceived social rank) include: being ultrasensitive to critical comments; always comparing yourself to another person's winning quality; submissive behaviour; perfectionism; procrastination and inaction; being secretly very judgemental of other people; and trying to hide your flaws.[9] Now, where have I seen these signs before? Do I see some of them in myself?

Validation never comes from directly or indirectly seeking approval from the ones we were told are superior. A nod from the 'superior beings' that says I am okay is not going to fix me. Healing must come from inside. I wish I could reach beyond the grave, look Sobukwe in the eye and lose myself in conversation with him. You saw it too, didn't you? That true validation is identifying with me as a fellow human being. A validation that has meaning only when you are able to shed the shackles of privilege and stand with me as a true equal. But, how can you stand with me when you have never experienced my reality, my pain? Recognise the privilege? Stand with me without offering patronising paternalistic help that takes away my dignity of self-determination? Is that what you saw, Sobukwe? I think, hope, I understand.

An unlearning and a relearning. Both of us. You the beneficiary of privilege and me on the back foot in a winner-takes-all game. But, I stumble on this truth; I need to understand how my brain works. Neuroscience.

They declared me free. How can I be free if my imagination is still trapped in their matrix? How do I get out of the matrix if I can't see it? How do you gain freedom from something that does not exist? Money is not going to set me free. Sure, it might make my life easier, but it will not set me free. The truth of who I am will set me free.

It is my own journey of discovering the depths of my pain, the awakening and the painful road to dismantling societal beliefs I had absorbed about myself and others, reimagining my own reality and reconstructing my own belief system devoid of the influences of others, based on fact rather than myth, that led to my digging deeper and seeking to understand the collective pain. The more I see it around me, the more I mourn for my people. We fight invisible demons.

In my search for answers, I have found more research conducted in the United States than in South Africa. However, the similarities in terms of the issues around race are strong enough for me to believe that the results can be applied here, in our context, in a country where the divisions are more often than not drawn along racial lines. From many of the studies that are conducted, one thing is crystal clear: racism harms children. It affects them in adulthood and the effects of those wounds cut across generations. There is a growing body of knowledge around the harmful consequences of racism and how it cripples its victims, not only mentally and psychologically, but also physically.

One study, conducted by researchers from Rush University and Yale University, concluded that children develop an awareness of racial stereotypes quite early, that is, between the ages of 5 and 11.[10] These stereotypes include academic ability and how intelligent certain racial groups are. The study concluded that when children become aware of the stereotypes people hold about their own racial group, it invariably affects how they respond to everyday situations. This includes how they interact with others and how they perform in tests. The study shows that those children who have been exposed to the belief that their own racial group is less intelligent tend to perform poorly in tests. The brain experiences discrimination as a stressor and in some cases as a threat to survival.[11] With advances in neuroscience revealing more and more about the workings of the brain, we are also becoming more conscious of the fact that so many of our responses are involuntary, uncontrollable and unpredictable.

In South Africa, children born with a darker skin and non-European features live with the overt and covert messages that are sent on a daily basis. You are less than them, and are consistently faced with outward manifestations of an inferiority complex. This is evident all around in those who look like them, and translates into submissiveness, the reinforcement of their 'place' in society and in brazen inequality cut along racial lines. It extends to the way they are treated, prejudice and where they are expected to live, the colour of their skin being associated with a propensity for crime, and so forth.

Perceiving discrimination against oneself significantly heightens stress responses and is therefore detrimental to mental and physical health.[12] If we look at this in the context of the fact that stress results in the loss of neurons in a brain region associated with learning and memory (that is, the hippocampus),[13] and we combine this with the effects of malnutrition, it is no wonder that many of our children battle to break out of the vicious cycle that keeps them on the lower rungs of the ladder.

Chronic stress and elevated levels of cortisol increase the production of oligodendrocytes (cells that protect and insulate neurons). It also decreases the number of stem cells that mature into neurons within the hippocampus. It appears that the overproduction of oligodendrocytes is responsible for long-term, and perhaps permanent, changes in the brain that could set the stage for later mental problems and difficulties with learning and memory.[14] In addition to changes in brain structure, the use of disdainful terms, such as 'affirmative-action appointee', adds to day-to-day stress among people of colour. You only got the job for political reasons and not for your capability. So, every day I work harder and expect more from myself than my white counterpart.

It has been demonstrated in research that race-related anxiety surrounding negative judgement about performance and dis-crimination is associated with lower cognitive performance among black participants (but not white participants). A number of cog-nitive processes, including attention/working memory, learning and memory, and executive functioning are impacted upon in the process. It could therefore be concluded that, in some cases, test performance may not represent actual brain functioning among ethnic/racial groups, but rather race-related anxiety about their test performance.[15]

Our brain makes it practically impossible for us to be colour-blind with regard to skin colour. Although newborn babies show no preference for the skin colour of faces, there are clear signs that from the age of around three months they spend more time scanning faces and start to show a preference for faces with the same skin colour as that of their parents and those who look like them.[16]

Recognising ethnic differences, therefore, already becomes preva-lent in early development. Children observe how these different ethnic groups, including their own, are treated and these stereo-types become hard-wired into their perceptions and biases. People can take in visual cues of race, gender and approximate age within milliseconds of seeing a face.[17] Our problem as *Homo sapiens* is not that we recognise that nature has divided us into groupings in terms of skin colour and typical features, but rather that we have a propensity to assign stereotypes to groups. If a child grew up seeing differences in appearances but was not conditioned to think that others are any more different than the surface of their skin, the child's brain would not create neural pathways that lead to an inferiority or superiority complex in relation to her race.

Studies in the field of neuroscience reveal that when we perceive people as other than us, we can even fear them, an emotion that is a powerful driver of thinking and behaviour. Thus, learnt fear extends to racial prejudice to the extent that feedback from someone of a different race is perceived as a threat. Therefore, a basic interaction can be influenced by the recognition of a face as an 'other'.[18] This response is involuntary, and often the person is not aware of what drives their fear. A psychology and radiology study conducted by researchers at Stanford University revealed that when European American males were shown faces of unfamiliar Caucasians, the first area of the brain that was activated was the fusiform gyrus, which is involved in facial recognition. However, when these same males were shown faces of people of colour, the fusiform gyrus response was delayed and the first area of the brain to respond was the amygdala, which is responsible for the fight-or-flight response. Interestingly, though, when they were shown faces of well-known people of colour, or they were given a few character details before the experiment, the amygdala response was annulled.[19] It's a sobering thought: these guys' first response to seeing my face would be fear. Not exactly the response I am looking for when I put my make-up on in the morning.

Similar studies using magnetic resonance imaging (MRI) scans show that when witnessing pain applied to members of their own race, the empathic neural response is stimulated in participants, and that it decreases when witnessing pain applied to other racial groups. The studies did show, however, that when members from other racial groups were considered as part of the individual's social group or team, the empathic response returned.[20] These are significant findings for a country like South Africa, where we deal with not only racial but also tribal issues. It is clear that if we have something that binds us together as one nation, our empathy across racial lines could improve and our fight–or–flight response could be eliminated.

I don't think that we have a choice in addressing this, as the consequences are now known. Experiencing the fight–or–flight response on a constant basis is harmful to our health. This goes both for victims and perpetrators of racism. The stress associated with fear increases our cortisol, which in high levels is associated with sleep deprivation, weight gain, hostility, hypertension, a weakened immune system and other negative health effects.[21] For me, this brings into question the reasoning behind the health statistics we are given for the South African population. According to The Heart and Stroke Foundation, ten South Africans suffer a stroke every hour, and 225 are killed by heart diseases every day.[22] These statistics are generally attributed to South Africans' diet and lifestyle. However, studies in neuroscience around the effects of racism on individual health brings another dimension that is seldom spoken of in our context. This made me ponder my own responses and health issues. In taking another look at how my body responds when I feel discriminated against, the penny dropped. Stress increases my cortisol levels, and that chips away at my immune system, which of course comes with a double whammy for me. Not only am I of a darker hue, but I am also a woman. Having travelled to many different countries, I cannot think of many places where I have not felt discrimination based on my colour, gender or both. I could fill a book with such memories, and now that I know what discrimination does to my body, it frightens me when I think about what it means for my health and longevity.

The bad news and the good news is that this is all in our brains. It's bad news because we respond involuntarily to hard–wired neural pathways created in the brain. But the good news is that with intervention we can rewire our thinking and reverse the effects of stereotyping in our thinking processes that affect our self-esteem and performance.

Epigenetic modifications to DNA can be reversed. In other words, neural stem cells can recover from high levels of cortisol if the stress is removed. Neuroscience clearly shows that it is possible to create new neurons and rewire circuits in the brain. By repeating certain thoughts and behaviours often enough, it is possible not only to undo negative racist behaviours and attitudes, but also to stop absorbing the negative effects of discrimination. Thus, by redirecting or rewiring circuits in our brain, we can free ourselves from being victims and restore the sense of self to a healthy level. This in turn would have the physiological effect of a healthier body.

It requires a concerted effort, as rewiring circuits in the brain does not happen without intervention. Key to such intervention is making the effort to get to know the people around us who may not look like us. As they become more familiar, we are less likely to go into fight-or-flight mode. This will also assist in dismantling stereotypes, although we need to take into consideration that, in the South African context, many have been deprived of a good education. A healthy response when two people from the extreme opposites in the education system meet is for the one to resist feeling inferior and to acknowledge the fact that the other has simply been exposed to more, and is not necessarily more intelligent, and for the other to resist feeling superior and realise that the system gave him an advantage, not a superior intellect.

The challenge to leaders in all spheres, be it in schools, universities, business, civil society, religious organisations, social spheres and all other domains, is to determine to what degree they are contributing to the rewiring of the minds of our people. How much are we doing to dismantle racism and the associated inferiority and superiority complexes? Now that we know the harmful effects, and the remedy, we can't plead ignorance. We are duty-bound to drive the right discourses. Becoming impatient with people who themselves do not realise how damaged they are is not what is going to propel us forward. Telling people to forget the past and move on is a futile exercise if we are not going to help everyone to become free. The truth will set us free. The truth is that we were all born equal. The third battle is exactly that: the battle for the freedom of our minds from the shackles of inferiority and superiority complexes. Only then can we become one nation and a prosperous one.

I too am wounded, but I am rewiring my brain. I can feel my wings grow again.

Radical politics, yes, but with civility and humanity

Adam Habib and Alexandra Leisegang

Professor Adam Habib is Vice Chancellor of Wits University. A professor of political science, he has over thirty years of academic, research and administration expertise, spanning five universities and multiple local and international institutions and boards. He is a member of the American Academy of Arts and Sciences, a fellow of the African Academy of Science and the Academy of Sciences of South Africa. His latest book is Rebels and Rage, *a reflection on the #FeesMustFall movement.*

Dr Alexandra Leisegang holds a PhD from Wits. She has worked as a research consultant in the NGO sector as well as in political communications for the Democratic Alliance (DA). Her primary interest is in political party behaviour, including party organisation and political marketing.

IN RECENT years, South African politics has been characterised by a distinct lack of civility and accountability. Racism and violent threats have become the norm and civilised, democratic politics is being replaced by the political mob. Some politicians and activists no longer engage in debate but rather vandalise property, threaten journalists and spew racial hatred – all in the name of radical politics. Many of those who draw on the inspiration of radical thinkers such as Sobukwe, Fanon and Biko invoke these names but act contrary to what they stood for.

It is during times like these that we should think back to the era of leaders like Robert Sobukwe, who championed a politics that was civil and disciplined. Sobukwe's legacy is increasingly being evoked, but we need to ask whether our society is being true to his memory. To borrow Benjamin Pogrund's phrasing, Sobukwe has been 'airbrushed'[1] out of the liberation history and, until recently, not much has been written about him. On the occasion of the renaming of Wits University's Central Block to the Robert Sobukwe Block, former Deputy Chief Justice Dikgang Moseneke remarked:

> It is ... deeply disingenuous to suggest that any of our valiant heroes may be discarded or hidden under the rubble of history. Their ideas will tend to surface and resurface because they are a vital part of a progressive knowledge system.[2]

Sobukwe's ideas are indeed resurfacing at a time when South Africans are calling into question the ANC's leadership over the past 25 years. However, it is not only his ideas that need to resurface but also his style of leadership.

Sobukwe, by all accounts, conducted himself with dignity and decorum and rejected the politics of militarism and spectacle that have come to define radical politics in South Africa today. The implicit assumption by some radical activists recently is that social mobilisation and progressive politics have to be undisciplined, threatening and violent if they are to be radical, a view that is at odds with the personal conduct of many of the grand leaders of the radical political tradition from whom these same activists draw inspiration. If these activists read widely enough, rather than relying on rhetorical statements and party memorabilia, they would know that Sobukwe, Cabral, Biko, Fanon, Alexander, Guevara and the like were often courteous individuals who underscored the importance of discipline. In their world, being ill-disciplined could cost lives.

The Economic Freedom Fighters (EFF) in particular have branded themselves as a radical political party, but are their actions truly in line with the radical politics of the past? Derek Hook argues that the EFF are 'in many respects Sobukwe's political heirs' as both the PAC and EFF are breakaways from the ANC Youth League (ANCYL) and some of their positions are similar to those of Sobukwe.[3] However, the similarities end there. The EFF, and particularly its leadership, favours a militaristic style of populism that operates more in the realm of spectacle than ideas. Further to this, Hook also points to the fact that Sobukwe had a 'pronounced distaste for wealth', which is hard to reconcile with the ostentatious tendencies of Julius Malema and others in the EFF leadership.[4]

Perhaps the most telling difference is the manner in which the EFF leadership conducts itself and encourages its 'fighters' to behave. Criticism of the EFF is met with vandalism, threats and violence by its leadership and members. However, this behaviour is not limited to the EFF. In recent years, we have seen several incidents in which a political mob has mobilised over racist remarks or criticism of a politician. Many people's response would be: this is just an act of political spectacle by a political party or radical activists. But to allow it to continue without protest is to enable the naturalisation of such political behaviour in our society. Even at the level of the hard-fought-for democratic Parliament, we are regularly treated to a politics of spectacle in which name-calling and fist fights are more common than robust debate on inequality in our society. These acts are not the evolution of a supposed progressive politics. At the core of the crisis in our democracy today is a lack of civility and accountability. We need to examine how this has developed and what the consequences are. We also need to look to how this can be reversed, otherwise the democratic foundations of our society will continue to be eroded.

Is civility important to democratic politics? The obvious answer is yes. But there are many in our democratic institutions who believe that civility is a bourgeois norm that has helped to mask the growth of inequalities in the last two decades. Civility is seen as being supportive of the status quo, a behaviour typical of older political generations who were unable to transform the economy and society. Too many young activists, and now increasingly politicians, speak with a sense of bravado about their politics being 'robust'. However, this has now become code for rudeness, uncivil behaviour, use of expletives, disruption and the violation of the rights of others, and sometimes even violence. Robust politics and engagement does not mean resorting to violent action.

Uncivil politics, as distinct from extra-institutional politics, has its roots in the politics of the right and fascist movements in the interwar years. These movements were marginal political entities that used the rights (and never took on the responsibility obligations) of their democratic systems to build their bases and subvert democracy itself. A less toxic, relatively more peaceful and non-racial, uncivil politics emerged in the student movements of the West during the 1960s and 1970s. These were extra-institutional and disruptive mobilisations but were on balance directed at bringing people together across racial and ethnic divides.

Yet there were strands within the movement that overplayed their hand and increasingly became racialised and violent, and were quickly suppressed by their respective governments. In the developing world, we did not have the luxury of such incivility: abuse was a part of people's daily lives, activists were abused by police and the state's henchmen, and radical politics was increasingly about inclusion both in our ultimate goal and in our daily practice. Ironically, those in South Africa who have recently adopted this behaviour subscribe to radical or leftist thinking but have really adopted the strategies and tactics of the right.

How is it that radical politics in South Africa has come to

be interpreted to mean uncivil engagement? To be fair, part of this has its roots in the liberation movement itself. Competitive liberation politics in the later years of the apartheid era produced a toxicity that led to violence in some parts of the country. But this was overshadowed by the widespread violence unleashed by the apartheid state against all strands of the movement and communities. Perhaps this, together with the fact that all of us were excluded from the state, ensured that the intra-party and intra-liberation incivility and violence was contained by a broader tradition of civility and comradeship within the liberation movement.

In the first decade of the post-apartheid era, the ANC went out of its way to cultivate civility in public discourse and parliamentary politics. A significant part of this had to do with Nelson Mandela, who took on the responsibility of building bridges across South Africa's multiple divides in order to buy South Africa the political space to transform itself. Thabo Mbeki also continued the civil tradition in public discourse and parliamentary politics, perhaps assisted by his own intellectual orientation. None of this must be interpreted to mean that political discourse was in any way easy or not divisive. The public discourse between Mbeki and DA leader Tony Leon was very polarising, as was Mbeki's public criticism of both intra-party and external dissidents. But these polemics occurred largely within the confines of the democratic system, even if they were unsavoury and may have affronted particular individuals. Where Mbeki was seen to have crossed the legitimate democratic line was in his treatment of some intra-party dissidents, particularly in the use of state institutions to settle party-political battles. But these democratic breaches were confined to the ruling party, and mainstream public discourse and parliamentary politics remained relatively free of this kind of uncivil politics.

Jacob Zuma changed all of this. The impetus came with the firing of Zuma as deputy president after he was implicated during the corruption trial of Schabir Shaik. This prompted Zuma to launch the succession race for the ANC presidency, supported by the ANCYL, the Congress of South African Trade Unions (Cosatu) and the South African Communist Party (SACP). The latter two were not natural allies of Zuma but mistakenly believed that they could control him and thereby effect a more social-democratic and inclusive political economy. Zuma and those around him fed the illusion by sprouting anti-neoliberal rhetoric. Suddenly all and sundry, including dubious business figures, state officials and mainstream ANC and Youth League activists became ardent socialists, at least until they were safely ensconced in public office.

But the more important effect of this succession battle was that Zuma breached all of the known ANC conventions in his use of strategies and tactics. Zuma, through the ANCYL in particular, pioneered a politics of spectacle that was mainstreamed into the popular discourse and in the broader public arena. This involved the advancement of an ethnic and/or racial politics, the public slander of individuals, threats of violence and a social mobilisation that trashed public facilities and private businesses and mythologised militarism. These tactics were most tragically deployed in the mobilisation outside the courts during Zuma's rape trial, particularly targeted at the rape victim, Khwezi, and were led in principle by leading ANCYL members at the time. The tactics perfected outside the courts were also deployed against leaders within the ANC, and particularly against those associated with Mbeki. Unruly behaviour that was previously typical of ANCYL meetings became a feature of ANC gatherings. This, together with the Cosatu-SACP alliance arrayed against Mbeki, and the latter's tragic miscalculation to stand for a third term as ANC president, delivered both the organisation's and the country's presidency to Zuma.

The unholy alliance around Zuma was soon to unravel. In

quick succession, one ally after another – Tokyo Sexwale, the Shaik brothers, Zwelinzima Vavi, Julius Malema, Floyd Shivambu, Blade Nzimande and the SACP – fell out with Zuma and were marginalised. Malema, Shivambu and the Youth League leadership initially held out and were alleged to have been involved in all kinds of tender irregularities in Limpopo province. But, in December 2011, as the scale of this corruption spread and the province was severely bankrupted, National Treasury, under then minister of finance Pravin Gordhan, was forced to intervene and clean up the mess. In the subsequent political fight, Malema and Shivambu turned against the Zuma leadership. As their antics became increasingly embarrassing to the party, they were tossed out of the ANC and went on to form the EFF from the remnants of the then Youth League.

Nobody expected the EFF to survive. It defied all predictions of demise and proceeded to become a thorn in the side of Zuma. Three features aided it in this regard – one structural and the other two agential. The structural feature was the increasing alienation of the youth, both within poor communities and among the emerging middle classes. This is a worldwide phenomenon but is more accentuated in South Africa by widespread poverty, increasing inequality within society and the toxic identity politics that this has spawned among black people in the mainly middle-class suburbs. The first agential feature was the financial support that Malema was alleged to have mobilised in some very dubious quarters, including among shady businessmen and tobacco smugglers. The second agential feature was the increasing divisions within the ANC, which came with an ever-increasing number of leaks that continually fed the EFF leadership. ANC factions of course believed that they were using the EFF to inflict damage on their intra-party opponents, but the EFF leadership used the leaked information strategically as and when it suited them to weaken the ANC and build their own capabilities.

If this had been all that the EFF did, it would have been perfectly legitimate. But the EFF went beyond this to perfect the politics of spectacle that they had learnt outside the courts during Jacob Zuma's trial and now deployed this within the parliamentary precinct and in the broader society. The politics of spectacle, reflected in the chants to Zuma to 'pay back the money' and in the continued haranguing of Zuma and other ANC leaders, was devastatingly effective. It wrong-footed ANC parliamentarians, whose overwhelming parliamentary majority was no antidote to the spectacle of disruption. Even when security measures were utilised and EFF parliamentarians were evicted, they would simply repeat the exercise on the next occasion. Focused solely on the unravelling of the Zuma administration and unconstrained as a result of having no desire to convince the electorate of their ability to rule, the EFF's strategies proved to be successful.

Gradually, other parties began to realise the value of the EFF's tactics. But, constrained by their own desire to rule (even at some future date), and perhaps by their own inabilities, none could replicate these tactics. So these opposition parties decided to do the next best thing: align with the EFF inside and outside Parliament to increase the pressure on the Zuma administration. The result was a series of broader campaigns within society that greatly enhanced the image of the EFF, especially among students and the broader youth. It also enhanced the image of the movement among journalists and analysts who had been at the forefront of exposing the corruption and ethical breaches associated with the capture of the state by the Gupta family, which Zuma had enabled.

But, while uncivil and spectacle politics may have been devastatingly effective in unravelling the Zuma administration, it has been found wanting in an era of reconstruction. This has become increasingly apparent as the EFF's spectacle politics and destructive potential are unleashed against the very partners, such as the

DA, who opportunistically aligned with it to keep the ANC out of power in Johannesburg, Tshwane and Nelson Mandela Bay. Journalists and analysts who only a year ago were gushing about Malema's political wisdom have also found themselves on the wrong side of the EFF's ire as they became increasingly critical of the party's destructive politics, including its propensity for racist attacks on individuals and the violent actions of some of its leaders and members. But some of its other partners – the United Democratic Movement (UDM) and the new South African Federation of Trade Unions (Saftu) in particular – still continue to find the EFF's tactics valuable because of a coincidence of interests in unravelling the DA administration in Nelson Mandela Bay and undermining outsourcing arrangements in selected corporates, such as South Point. But they too are likely to be turned off when the EFF's propensity for destruction is unleashed on occasions that compromise their interests.

Either way, both motivations – the personalised form of politics through the vilification of Pravin Gordhan (and previously of Zuma) or their racialised character, in which allies and enemies are determined on the basis of the pigmentation of their skin – indicate why the EFF is such a destructive force in democratic politics. Couple this with their propensity to hunt their critics in packs on social media, their violent demeanour reflected in the altercations with journalists by Shivambu and Malema, the frequent destruction of property by members, and their predisposition to spectacle, the intention of all of which is often to silence individuals and frighten them from openly participating in a critical democratic engagement. Habib has previously described these characteristics as proto-fascist, suggesting that the EFF is akin to parties of the far Right in Western Europe and North America – the AFD in Germany, Le Pen in France, the Northern League and Five Star Movement in Italy, and Trump in the United States – all of which have mobilised the legitimate grievances of people to establish a politics of hate that divides rather than unites, and destroys rather than builds anything of substance.

To be fair, the EFF is not the only manifestation of this kind of politics. Much of this was evident in the ANC YL of the last few years or in the Black First Land First (BLF) movement. It is also worth noting that much of the current cohort of politically active youth grew up and learnt their politics in the era of Zuma and Malema. Is it any wonder, then, that there is such a penchant for a politics of spectacle that crosses party boundaries? Yet, despite this, the politics is most cogently expressed in the EFF from where it has the greatest influence and ability to scale up the spectacle. This in part has to do with the EFF's direct presence in Parliament, and its leaders' abilities to capitalise on this and project a profile far larger than their modest representation implies.

The lack of civility and the growing politics of spectacle is fuelled by an increasing lack of accountability in our society. Over the past few years, we have seen the growth of the political mob that resorts to vandalism and violence. Whether it be service-delivery protests or social outrage on Twitter, the growing reaction in South Africa is to hunt individuals down (virtually and in real life) or to burn infrastructure and vandalise property. And yet no one is held accountable for these actions. In many cases the outrage is legitimate, but resorting to mob justice is not, and there is no place for it in a democratic country with the rule of law.

Racism, corruption and violence should not be tolerated in a democratic South Africa, and individuals should face the proper sanctions. This must, however, be done by the appropriate officials of the police service and prosecuting authority, not by a group of self-appointed activists who effectively constitute a political mob. These kinds of actions do not enhance democracy and account-ability. They undermine it because they promote mob rule and mob justice. We have seen this before when groups of activists mobilised to defend Jacob Zuma and to attack all those who questioned his credentials to rule. We have seen it when political mobs decided to trash certain well-known stores or, even worse, when altercations occurred in schools. Imagine if, in one of these incidents, someone felt threatened, pulled out a firearm, and someone was killed. All hell would be unleashed. And yet the police, and the state, have allowed this kind of mob justice to prevail and even to spread across society.

It is perfectly legitimate for there to be social outrage at racist remarks and corruption. And it is even legitimate for this social outrage to be directed to the boycotts of businesses that employ and defend racists and corrupt individuals. But this form of protest should not be allowed to transform into a political mob identifying family members, visiting them at their homes and businesses, and threatening to harm them. We allow this at our peril. All citizens in our country, even ones we don't like, are entitled to security. If they have violated the norms and rules of our society, they must be subject to sanction, but by the appropriate authorities, not by self-appointed vigilantes. Otherwise, we run the risk of individual citizens deciding that they have to protect themselves, and then our public space simply becomes an anarchic arena ruled by those with the biggest muscles and guns.

The structural inequalities in our society are partly the cause of the violence we experience on a daily basis. This affects especially those who are young, black and female, and who continue to be socio-economically marginalised. But structural inequality alone cannot explain the levels of violence in our country and the violent reaction to some political situations. After all, there are other highly unequal societies with far lower levels of violence. The additional distinguishing feature of our society is the widespread belief that there are no consequences for violence. This is especially true of activists in political parties and community organisations, many of whom believe that one has to be violent and to commit arson to be heard. This neatly dovetails with the politics of spectacle that has become the strategic orientation of some political parties and increasingly that of many young activists across all political lines. The strategic orientation and the propensity to engage in violent actions has consolidated itself because of a widespread belief that there are no severe consequences for such crimes. This is why so many of our protests and strikes become violent. And we can wring our hands as much as we want: we will not arrest the violence in our protests until we develop the political will to impose serious consequences on those who commit violence and on those who promote it.

In 2018, #FeesMustFall activists were calling on President Cyril Ramaphosa to provide amnesty for those who had been charged and found guilty of violence during the student protests. The call for amnesty was made on the grounds that the protests had been a political act for a progressive cause. The assumption implicit in this argument is that progressive activists are somehow entitled to commit violence and break the law because their cause is legitimate. But is this not establishing two sets of laws, one for political activists and another for ordinary citizens? Is this not reproducing another generation of unaccountable political elites? And, if this is the case, how are we ever going to bring an end to the rot of political elites who engage in state capture, fraternisation with known criminals, corruption, the destruction of public institutions, and ultimately the erosion of state capacity? This is not to say that these young activists should be condemned for the rest of their lives. If they can take responsibility for their actions and acknowledge wrongdoing, then they should be allowed a second chance. However, this requires that they be held accountable.

President Ramaphosa has called for increased investment to

enable inclusive growth. But this is never going to happen as long as we allow violence, extrajudicial action by political mobs and vigilantism to prevail in our midst. Indeed, if matters continue as they are, we risk not only not attracting the required amounts of investment for inclusive growth but also feeding a belief in society that you cannot trust the state to protect you, and that you need to procure your own muscle to be safe. This would of course undermine the social pact – the philosophical foundation – on which any democratic society is founded. It would essentially enable the beginnings of a gangster state.

What, then, is to be done with this kind of politics and how can it be contained? It would go without saying that this uncivil and spectacle politics is dangerous for our democracy. Not only does it fan ethnic and racial hatred and deepen divides in our society, but it also continuously violates the rights of others, and on many occasions turns violent. How often have businesses and public institutions been trashed and individuals assaulted without any firm consequences? The lack of accountability also enables the spread of such behaviour, which erodes confidence in the criminal justice system and weakens citizens' commitment to the social pact of our democracy.

We need to restore accountability in our country. This must entail a firm response to the violence and violation of rights per-petrated by the EFF and others within the ANC. Violent actions must have consequences, as must the threats that critics are regularly subjected to. It is also unacceptable that public institutions and the courts respond firmly to the racist diatribes of individual white citizens and then remain silent when the same is done by political leaders and activists. Our Constitution and the law are meant to apply to all, and this must be seen to be the case.

There were many progressives in the 1990s who warned the ANC and the newly ascendant leadership that the adoption of a neoliberal economic programme would have the consequence of socially and politically polarising society. It was a warning that went unheeded, and today we are living with the consequences of that choice. Similarly, 15 years later, there were many who warned about the dangers of electing an individual as corrupt as Jacob Zuma. Again that warning went unheeded, and we are living with the consequences of widespread corruption in our public institutions and state-owned enterprises, and the economic effects of state capture.

There are many who are warning about the dangers of uncivil and spectacle politics. If this warning again goes unheeded, South Africa will pay the consequences through the emboldening of a proto-fascist party practising an uncivil politics that divides rather than unites, destroys rather than builds. This will ultimately erode the democratic foundations that were so painstakingly built and paid for with the lives of so many previous generations of South Africans, such as Robert Sobukwe.

Radical politics is necessary to overcome the challenges our country still faces, but it should be a return to the radical politics of Sobukwe and others, which was characterised by humanity and civility. In order to move forward, we need to understand our history, and Sobukwe was one part of that history. His form of radical politics must live on, but it should not be allowed to be mischaracterised and adopted by those who seek to destroy rather than to build on the progress that has been achieved.

Rise like an eagle:
Reinterpreting Sobukwe

Thandeka Gqubule–Mbeki and Duma Gqubule

Thandeka Gqubule–Mbeki is economics editor at the SABC, across TV, radio and digital. She holds a master's degree in journalism from Columbia University, New York. She was previously associate editor at the Financial Mail, *and has taught journalism at Rhodes University and Monash South Africa. She was awarded the Nat Nakasa Press Freedom Award in 2016. She is the author of* No Longer Whispering to Power: The Story of Thuli Madonsela *and* Semane Queen of the Peaceful Crocodile.

Duma Gqubule, at 16, was found guilty of treason and released into parental custody. He moved to Scotland and obtained an MA in economics from the University of Aberdeen. He has been a financial journalist with The Star *and the* Financial Mail. *He is among the authors of Cyril Ramaphosa's* Black Economic Empowerment Report. *He founded KIO Advisory Services, a black economic empowerment advisory service to government and business, and is author of* Making Mistakes Righting Wrongs.

THERE IS A TRAIN that travels through the Eastern Cape of South Africa. This can be said to be the train of good fortune. It is the train that for decades took hopeful young black South Africans to the powerful centres of education in the Alice and Fort Beaufort areas. It snakes around small, scraggly, forgotten towns and heads northeast towards the town of Alice – leaving behind failing local economies, shattered social arrangements and dismal family financial circumstances. The young people rode the train to leave the bleakness behind.

But there was a price to pay. Indigenous religions and epistemologies were to be left behind, as were African traditional practices. Ahead, the youngsters were to be inaugurated into a new way of being black in the world. They were leaving home to be fashioned into the likeness of boys learning in England. The teachers at Healdtown school in our father and Robert Mangaliso Sobukwe's day were white and mainly British. It was only later that some racial diversity was introduced into the staff complement, and only later that the school's alumni would forcefully reclaim their Africanness and teach generations of Africans who came after them the lessons of self-love and pride in being black African.

But, back on the train, much fun was had by all — at least by our father's account. The train stopped to pick up youngsters at many stations along the way. The boys looked out for new girls going to Healdtown for the first time. Our father recounted to us tales of teasing young girls on the train, swapping books and singing. The boys would impress girls by reciting poems from their English literature curriculum — Shakespeare, mainly. Can you imagine these sons of the African countryside saying to a beautiful black girl:

Shall I compare thee to a summer's day?
Thou art more lovely and more temperate.
Rough winds do shake the darling buds of May,
And summer's lease hath all too short a date.

The train trip to Healdtown was the ride to turn the fortunes of black folks. As history would have it, those many rides turned the fortunes of South Africa and gave rise to a golden generation of nationalists who mounted a formidable challenge to white supremacy and apartheid. This golden generation rose up after the Second World War.

Port Elizabeth railway station was where they assembled to get on the train. The station building was, like their futures, bright, impressive and vast. The architecture was ornate and stately. The pillared white building was as imposing as it was quintessentially European in style.

It was in 1873 that the then prime minister of the Cape Colony, John Molteno, began construction aimed at extending the colonial railway network. Port Elizabeth station was built next to the port, where ships from Europe and Asia arrived and departed. The port was a hive of business and trading activity, and was so prosperous that the city was nicknamed the 'Liverpool of South Africa'. Those whose lives intersected at the station or the port, whether for commerce or for study, became comparatively prosperous and played a significant role in the emergent nation of South Africa.

Departing from Port Elizabeth station and heading to Heald-town signalled a life of promise for young black teenagers. It was this train that took our father, the future Reverend Dr Simon Gqubule, and Robert Mangaliso Sobukwe to school at Healdtown. Our father came from the town of Uitenhage in a township called KwaLanga – where police shot and killed 35 people after a funeral on 21 March 1985 – while Sobukwe came from a town a little further north, Graaff-Reinet.

The train that they took to Healdtown twice a year took poor black boys to the African equivalent of Eton of their time, de-proletarianised them, and returned them to their homes and societies as emerging leaders of a new Christianised African elite.

Many young rural and urban black boys set out from various stations around southern Africa and beyond. They included the likes of Nelson Mandela, Govan Mbeki, John Tengo Jabavu and Raymond Mhlaba – among them a future president of South Africa and the father of a president of South Africa. Three of them would be Rivonia trialists, who spent decades together on Robben Island after being convicted and sentenced for seeking to overthrow the apartheid government. There was clearly something in the water at this school where our father, Simon, met Robert Sobukwe.

Sobukwe arrived at Healdtown at the beginning of 1940. He was held back slightly until a church scholarship was found for him to attend the school. As he arrived, Mandela was being elected to the student leadership at the University College of Fort Hare (now the University of Fort Hare) in the valley beneath the hills in the small town of Alice, close to Healdtown. In 1939, Mandela arrived in this basin of influential schools – what the legendary Healdtown-trained poet, the great Mqhayi, called 'the place where the national trails [are] and the rivers of knowledge'. That year, Mandela, who was studying law, met Oliver Tambo, who was to be for several decades the leader of the African National Congress (ANC) in exile.

Our late father-in-law, Govan Mbeki, also an old Healdtown boy, explained what it was in the educational formula and environ- ment created by the Methodist Church at Healdtown: 'It was a place where we learned that discipline and initiative are linked, although as young people we did not always understand this. We were required to work hard and came out of there ready for the challenges of life.'

Intense relationships often developed because Healdtown was a boarding school. The students needed each other, for they had very little and often had to share. It was, in its time, the biggest black and Methodist educational centre in southern Africa, with 1 400 students, most of whom were boarders. The majority of the staff came from Britain and were professional teachers rather than Methodist ministers.

Since our father was slightly younger than Sobukwe, he looked up to him. This was not only out of normal Xhosa deference to elders, but also because Sobukwe was academically a top performer, held up by the leadership of the school to be admired and emulated by the younger boys. My father emulated Sobukwe. He too was a top academic performer. He even acquired Sobukwe's taste for theology and English literature, and his love of history. Sobukwe was head boy in his senior year. Thus, my father and his peers were led by him. It was Sobukwe's leadership style, serious yet easy-going, thoughtful though not lacking in humour, disciplined yet compassionate, that made our father a lifelong admirer and emulator of Sobukwe.

But our father became a friend, and we suspect a bit of a groupie. Together they formed a mutual society of shared passions, such as English and African literature, and a deep spirituality honed and chiselled in the Methodist Church of Southern Africa. They were souls who bristled at the thought of injustice.

Simon Gqubule and Robert Sobukwe had similar family backgrounds and came from neighbouring parts of South Africa – arid rural backwaters of the Eastern Cape, the forgotten frontier towns of Uitenhage and Graaff-Reinet. It is said that Sobukwe was 'unashamed of his humble beginnings'. He often declared, 'I am the son of Sobukwe, born in Graaff-Reinet, that land of goats …'

Towns like these prove that South Africa has two economies. They show the structural inequality of the South African economy. The impact of unemployment is visible everywhere. It was not much different in Sobukwe's time.

The Second World War brought about certain changes in values and attitudes worldwide. In Africa, the issue of racism came into sharp focus, and across the continent a challenge to colonisation was mounted. Along with the movement to decolonise Africa, nationalist movements of various hues arose. Nativism took root, as did other related ideologies. But South Africa had already gone through its own bizarre form of decolonisation when a retreating Britain handed over power to Afrikaner nationalism, which in turn opted to introduce rigid racial policies. These became increasingly restrictive until the introduction of total apartheid in 1948.

Under apartheid, jobs were racially awarded, as were opportunities. Thus, in Graaff-Reinet and Uitenhage local economic development in the black neighbourhoods was just about nonexistent. Small enterprises were, and are, lean and small. Spatial inequality is glaring in towns that had strict separation between white and black areas, the legacy of the 1913 Natives Land Act. Access to education, health and other services remains unequal to this very day.

Our father became a leader in his own right, one of the golden generation. He rose to become one of the first black presidents of the Methodist Church that had reared him at Healdtown. He also became a political and social leader, rising to become the president of the United Democratic Front (UDF) at a very turbulent time in the history of South Africa. He occupied this leadership position during the stormy 'ungovernable' years of the early to mid-1980s, during which an insurrectionary fervour gripped the nation.

In townships, latter-day youth have affectionately nicknamed the elders of this golden generation 'abo-topi-royal' because of their regal bearing, their strict rules of conduct, their self-discipline and their nearly British way of speaking English. Their polished, modulated tones reflected the influence of the *Royal Reader*, the textbook on which they were reared.

Throughout our father's life, he told stories about Sobukwe. These were mingled with boyish memories and nostalgia for an iconic and destiny-defining alma mater. Often, after evening prayers in our father's lounge, and after singing hymns from the Xhosa Methodist hymnbook, our father would stretch out his legs, close his eyes, and throw back his head. Then he would draw on a lifetime of memories and narratives, many of them harking back to the Reverend Seth Mokitimi or a man by the name of Setiloane. Then would come the inevitable worries and longing for Sobukwe. He would shake his head and say, 'My children, apartheid is an evil thing.' Seth Mokitimi had been their chaplain at Healdtown and a Methodist minister. He was influential in Sobukwe's life too.

Being mere children, we were often bored by these tales. Our father had a habit of telling the same story too often, and then of watching our faces, hoping for a favourable reaction each time. It was only later that we learnt the leadership lessons of Sobukwe that our father so fervently tried to instil in us. It was only when we reread the history, and reinterpreted it through the eyes of our own generation, that we understood that South Africa's long, long history has been propelled by waves of activism, each of them significant in the way they shaped our society and future. But some have been more significant than others. The Sharpeville wave was more significant in modern history, for it ensured that the United Nations and the world took notice of the draconian turn of events in South Africa, and a global hardening of sentiment towards the apartheid regime occurred.

In the black community, a new style of politics was born – not only in the pan-African camp but also across all political persuasions. This new mood can be summed up as a moment of revelation and reckoning, when black people realised that armed struggle should be placed on the table for consideration in the arsenal of means of struggle against apartheid. In Mandela's words, we had only two choices: 'Submit or fight.'

Our father chose to fight. This, then, is the lesson of Sobukwe. Whereas Sobukwe had asked the activists and followers who were to hand in the dreaded passbooks at the nearest police station to be peaceful and observe strict rules of conduct, the regime responded with brazen barbarism.

Sobukwe's pain after leading the march was my father's pain. Sobukwe was persecuted. He was silenced, jailed, and viciously isolated. Special clauses and laws were made just for the incarceration of Sobukwe, yet he endured and never yielded his faith in himself and his belief in the liberation of the Africans and their capacity to govern themselves and create just societies.

Our father corresponded with the family and tried to keep hope alive. But these were bleak days and there were terrible consequences for solidarity. It had to be expressed in secret, and it was.

Our father felt that the nation had not fully appreciated the quality and values-based leadership of Sobukwe, which had inspired and formed him at Fort Hare. He hated, in particular, leaders who did not have a sense of history or a reverence for the study of history. It is often said that great leaders are first great students of history. This love of the subject of history was something our father shared with Sobukwe at Healdtown. 'Leaders must study history,' our father would teach. He would ask how on earth leaders sought to lead if they had no understanding of where those whom they wished to lead were or where they had been.

It was then that he told us that Robert Mangaliso Sobukwe was a brilliant and honest fighter. He said that he was the hero of Sharpeville, if heroes could be identified – he and the 69 people who perished and lay bleeding to death after the apartheid regime opened fire on peaceful protesters.

He told us that Sobukwe became one of the most feared men in the country. He told us about 1960; the stand Sobukwe and many others took marching to police stations all over the country. He said the march to Parliament in Cape Town was electrifying. He told us that Sobukwe was jailed and locked away so that he would never again attempt to awaken our consciousness as a nation to the dangers of injustice and brutality.

We thought that house number 53 on Robben Island must have been the saddest house on earth. He told us that his head boy from school was a courageous man who waged a just and determined struggle. He told us how much he admired and loved him. He told us in not so many words how to endear ourselves to him by standing up to injustice.

It was not so much the dates and details of history that gripped our father's generation, but rather the history of decisions taken and the solutions chosen, and the context that gave rise to these. It was the education contained in knowing what was previously chosen as a preferred mode of thought or as a course of action that seemed important to them. This seemed to hold lessons of caution for them, and was an education in how decisions have consequences and how complex reality really is. They believed that the study of history not only held cautionary tales, but also inspired great leaders coming out of nowhere, from desolate circumstances, to lead great nations and accomplish great feats. After all, their motto at Healdtown was founded on the biblical scriptural promise: 'They will rise up with wings as eagles.'

In many senses, they were a generation who learnt how to make something out of nothing. They came from homes with no money yet they led nations. They created social movements when there was nothing but despair. They created political institutions – like the nationalist organisations – where previously there were none.

The mental toughness and fortitude demonstrated by Sobukwe in prison is legendary. He found solace in his studies and in the love of a few friends who were able to visit, such as Benjamin Pogrund. Mental fortitude and steadfastness is a feature or a characteristic that is sorely missing in our political culture at the moment – as South Africa has lost its way in a morass of theft and an orgy of gorging on state funds and corruption.

Our father despised muddle-headedness. Healdtown taught

its sons and daughters to be precise, methodical and visionary. Sobukwe, as a young student leader, had that kind of leadership clarity.

––––––––

Sobukwe demonstrated the force of this demand for mental clarity in his generation during an interview in Kimberley with Professor Gail Gerhart, when she was a graduate student at Columbia University. He told her about another contemporary, AP Mda, of whom he said: 'Mda was one man we have always admired for his brilliance and clarity of thought. He has a great gift for language, a way of using words to express ideas with complete clarity. He can untie mental knots … One could go to him with any problem, and he would analyse it for you, untie it … Compared to Mda, all of us were political babies.' Sobukwe told Gerhart that Mda appeared to him to be 'very much influenced by the writings of Lenin'.[1]

Sobukwe's own clarity and brilliance are contained in his seminal leadership moment, when he appeared to be at the peak of his vision and leadership. This is demonstrated in the directness and simplicity of his call to South Africans to rid themselves of passbooks in a mass, powerful demonstration of civil disobedience. The response was profound and reverberated throughout the country and beyond, proving that leaders must be clear-minded and direct.

Leaders must be frugal and not wasteful. Healdtown itself was founded in 1855 during a worldwide economic depression. It was a time of devastation for the Xhosa people too, following the last of eight frontier wars fought by the Xhosa people against the British. In the following year came the Nongqawuse cattle-killing episode, in which a young Xhosa prophetess managed to convince great swathes of the remaining population, desperate to defeat the British in defence of their land, that if they killed all their cattle the ancestors would rise and drive the whites into the sea. After the defeat of the indigenous people, many sought to re-ennoble themselves and redeem their fortunes through education. Thrift was a great value and extravagance was considered gauche and vulgar.

Our father told us that he hated the African meal of samp and beans because he had had too much of it in the austerity of wartime and poverty while he was a student at Healdtown. As head boy, Sobukwe was an enforcer of the no-waste rule. Extravagant and greedy leaders are dangerous. This is the lesson that beckons to us from a rereading of Sobukwe. This may appear to readers from other countries to be a trite comment on our part. But we beg their indulgence, for we have been through a period during which a grotesque administration lost our country billions of rands in an avaricious binge that wrecked the economy, significantly weakened infrastructure, and devastated the social fabric of the country.

Africa is in the grip of capricious and avaricious elites that have destroyed the golden generation's dreams of egalitarian democracy. The root of the idea of never taking more than one gives into the circle of life is an old communal African notion that has been effectively eroded by latter-day neocolonial ideologies.

———

In our day, there have been waves of anti-intellectual ideologies and practices, especially over the past decade. For these, struggle had to be radical and brutal. Politics was to be practical and muscular. But Sobukwe always saw a role for intellectuals, in the Gramscian sense of an engaged intellectual.

Here, we again turn to the Gerhart interview, in which Sobukwe says: 'At the time I first came to Johannesburg, I still didn't see myself as an activist particularly, not of the Leballo type anyway [a reference to the PAC's Potlako Leballo]. I saw myself more as an intellectual who could help back up this movement and give it some theoretical strength.' He goes on to explain that Leballo and his group were 'mainly emotional in their nationalism. They needed firmer theory, more academic grounding.'[2] At the time, Sobukwe was on the faculty at Wits University and he had offered to edit the publication called *The Africanist*.

In this extract we see a Sobukwe who believes in reasoned struggle and who cautions against crude and emotional nationalism. In this sense, he is the ultimate Enlightenment man. He believed in the importance of reason and reasoned action. He believed in the importance of being a rational agent of change, and that this would save activists from being involved in all manner of controversy and contradiction. The identity politics of our day are based on emotion and not on reason and often operate in the realm of post-truth populism.

Central to Sobukwe's self-identification was his idea of himself as an intellectual. This had been so since his intellectual and academic prowess was first identified at Healdtown. Reason and the importance of thought and ideas were central to his leadership ethos. This holds lessons for present-day leaders. Sobukwe's reputation for good, solid academic work was so strong that it had a profound effect on Healdtown, long after he had left the school on the hill. Reverend Stanley Pitts, who became Healdtown's principal four years after Sobukwe left, said that he was 'the brightest student we ever had'.

His family background and identity politics are important, and cannot be ignored. But there is more to politics than identity. This is what Robert Mangaliso Sobukwe sought to teach us – if only we would have listened during his lifetime. Today there is a resurgence of movements of young people who would have us believe that all the injustices in our society should be understood in the language of ascribed identity. Indeed, reactionary identity politics are back with a vengeance and are fuelling the rise of the right wing throughout the world.

We have read and reckoned with the assertion that contemporary identity politics is less about confronting injustice, as Sobukwe's identity politics were, and more about rebranding injustice. Only by challenging reactionary and racist identity politics can we truly challenge inequality and injustice, as Sobukwe did when he declared: 'There is only one race to which we all belong and that is the human race.'

Sobukwe was a gentle path of light. He taught us that leaders should have the highest of humanist values and the very best standards of conduct. In the end, we also learn that universalism does not succumb to relativism in Sobukwe's view, as he believed we are all members of the human race.

He teaches us today not to sacrifice reason, objectivity and the search for a just truth on the altar of political expedience or even of theoretical subjectivity. He teaches us that emotional attacks on reason will not serve us well. Reason must be met with reason. Action must be rational and well considered. We learn that while we should be proud of ourselves as Africans, fetishising our identity is a route to nowhere. We learn that we must pay greater attention to class inequalities and injustice.

The lesson of Sobukwe is to be wary of the re-emergence of anti-Enlightenment ideas, which would have us believe that different racial groups are different cognitively and have different values. He also taught us to rage on through the ages against injustice and inequality and the degradation of one human being by another. Finally, self-appropriation and self-leadership lead to the leadership of society. This is evidenced in Sobukwe's statement:

'True leadership demands complete subjugation of self, absolute honesty, integrity and uprightness of character, courage and fearlessness, and, above all, a consuming love for one's people.'

———

Healdtown was a casualty of apartheid. The Methodist Church refused to hand over the hostel buildings when the government imposed Bantu Education in the 1950s and they fell into decay.

The road map that still helps to guide us

Barney Mthombothi

Barney Mthombothi is a newspaper columnist with a career in journalism spanning four decades in print and broadcast media. He began his career at the Rand Daily Mail, *and has worked for the* Sunday Express, The Star *and the* Sunday Tribune. *He also worked as a producer at the* BBC World Service *in London. Mthombothi is a former head of news at the* SABC, *editor of the* Sunday Tribune *and of the* Financial Mail *in Johannesburg. He was a Reuters Fellow at Oxford University and a Nieman Fellow at Harvard University.*

FOUR DECADES AFTER his death, Robert Mangaliso Sobukwe, the former leader of the Pan Africanist Congress of Azania (PAC), is at last emerging from the shadows, his ideas now sought and closely scrutinised as South Africa continues its search for a lasting solution.

Land, the issue that fired his political passions, is back in the spotlight, and a solution to satisfy all shades of opinion is still elusive.

Sobukwe, 'Prof' to his admirers, was 35 years old when he was convicted and sentenced to three years in prison for leading the anti-pass campaign in March 1960. He never had a public nor a normal life after that. At the completion of his sentence he was kept, without charge or due process, in solitary confinement on Robben Island for six years before being banished to Kimberley, where he died of lung cancer in February 1978.

For the last 18 years of his life, he had a banning order slapped on him, which meant that his movements were severely curtailed and monitored. The media were not allowed to quote him, even in death. Very few of his compatriots have actually heard him speak or have any recollection of the sound of his voice. He is the only prisoner known to have been kept in custody well beyond the expiry of his sentence.

Then justice minister John Vorster's explanation to Parliament of why extraordinary measures had to be taken against Sobukwe sounded almost as if he was paying him a backhanded compliment: 'For here we are dealing with a person – let me say this – who has a strong magnetic personality, a person who can organise, a person who feels that he has a vocation to perform this task well knowing what methods will be applied.'[1]

But it seems that the National Party were not the only people fearful of Sobukwe. Since taking over government, the African National Congress (ANC) has seemed determined to keep Sobukwe in the obscurity to which the Afrikaner Nationalists consigned him. His supporters believe that there has been a deliberate attempt by the current government to have Sobukwe, who ranks alongside Nelson Mandela as a giant of the liberation struggle, airbrushed from the country's recent history.

Sobukwe had been politically active for only a little over ten years before he was silenced. Apart from a few speeches, there is very little of his writing available. Nor are there any recordings of his voice. It is therefore remarkable that his ideas have not only survived – despite all the attempts to suppress them – but also seem to be enjoying something of a renaissance, decades after he was cut off from the people he saw as his life's mission to serve. His life was cut short at just 53, but his ideas endure.

Ideas are like seeds. Once planted, they need to be constantly nurtured and watered in order to germinate and grow, and then to bloom and bear fruit. Without proper nourishment, they don't germinate, or if they do, the plant becomes stunted, withers and dies.

The extraordinary thing about Sobukwe is the fact that his ideas, having been ignored for decades, or sown on what seemed like barren soil, didn't perish. They are sprouting anew, despite the fact that he was not around to tend the orchard, and nor was his party, the PAC, which never recovered after it was outlawed following the Sharpeville massacre.

Sobukwe had warned before the campaign – he described the 'dompas' (passbook) as the distinctive badge of slavery – against using ordinary people as cannon fodder: 'When we embark on a campaign, it will be the leaders who will be in front. They will not remain behind while the masses rot in jail.'

The sentiment was well-intentioned, but it was to prove to be the party's undoing. And so, on 21 March, the leaders led marchers to various police stations, where they were duly arrested and many convicted. The PAC never recovered from that blunder. The leadership was almost eliminated. Because the party was hardly a year old when it took on the state and was crushed, it meant that, when its leaders were sent to jail, there were few cadres, if any, who could step into their shoes. Those who were able to elude the dragnet went into exile, where the party spent years fighting damaging internal battles. This infighting further undermined its ability to spread its ideas.

It is not generally known that the PAC in fact had a higher public profile than the ANC in the immediate aftermath of the crackdown. Poqo, its armed wing, formed after Sobukwe's imprisonment, continued for a while with acts of sabotage, especially in the eastern Cape. But the tables were turned in exile, thanks to the divisions within the PAC. The organisation was also seen as more radical and anti-white, a message that was obviously difficult to sell in Western capitals.

The ANC, meanwhile, capitalised on the PAC's difficulties, appointing itself as the sole authentic representative of the people of South Africa. It even used to refuse to share a stage with the PAC, or to attend any function involving the lesser-known South African exile groups. The ANC's aim, it seems, was not only to isolate the South African government but to throw the PAC into the bargain as well. It also used this tactic to good effect once in power.

After the banning of the two organisations, black people were left without a credible voice. The government moved quickly to fill the void, implementing its Bantustan policy wherein each tribe or so-called nation would exercise its rights or opt for independence as a 'free nation'. However, such a policy did not find favour with the black majority and the leaders of these 'homelands' were largely dismissed as apartheid stooges.

It was not until the emergence of Steve Biko's Black Consciousness Movement (BCM) a few years later that a semblance of resistance to government policy took shape. The BCM had a close ideological affinity with the PAC. Like the PAC, the BCM also referred to South Africa as 'Azania'. Biko, although banned, could have visited Sobukwe in Kimberley. The two leaders had a lot in common. Most of the BC ideas are no different from those espoused by Sobukwe. As Benjamin Pogrund, Sobukwe's biographer, correctly stated in a tribute, which was never paid: '[It] was he who took the ideas of Black Consciousness – so vital towards the gaining of freedom for all our peoples – and developed and refined them.' The ANC handily won the propaganda war as the representative of the people of South Africa. Although its armed struggle against the government didn't amount to much, that too was useful for its propaganda value. And Mandela, imprisoned on Robben Island, became a potent symbol of resistance.

With Sobukwe silenced and his party involved in self-destruction, there was bound to be one winner when the liberation movements were finally unbanned and negotiations for a new dispensation began. The PAC was literally drowned out. Its mediocre leadership had very little impact on negotiations. Its ideas or policies hardly featured.

The attack on the St James Anglican Church in Kenilworth, Cape Town, by members of the Azanian People's Liberation Army (Apla), the PAC's military wing, in July 1993, in which 11 worshippers were killed and many were wounded, was a turning point. The attack was seen by some as an attempt by the organisation to boost its negotiating muscle at the Codesa negotiations. If so, it backfired spectacularly.

The hostility between the two organisations was such that, during the Codesa negotiations, the ANC initially came out against the inclusion of 21 March (the day of the Sharpeville massacre) on a new list of public holidays, because it was viewed as giving credit to the PAC, only to back down after a public outcry.

Winston Churchill was right: history is written by the victors. Once in power, the ANC went about renaming just about everything after its leaders and their friends – streets, dams, universities, squatter camps, airports, municipalities. This has extended even to national awards, such as the Order of Luthuli, the Order of the Companions of OR Tambo, etc. African leaders such as Kenneth Kaunda and Samora Machel were also similarly immortalised. Even lesser-known political activists have been honoured. But not Sobukwe. He was a threat even in death.

The ANC wanted to emphasise what they regard as an indisputable fact: that they were the only liberators. The sacrifices of Sobukwe and others who paid with their lives were ignored and forgotten simply because they were of a different ideological stripe. This has been a sore point for many of Sobukwe's supporters. Freedom was supposed to be inclusive. But the ANC government's decisions and actions in this regard have been divisive.

But the situation is changing. There is a renewed interest in Sobukwe and the issues that defined his political life, especially the land question and the reunification of Africa.

What is it, then, that makes people take a shine to Sobukwe? Various factors. After 25 years of freedom, people have suddenly discovered that their new leaders have feet of clay. They are as fallible as the apartheid lot they replaced. The condition of ordinary people has not changed much; in fact, in some respects it has worsened. Unemployment stands at just under 30 per cent, and over 50 per cent among the youth. Apartheid used to be the biggest cause of emigration. People are still leaving, but now rampant crime is the trigger. And it shows no sign of abating.

But perhaps the biggest downer is the level of corruption, especially involving cabinet ministers and other senior government officials. Corruption, which reached epic proportions during Jacob Zuma's presidency, has seriously undermined public confidence in government. Even more dispiriting is the seeming lack of consequences for wrongdoing.

Probably due to its long stay in power, the ANC has also been affected by ideological confusion or dissonance. The party has lost its swagger and certainty. Power – and its perks – is the only glue that seems to be keeping the party together.

The old veterans involved in the ideological skirmishes that led to the breakaway of the PAC from the ANC have long departed the political stage. The acrimony of that separation is now but a distant memory. The younger generation carries no such scars or burdens. Unlike their elders, who are already set in their ways, the youth tend, if anything, to be more receptive to new and radical creeds and ideas for solutions. Leaders such as Sobukwe, Biko, Che Guevara, Thomas Sankara, etc, are viewed as idols, not as outcasts to be shunned. There is also a misguided belief gaining ground among a significant section of the youth that the 1994 agreement that ushered in South Africa's new democracy was a fraud and a sellout, and should therefore be supplanted.

Public disillusionment therefore causes people to look around for alternatives. People are rediscovering Sobukwe's ideas, and they find them appealing.

Apart from the old guard sauntering off into the sunset, thus allowing the younger generation space to look at Sobukwe with new eyes, Thabo Mbeki, as ANC leader, also started blurring the ideological differences between the two organisations. He made clear his intentions to embrace a more pan-Africanist approach when, as deputy president, he delivered his now-famous 'I am an African' speech at the inauguration of the country's new Con-stitution in 1996.

Taking over from Mandela three years later, he moved the party firmly into territory previously occupied by the PAC. He not only saw himself as the voice in global affairs of a derided continent and its diaspora, but also, in a sense, became the obvious inheritor of the mantle of Sobukwe, encouraging South Africans to embrace an African identity and to reject a so-called South African exceptionalism – just as Sobukwe had done four decades before.

Mbeki's ideological outlook was closer to Sobukwe than it was to Mandela, Albert Luthuli and even Oliver Tambo – for years his mentor in exile. Mbeki's passionate championing of what he called the African Renaissance, an attempt to reintegrate Africa into the global agenda, also harks back to Sobukwe's vision – and to Kwame Nkrumah's before him – of a politically united and centrally administered continent, speaking with one voice. 'World civilisation will not be complete until the African has made his full contribution,' Sobukwe had said in that speech at Fort Hare in 1949 that announced him as a star of the future.[2]

Nothing preoccupied Sobukwe's mind more than the land question. The African, he insisted, would not truly be free until the land was returned to its rightful owners. It was the Freedom Charter that led to the Africanists leaving the ANC because, they claimed, the Charter was an imposition by the (white) Congress of Democrats.

Potlako Leballo, who became PAC leader after Sobukwe was jailed, expressed the general sentiments of the Africanists when he was quoted by the publication *Contact* in November 1958: 'The African people in general do not want to be allied with the Congress of Democrats. They know these people to be leftists and when we want to fight for our rights, these people weaken us. We also oppose the ANC's adherence to the Freedom Charter. The Charter is a foreign ideology not based on African nationalism.'

But the Africanists' bitterest animus was reserved for a section in the Charter's opening sentence that says, among others, 'South Africa belongs to all who live in it, black and white ...' That, ultimately, is what led to the split – the land question. Sobukwe said the land was being 'auctioned for sale'.

'We have come to the parting of the ways,' he said, 'and we are here and now giving notice that we are dissociating ourselves from the ANC ...' Land therefore became the PAC's rallying cry. 'I-Afrika, izwe lethu! Izwe lethu, i-Afrika!' (Africa, our land! Our land, Africa!) became a very emotive slogan, and in it is encapsulated the two dominant pillars of Sobukwe's ideology: the return of the land to those he regarded as its rightful owners; and the freeing the continent from foreign rule, leading ultimately to what he hoped would be a united and prosperous Africa.

John Vorster may have been mesmerised by Sobukwe's magnetic personality, but probably what frightened him the most was the appeal – and the directness – of Sobukwe's message and the uncompromising language he used. '[W]hite supremacy, under whatever guise it manifests itself, must be destroyed,' Sobukwe had said in his inaugural address as PAC president in 1959. He could not have been more unambiguous.

Sobukwe was not only throwing the lot of black South Africans in with the rest of the continent but he was also linking it with the struggles for black emancipation in other parts of the world, approvingly quoting George Padmore, a radical West Indian communist and one of the drivers of the pan-Africanist movement at the time. Such a breadth of thinking must have sent a chill down the spines of apartheid's ideologues.

He was nobody's poodle either, decrying Soviet communism just as fiercely as he detested Western imperialism.

Land – or landlessness – has always been the fuel that has fired up black resistance to apartheid. Although it was the exclusion of any black involvement in the Union of South Africa in 1910 that led to the formation of the ANC two years later, it was in fact the 1913 Natives Land Act that galvanised black opposition to white rule. Until that point, some black opinion-makers were still hoping for a change of heart among the new rulers. But the Land Act was a game-changer. It restricted the black majority to only 13 per cent of the land for the first time in the country's history. The psychological impact of that reality cannot be overstated.

But the ANC leadership at the time persisted with a policy of persuasion, working within the system and sending delegation after delegation to London to plead their case with the Crown. These efforts bore no fruit. It was not until the adoption of the Programme of Action in 1949, at the instigation of its Youth League, that the ANC embarked on more radical mass action, in the form of strikes and boycotts, and eschewing participation in state-created institutions.

Two seminal events were the direct results of this new approach: the Defiance Campaign of 1952, which in turn led to the wholesale arrest and prosecution of the entire leadership of the Congress Alliance in what became known as the Treason Trial; and the adoption in 1955 of the Freedom Charter, the ANC's policy bible.

It was of course in response to the Freedom Charter that Sobukwe led the Africanists out of the ANC in 1958 to form the PAC. And land, or its repossession, became the new party's stock in trade.

By the time the liberation movements were unbanned and negotiations began in earnest in the early 1990s, the PAC was already a spent force, having cannibalised itself in exile. But land as an emotive political issue didn't go away. It was as though Sobukwe was speaking from the grave.

The constitutional compromise reached at Codesa seemed for a while to be holding. Property rights were guaranteed, but the government would buy land from white farmers for distribution to black people on the basis of 'willing buyer, willing seller'.

The restitution programme could have worked, but there were too many obstacles. It was underfunded. Corruption meant that many farms ended up in the wrong hands, especially those of government bureaucrats. Many of the beneficiaries lacked basic skills, and as a result many of these farms lay fallow and agricultural production suffered.

It was a matter of time before somebody made political hay out of these shortcomings. In 2010, Julius Malema, as head of the ANC Youth League, visited Zimbabwe and was charmed by Robert Mugabe's ruinous land policies, suggesting that they held an important lesson for South Africa. Malema was later expelled from the ANC, but for reasons that were unrelated to being Uncle Bob's eager praise-singer.

When Malema founded his own party, the Economic Freedom Fighters (EFF), land was at the top of his agenda. He rubbished the Constitution, describing Mandela as a sellout for agreeing to allow white people to hold on to their property. The EFF, he said, would campaign for expropriation of land without compensation. The idea seemed so far-fetched that at first nobody gave it any chance of success. And it would have been a dud but for the ANC leadership contest at the end of 2017. In fact, when Malema brought it up in Parliament, the ANC voted against the resolution. But Jacob Zuma, in a desperate effort to derail Cyril Ramaphosa's bid to succeed him, stole Malema's line and urged the ANC conference to vote in favour of expropriation without compensation. Ramaphosa went on to triumph against Nkosazana Dlamini-Zuma, but he lost the battle of ideas. Land expropriation without compensation became ANC policy. When the EFF reintroduced the motion in Parliament, the ANC had no alternative but to vote for it.

But the resolution has left Ramaphosa with a headache. His appeal stems from the fact that he is seen as the leader best qualified to revive the economy. No investor in his right mind would want to put his money where property rights are not guaranteed. Ramaphosa's indecent rush to assure King Goodwill Zwelithini that Zulu land in his trusteeship would not be expropriated – after the king had threatened to go to war – then begs the question: which land then will be expropriated? What will be the criteria? Will such a discriminatory law pass constitutional muster?

The move also seems to be dividing the ANC. In a blistering 30-page document, Thabo Mbeki accuses his party of abandoning its 'historical mission' of uniting the people of South Africa, and is now no different from the PAC. He sarcastically says this is tantamount to the ANC rewriting the Freedom Charter to now say: 'South Africa belongs to all who live in it, black and white, except as this relates to land; and, all national groups are equal before the law, except as this concerns land.' Meanwhile, the EFF, pleased by the fact that it is punching above its weight, has adopted Sobukwe as its new hero. In 2017, marking 40 years since his death, the party said it celebrated 'the revolutionary life of Sobukwe with immense reverence. Sobukwe's stance on the expropriation of land with no compensation is one that is encapsulated in the EFF's seven pillars. His moral compass is undeniably the ground on which the country should walk.'[3]

The EFF is claiming Sobukwe for itself, but I don't think Sobukwe believed in the wholesale nationalisation of the land, as the EFF does. The EFF wants all land to be owned by the government. There would be no private land ownership if it were to come into power. People would have to lease land from the government. Under such a scheme, even black people would be worse off than they were under apartheid. There would be no economy to speak of without the right to own property.

Sobukwe was a sober, rational man. He obviously wanted African people to get their land back. But he was also aware that the economy needed to grow if people were to be lifted out of poverty. The cake needs to rise before it can be shared equitably. Responding to pessimists who feared chaos and savagery after freedom was attained, he said he instead foresaw 'the creation of a United Africa and the advent of a new era of freedom, creative production and abundance'. It is difficult to imagine how abundant productivity could be achieved in an environment where private property barely exists or private initiative is either curtailed or discouraged.

But the PAC was very young and its policies were still evolving or at a formative stage at the time it was banned. Sobukwe's subsequent incarceration, exile on Robben Island and banishment didn't help matters. The natural growth process was stifled.

———————

Sobukwe was as forthright with regard to South Africa and Africa's destiny as he was on the land question. Even during those early years, with struggles against colonial rule mushrooming in many parts of the continent, he envisaged the creation of a united Africa under one administration.

In a speech in May 1959, a month after the formation of the PAC, he called on his compatriots to reject what he called 'South African exceptionalism', that is, the notion that the country was different – and even better – than the rest of the continent: 'We who are Pan African in outlook do not subscribe to the doctrine of South African exceptionalism and are committed to Pan Africanism and a Union of African States, which we would like to see as a unitary, centrally controlled organic whole.'

Elsewhere, he was blunter, almost provocative, saying it was 'the sacred duty' of every African state to strive ceaselessly for the creation of a United States of Africa, stretching from Cape to Cairo, from Morocco to Madagascar. 'The days of small, independent countries are gone,' he said.

It was quite a bold statement to make. But he was not only putting the cart before the horse; it was also pie in the sky. Fanciful. It may have been an ideal, but it is still not feasible. At the time, only a few African countries, such as Ethiopia, Liberia and of course Ghana, were independent. The rest were still waging freedom struggles against colonial rule. It was inconceivable therefore that these countries would get rid of their colonial masters at great human cost only to sacrifice their newfound autonomy on the altar of African unity. It simply defied logic. Sobukwe argued that the creation of a centrally controlled unit would make it easier for the continent to solve the massive challenges it faced. Not so. In fact, it would make the task even more difficult. A united Africa would be huge and cumbersome, distant and even aloof from the people it serves.

As recent history has shown, it has been difficult even for neighbouring countries to unite for their common good, as was the case with Senegal and Gambia. Tanzania (Tanganyika plus Zanzibar) has so far been a success, but many countries have found it difficult to hold together, for the simple reason that people who don't belong together were thrown together by colonial diktat. Some countries, such as Ethiopia, Sudan and Somalia, have had to be broken up due to civil wars. Others, such as the Democratic Republic of Congo, Cameroon and even Nigeria, are barely holding together. Civil wars have created instability that has set back the continent's progress by many years.

Black South Africans have shown great antipathy towards the African migrants who have flocked to this country since it opened its borders to the continent. Xenophobic incidents occur regularly, in which foreigners, mostly Africans, are killed. Such scenes would have shocked and distressed Sobukwe. Expressions of African fellowship by leaders are not always shared by ordinary people on the ground. A continent-wide government is therefore out of the question. So many factors would militate against its success. It would contain within it the seeds of its own destruction.

Moreover, what Sobukwe referred to as South African exceptionalism is what many people would regard as simple patriotism, that is, love of one's country. He conflated his country's interests with those of the continent. As far as he was concerned, South Africa did not necessarily come first. It's a sentiment that can be discerned in Thabo Mbeki's African Renaissance. South Africa is never a stand-alone; it is always seen within a continental context. But one can love one's country without being jingoistic about it. One cannot be of a continent without belonging to a country. The country is the origination of one's continental affinity or affiliation; it therefore must take precedence.

Sobukwe correctly intimated that Africa should avoid aligning itself with either the West or the Eastern Bloc, but instead seek to serve its own interests, an echo perhaps of Lord Palmerston's famous injunction that in international relations a country has no permanent friends or permanent enemies, only permanent interests. The need to speak with one voice does not mean that 55 sovereign states should be bound by one government. Cooperation rather than integration can in fact achieve better results.

And indeed, in 1963, in Addis Ababa, 32 African countries, in pursuit of the goal of speaking with one voice, founded the Organization of African Unity (OAU). But the OAU, which became the African Union (AU) in 2002, has dismally failed to live up to its original billing. It tends to see its role as the defence of despots and dictators rather than the advancement of the interests of its citizens. More useful and relevant to the needs of its member states are regional bodies such as the Economic Community of West African States (Ecowas) and the Southern African Development Community (SADC). In March 2018, African leaders signed a framework establishing the African Continental Free Trade Area, which aims to create a single market for goods and services. It is hoped that such a treaty will encourage intra-African trade, which is still surprisingly weak after decades of independence.

Arrangements such as these, fostering better relations and co-operation between independent nation-states, are likely to be more fruitful than collapsing the entire continent under one centrally controlled government, as suggested by Sobukwe. As Tip O'Neill, legendary Speaker of the US House of Representatives, was wont to say, all politics is local. Government has to be closer to its people in order to be effective and more responsive.

Sobukwe was optimistic, bullish even, about the future after Africa attained its independence. He did not mince his words: 'By the end of the century,' he wrote, 'the standard of living of the masses of the people will have risen dramatically.'

Probably by talking a good game, he was hoping people would behave accordingly. If that was the case, the trick didn't work.

He could not have been further from the truth. But we have the benefit of hindsight. The colonialists are gone, but instead of rebuilding their countries, the natives have turned on each other. Civil wars have killed millions, and millions more have sought refuge in neighbouring countries and beyond. The continent has the highest number of displaced persons on earth. The new rulers are even more corrupt than the colonialists they replaced. South Africa, which stood a better chance than most of a brighter future, is almost on its knees due to corruption of epic proportions. Sobukwe would have been disgusted by the scale of the looting. This surely is not what he struggled and sacrificed his life for.

With his active political life drastically curtailed by imprisonment and official restrictions, Sobukwe was nevertheless able to leave us a road map that helps to guide us. The issues he raised still cry out for attention. It is a pity, though, that we have been deprived of the benefits of his thoughts and insights later in life. Being the restless spirit that he was, he must have spent those solitary years – he was in virtual isolation for the last 18 years of his life – mulling over the issues confronting his country. Were there any tweaks, twists and turns from his original thinking? And how could these have influenced the course of events? Sadly, we shall never know.

Making our way through expectations, demands, fears and hurts

Paul Verryn

Paul Verryn was ordained as a Methodist Church minister in 1973, and was Bishop of the Central District from 1996 to 2009. He works extensively with vulnerable communities across southern Africa. During apartheid, he gave refuge to young people threatened by the security police. He champions the rights of migrants and victims of South African xenophobia and works with prisons to provide victim–offender dialogues. He was awarded an honorary doctorate by Nelson Mandela University in 2009.

MANGALISO SOBUKWE is hailed as the icon of the Pan Africanist Congress (PAC). At a time when many are idolised and revered as almost perfect, his legacy of humility and bold servant leadership offers a stark contrast. His contribution in his context is remarkable, particularly in light of the fact that apartheid assumed that blacks knew and understood their supposed inferiority as a fact of life. He enabled a completely different imagining of his humanity: in the face of humiliation, he offered an assertiveness that was surprising for all who encountered him. This clarity of his truth broke the chains of his oppression.

He regarded himself as equal to everyone and therefore enabled everyone to be rescued from self-inflicted negation. His fundamental point of departure was that all were created in the image of God and that all deserved to be treated with respect. In a context where this concept was anathema to some, his insistence on it as a fundamental construct of relationships was revolutionary. In a country where segregation because of race was the norm, his philosophy, or theology, was absurd. His invitation to all people to see the other as equal was preposterous. How dare this less-than-human claim the same dignity, the same rights, the same essence for black and white alike? How dare he?!

I can remember sitting at the feet of Julia Nkadimeng, who worked for my family, and being told about the pass laws. She would describe to me the fear of ordinary people of the police as they began to scrutinise the passes, arrest defaulters, and force them into their vans for trial and imprisonment. I can recall the feelings of disgrace and humiliation at being imprisoned. I can remember as a boy being outraged at this bullying intimidation, and at the same time being frustrated that I could do nothing about this injustice. I understood why, at times, Julia was late for work. I would argue with my mother, who had no clue at that stage of the ramifications of this legislation and who would complain endlessly of Julia's irresponsible lateness.

The pass legislation was degrading to everybody. To black people, it carried the implication of illegitimacy in the land of their birth; to white people it proved their illegitimacy in terms of their humanity. Furthermore, the so-called system of law and order was used to perpetuate lavish injustice. The system also succeeded in ensuring that blacks were seen as criminals, really just because they were blacks. No such legislation was in place for whites, because they belonged. What enabled this madness?

Mangaliso Sobukwe was not bewitched by this construct of humanity. He refused to accept this nonsense as legitimate or true and began to raise consciousness around this matter, firstly, for black people. He dared to spark their awareness in a way that asserted the dignity of all people. In an unequal society, this was outrageous! He dared to break the shackles of oppression by initiating a campaign that encouraged the destruction of passes. After this act of defiance, people would make their way to police stations for voluntary arrest. They had broken the law! They were no longer going to participate in their oppression voluntarily. This demonstration of passive resistance incensed the authorities, who unleashed the full force of their vindictiveness. More than 60 people were assassinated in Sharpeville. Most were shot in the back as they ran for protection from the police. Sobukwe was deeply pained by this loss of life. He was profoundly committed to nonviolence in his search for freedom.

About thirty or more years later, I was conducting hearings in Sharpeville, in parallel with those of the Truth and Reconciliation Commission (TRC) and intended to capture what the TRC, because of its constraints, was not able to capture but which carried significant pain for communities. Some NGOs initiated the opportunity, particularly in the Vaal, where the devastation of slaughter still left huge scarring on communities. People gathered in the hall of the Catholic church, recounted their stories, and tried to find some closure for their pain. An elderly widow began recalling the fateful day. She remembered watching her husband, a teacher, leave for school and wondering, as she saw him walk out of the yard, whether this might be the last time. She knew that he was involved in organising the protest against the pass laws and was concerned for his safety. She waited that afternoon for his return. They had heard what had happened and that people had been killed by the police. That was as far as she could speak on that first day. It was the first time she had told her story in a public forum since it had happened.

She returned weeks later and resumed her narrative. He had not returned home and she and the rest of the family began their search. She checked with work colleagues, with political connections and with anyone who could throw some light on his whereabouts. All to no avail. She then began to go from clinic to clinic, from hospital to hospital. He was nowhere to be found. There seemed to be no relief to her dreadful anxiety. Had her premonition come true? She again stopped the narrative ...

She returned a few weeks later, reminded us of her previous account, and continued. Eventually, she had made her way to the police station with part of her family and waited for attention. She was shown to the back of the station by a rather abrupt official who opened the door to a room that was full of bodies. He kicked the head of one of the bodies and told them that if they made a noise or cried they would join the dead. The head that he kicked was that of her husband. Her ravaging sadness filled the room as if the tragedy had just happened.

No words can adequately describe this cataclysmic disgrace. And that this could happen in a country that claimed to be so profoundly religious! In that moment of history, whites lost their right to govern in the way they had imagined. They abdicated the sacred responsibility they had for the care of the people of South Africa, both black and white, and gave vent to the darkness of their racist fear and bigoted ideology. The most dangerous dimension of what was unfolding was an entrenching of hatred between black and white. To think that this happened just 15 years after the devastation of the Second World War. Were whites unable to remember the shameful horror of what had happened because of a fascist regime?

———

So often the Black Consciousness movement is misrepresented as a movement that rejects whites out of hand. However, Sobukwe very clearly articulated a new consciousness as a paradigm that would confront what was diminishing for whites and simultaneously affirm the sanctity of black and white alike. What was meant in this journey was an affirmation of diversity and a restlessness in our being until that diversity asserted itself – radically.

I cannot be fully white unless I include my black counterpart as equal in every respect to myself. I cannot be fully black unless I include my white counterpart as equal in every respect to myself. One of the reasons his white counterparts despised Sobukwe so profoundly was that he refused to recognise them as unquestionably superior. They were his equal and he insisted on living that truth without remainder. This attitude threatened the very ground of their existence, their sacred politics and, therefore, their belief that they had sole right to the riches of South Africa. He confronted them with a gigantic existential crisis. They could not, and would not, confront their insecurity and vulnerability. The use of violence on that awful day in March 1960 betrayed the fact that the state had very few resources to imagine anything other than the stale and uninventive use of violence to defend the indefensible. In that moment they lost all authority.

Fortunately, we have matured remarkably and miraculously since those very foolish days. Perhaps one fact could disturb our seamless equilibrium. Since the turn of the century, South Africa has been flooded by refugees and migrants from all over Africa. The issue of legitimacy is a great challenge for these vulnerable and sometimes deeply traumatised people. In roadblocks and raids that are reminiscent of the 1950s and 1960s, officials scrutinise the documents of our visitors, and the results lead to incarceration in Lindela, our deportation centre, and a speedy return to their country of origin. The return is often not as benign as we may think, particularly when the reason for their coming to South Africa has been to escape horrendous persecution.

What is puzzling is that this kind of treatment is not the

experience of white migrants or refugees. When, in the recent release of figures claiming success in Operation Fiela (literally, 'Clean Up'), success was claimed by the police for having identified many undocumented migrants, who could now probably look forward to deportation. The 'clean-up' was intended to pursue criminals and deal with them through due process. What has effectively happened is that black migrants have been targeted and identified as the unwanted criminal element in society. In an already damaged society, xenophobia is predictable, and it seems as if a ghost from our past has resurrected itself. Just as in the days of the pass law, when blacks were regarded as essentially criminal, so too now the narrative reflects the same prejudice.

Of course, for the asylum seeker or the refugee, indeed the migrant, the constant alienation and rejection have sustained traumatic effects. One of the church buildings at one stage housed over 3 000 displaced people, mostly foreign migrants, when it was decided to evict them. The event was very painful for the community. They had been warned that the situation was untenable and also that, for the church, the season for housing them had come to an end. One small family, a South African mother and her five children, found themselves homeless and in the next years moved from one place to another. The youngest children were twins. On one fateful day, one of the twins was killed by a falling wall – part of a building that should no longer have stood because of its precarious condition. The mother sat for hours clinging to the lifeless body of her child and did not want the ambulance to remove the sacred trust she had lost. Somehow, the fragility of our humanity and the carelessness of our relationships stands in stark contrast to Sobukwe's insistence that all human beings must have a place of belonging and be protected against a politics that inadvertently prefers one kind of person above the other.

An obvious feature of Black Consciousness emphasised the

intrinsic value of the cultures of all who live in Africa. One of the effects of the colonial era was to annihilate local culture as barbaric. At one stage, the politically correct culture was white, English and Western – whatever that entailed. An interesting rebellion against the English colonial was the emergence of an Afrikaner consciousness and the development of its own brand of belonging. In this community there certainly was a resentment of British arrogance and dismissiveness. Although the seedbed of apartheid was the Afrikaner community, the English embraced the anomaly wholeheartedly. The common enemy was black people. Sobukwe's resistance to the demolition of his culture was an affront to those who could not conceptualise anything other than their own stereotype.

Black people found in this affirmation of the intrinsic wisdom and truth in black culture a life-giving vision of an identity that could not be smothered by another apparently dominant system. Black became beautiful. Black mattered. Blacks had an enormous contribution to make to the formation of a new humanity. In fact, if humanity chose to ignore what it meant to be black and human, it would compromise its integrity. Generally, white people could not conceptualise a black person as having any rights at all, and saw this assertiveness of value as cheeky and absurd.

This affirmation of the practice of black culture sustained sanity in a world that disrupted family life. For instance, in a system of migrant labour, the cultural rhythms of the community often affirmed the dignity of the human being. In initiation rites, people's worth was assured in the face of constant degradation and disrespect. A wonderful network of practices secured black identity as right and good and exceptionally enjoyable!

No wonder that the clarity with which Sobukwe saw the worth of black people challenged the validity of a policy that was so monumentally short-sighted. He was inviting the world to a completely new opportunity. For most, this was a revolution in the truest sense of the word. He epitomised what fascists most feared – the sacred equality of all people. He exposed the nonsense of their politics – its gross inefficiency and absurd waste of human potential. He ridiculed the tenuous nature of the economy and the madness of alienating 80 per cent of the country's people from being able to realise and use their gifts for the benefit of all the world, and particularly of Africa. He insisted that the black person should participate fully in all aspects of life – politics, the economy, education, health, sport, life in all its dimensions. He warned strongly against any form of dependency, insisting that the begging bowl was an insult to one's personhood. He despised servility, but insisted that servanthood, in the biblical sense, was noble. He showed respect to all, and this left those who persecuted him with no valid reason for their actions.

———————

The Methodist Church proudly claims Sobukwe as one of its preachers. His journey in faith was not a separate dimension of his politics. In fact, some might be so bold as to claim that part of his insight derived from his faith journey. If one visits the Methodist church in Galeshewe in Kimberley, those who remember Sobukwe will show you where he sat for worship every Sunday.

He struggled to sustain his relationship with God in the face of years of meaningless incarceration and humiliation. Although this kind of treatment is still part of the political experience in many countries today, it nonetheless remains a particularly spiteful way of engaging those whose insights carry the foresight needed to craft the future political landscape of a nation. The separation from those he loved, and the waste of his potential as a leader, will always represent some of the more serious crimes against humanity. His loss of faith is one of the sacrifices he made for his fight against a system that justified its existence by using the very same scriptures that enabled his preaching. He was critical of the Methodist Church for its complicity in the racist narrative. When one would have expected something different from the Church, it cooper-ated with the apartheid system by placing only white ministers in white congregations and black ministers in black congregations. Even after the demise of apartheid, the Church still struggles with its divisions along lines of race. Although some exceptions are made, the Church has a long way to go in celebrating this legendary teacher who insisted on the inherent dignity of all and insisted that our integrity be found in our learning to respect our diversity.

Of critical importance to Sobukwe's political discourse was his insistence that the land needed to be justly redistributed to include very specifically the marginalised black community. Some of the most painful memories of the oppression of the black communities relate to the land expropriation that formed part of the apartheid mechanism. In our present journey as a nation, this injustice still haunts our leaders and promises to be one of the most vexed problems to be resolved. A cursory glance at the geography of the country will show millions of black people still living in shack towns and villages everywhere. Of course, the memory of the land grabs in Zimbabwe loom large on this horizon and people do understand the fact that if there ever could be a reason for a civil war, this would be its starting point. There are still stories that punctuate our present news of communities being moved, but fortunately our human-rights laws prevent, or should prevent, eviction into homelessness.

A court record exposes a community in Marievale who were evicted from their homes at 3.30 am in November 2017. The eviction took place at gunpoint and no alternative accommodation was offered. Needless to say, the community has been shattered by the cynical approach of the authorities, and the slow process of the courts has further exacerbated the pain of the community. The old tactics have been used to divide the community by giving access to water, for instance, to some. Many in the community speak of a 'futurelessness' and loss of dignity. Two members of the community have committed suicide, and their deaths have been understood as being directly related to these events.

Another incident is recorded in the Western Cape, where a grandfather was speaking to his granddaughter about the history of the family. He was telling her about a forced removal that had hurt the family deeply. They travelled in his motor vehicle so that he could show her the exact place of his birth. They arrived at the spot and he pointed across the road to the house where he began his life's journey. They parked for a while just opposite the house and absorbed the atmosphere of the place. It was a sacred moment of remembrance. A woman came out of the house and shouted at them across the road: 'Please remove your car. That is where my husband parks his car when he comes home for lunch.' They moved off. Identity, land and belonging will have to be unravelled if we are to find a sustainable peace.

A central question in this matter is how we negotiate our way through many, many expectations, fears, demands, hurts and betrayals. Options to consider might be whether opening a tribunal to listen and discern a way forward is best, or whether we first need to chart a course of healing that enables some of the poison of our past to be expunged. There are those who hope that the status quo will remain indefinitely and others who think that war is the only way to solve a matter as intricate and intractable as this one. The frustrations are escalating. Sobukwe somehow predicted this moment in time.

————

Another feature of Sobukwe's wisdom was in envisaging a new definition of nationhood. Aware of the heritage of colonialism, he proposed a cooperation, particularly in the subcontinent, that would imply a blurring of the given boundaries. One of the results, intended or not, of the present divisions in nationhood has resulted in South Africa being quite isolated from the rest of the continent. I have heard a Kenyan alleging that South Africa, in a sense, is not really part of Africa. We don't seem to understand the continent on which we find ourselves.

One of the benefits of the journey of so many migrants to this country is that we have been exposed to the music, the food, the languages, the intellect, the cultures, the children, the colours, the dancing and, of course, the stunning, undisclosed beauty of the continent. As noted before, one of the most tragic phenomena that has blighted South Africa in recent years has been the scourge of xenophobia. The government has reinforced the narrative not only through its pursuit of black foreign nationals as if they were criminals, but also in the monumental inefficiency of government departments in processing their struggle for legitimacy. In addition, the national protests against poor service delivery have been characterised consistently by attacks on foreign nationals' businesses and the looting of their shops.

These aberrations have also been consistently ignored by the police. The shocking criminality has gone unchecked and, worse still, has reinforced the victimisation of some of the most broken in our midst. Sobukwe's pan-Africanist philosophy opens all sorts of possibilities for the future economic development of this continent. Unfortunately, the global suspicion of foreigners militates against this new way of seeing the other. It is far easier to build into the consciousness a wall that excludes and vilifies the Mexican, say, than to understand the causes of wanting to escape a context of hopelessness. It is far easier to suspect and reject the other than to seek a harmony in our differences. It does seem as if a separatist mindset controls our imagination, and what seemed so reasonable about our divided history has embedded itself in our future. The other epitomises the enemy.

To illustrate: after the xenophobic camps had been closed in the Johannesburg area, many young people found themselves homeless and on the streets. A school was opened in Albert Street, close to the city centre, to try and ensure that the lives of these young people would not be wasted, and more importantly, that they would not learn their future from the streets. The school has had constant difficulties with registration and funding. Teachers have taught 'sacrificially' and the school has achieved quite outstanding results in the final examinations. In 2017, it achieved the top position as a school in the O-level Cambridge examinations. The school caters for South Africans as well as foreign nationals. It makes special provision for the children of disabled parents. This constitutes a glimmer of hope in a desert of despair.

Sobukwe's vision of the unlocking of the potential of this continent can begin an endeavour that could breathe new life into a tepid and stale politics. In many of the countries in the southern African region, divisions along tribal and ethnic lines threaten political stability and economic development. Some of the most dreadful records of human-rights violations impede sensible progress and disable the trust needed to address the problems of social and economic inequity. The political impact of our different cultures, value systems, developmental priorities, intrinsic wisdom and unspoken prejudices needs to be unravelled, analysed and understood. Careful and deliberate healing processes need to be negotiated so that relationships of integrity can be forged for the future. Sobukwe seemed insistent that we should not blur over our differences, but that difference must be acknowledged and respected to open a new way of interaction. The temptation is to overlook difference for the sake of progress. The premise is that the focus on difference necessarily divides and alienates. The argument is that this paradigm stresses a competitive confrontation and undermines efficient advancement. The alternative argument is, of course, that ignoring difference escalates tension and builds mistrust. The present political milieu suggests that much of our identity is found in our difference from each other. However, the proper affirmation of our unique difference is where our true strength resides.

The unnamed tensions that exist between the Shona and Ndebele in Zimbabwe are far worse than the acrimony between the black and white tribes. Deep wounds still survive the Gukurahundi genocide, and until some closure is negotiated, the subtext of that country will continue to be broken. The divisions in Somalia between the Bantu tribes and the Pastorals alienates the disenfranchised and drives them into exile. The pan-Africanist vision opens a new political space that insists that Zimbabwean, South African, Angolan and Somalian can create a better future together. The will to do this is imperative for our future. The anxiety is clearly the great demand on time that this process implies. One wonders whether a smaller, test-case approach would give lessons for the wider endeavour or whether there is an imperative to go for broke and include all from the start in a United States of Africa where boundaries between countries are irrelevant and where the resources of all involved are pooled and managed together. Issues of governance and authority would need to be newly imagined.

———————

One of the most contentious dimensions of Sobukwe's philosophy must surely be his views on race. The violation of one's culture, the alienation in the country of one's birth from a sense of belonging, the grinding poverty in a country of massive wealth, the oppression that even today is somewhat relentless, the humiliation of anyone with an alternative paradigm, and much more – all because of being black – must surely spawn an anger that cannot subside. Of course, hatred makes eminent sense, but hatred can enable becoming the very essence of what has caused such pain for oneself. Assertiveness does not necessarily imply the outright rejection of the one who has caused such profound pain.

Sobukwe understood profoundly this dark struggle, and his determination to free himself from a more devastating fate gave birth to his philosophy of pan-Africanism and Black Consciousness. This entailed claiming his rightful dignity as made in the image of God. He regarded himself in every respect equal to the white man. This intrinsic truth was obviously the most threatening fact to the peculiar lie of apartheid. This was true, as essentially apartheid claimed a biblical authority for its nonsense. This approach heralded fundamentally the end of 'baasskap' and opened up the space for black and white to engage honestly with one another. The journey could not be easy, but it offered the choice of life instead of death.

This truth implied a decision as to how the new paradigm was to be lived. So much of the accepted norm was subversive and conspiratorial. State power was enforced by a system that engaged intelligence networks operating in the world of secrets and darkness. Knowing what the other thought and planned, before they knew that one had this knowledge, was considered powerful. The devastation that was caused to the psyches of thousands in torture cells reinforced this way of operating.

Sobukwe refused to comply with this way of being. Instead, he insisted that a human being should determine to relate in openness to the other and so design a politics that was intrinsically born from a platform of human rights. The difficult struggle of hearing the viewpoint of the other, and of struggling to find resolution through including all the nuances of our diversity, would be the only way forward.

There are three ways of engaging the racial dialectic. First, there is the outright dismissal of the other – from a black perspective – which entails the deserved rejection of whites as the scum of the earth and as those who will never again have the right to participate, let alone share in the leadership of South Africa. This is a 'deserved' approach and gains its narrative from the enormous pain suffered by blacks for centuries. The hatred is justified and will continue to be justifiable. The anger is tangible and dismissive and any talk of reconciliation is viewed with contempt. Part of the reason for this contempt is that reconciliation has consistently been used to further subjugate the black voice and to silence any effort at real change for the marginalised. It is thought, for instance, that the TRC was guilty of enabling a liberation for those whose economic paradigm perpetuated white privilege and, by and large, left the vast majority of blacks impoverished. The danger of this decision is that the abused becomes the abuser. Hatred infects the imagination and has the power to perpetuate fascism.

The second approach for Black Consciousness is to engage with whites and keep them in the loop, as they are at present, but while being polite and gracious, to remain rejecting and vengeful. This could be seen as a passive-aggressive way of engagement, but ultimately is completely dismissive of the other. It is a way of being that is not unlike the way in which the former intelligence operatives in the white bureaucracy would use blacks to further their own ends. This approach relies on the setting of the other firmly in the enemy camp. It is essentially devious and conspiratorial.

In the church setting, for example, this type of engagement is not unlike that of the infamous Afrikaner-Nationalist Broederbond, which was seen as the ultimate power behind the throne.

It consisted of arch-conservative racists who manipulated those in office to ensure the white stranglehold on power. All was done in the name of the Messiah and for the cause of sustaining freedom for whites in South Africa. The great irony was that the longer this movement remained unchecked, the more precarious the safety of white people in South Africa became. Sobukwe's confrontation exposed evil head-on, and forced the powers that be to face the consequences of their brutal injustice.

In the church, for instance, there are black cabals that conspire to address their allegation that the church is still ruled by white money. Although the constitutions of the churches seem to deny this unjust stereotype, the caucuses are determined to destroy white dominance. In this endeavour, there also seems to be a determination to remove white participation. The same perversity of apartheid rears its head again in the churches and bedevils the real work that should herald a new dispensation.

Sobukwe opened a new conscience for this nation: black is beautiful and we are not going to be diminished by white violence. He also implied by extension that white was beautiful and could find an alternative to hatred and corrupt greed.

The third way that Sobukwe espoused was to confront white arrogance with the assurance of his own value. He refused to be diminished by the false politics of apartheid and claimed the right to confront its evil. He set the example of asserting his truth openly, knowing that he had nothing to hide. He was not naive enough to think that freedom would come without the sacrifice of blood, but he stubbornly affirmed the wisdom of his blackness and the legitimacy of the fact that our strength is located in our diversity. Black and white belonged and had to be included for a safe future. We are still struggling to realise this ideal.

Sobukwe lives beyond his years. The relevance of his insights remains undiminished. Confronting the fascism and insecurity of the apartheid illegitimacy was courageous and prophetic. The ongoing fractures within the PAC, which hails him as *its* leader, are no less than a tragedy. It is an irony that a philosophy that has the potential to unite South Africa essentially has followers who are driven asunder by divisions that struggle to be resolved. What will heal this land and nation while the poor remain in unresolved poverty and our records show a corruption that curses the integrity of people like Sobukwe, who have sacrificed their lives for something different?

Sobukwe as an inspiring metaphor for business

Bonang Mohale

Bonang Francis Mohale is the former CEO of Business Leadership South Africa (BLSA). He was previously chairman and vice-president of Shell South Africa and Sapref, and before that CEO of Drake & Scull Facilities Management. He has held CEO positions with Sanlam, South African Airways (EVP) and Otis, and earlier, after studies at Wits Medical School, with Pfizer & MSD Pharmaceuticals and Sandoz. He sits on the boards of Hollard Insurance, Swiss Re Africa and RMB.

We, the people of South Africa,

Recognise the injustices of our past;

Honour those who suffered for justice and freedom in our land;

Respect those who have worked to build and develop our country; and

Believe that South Africa belongs to all who live in it, united in our diversity …

> – Preamble, the Constitution of the Republic of South Africa, 1996

FOR ME, THE ESSENTIAL QUESTION IS: what can today's South Africa learn from Robert Mangaliso Sobukwe's profound life (and premature death)? Why was this gifted student, national secretary of the ANC Youth League (ANCYL), teacher, lecturer, lawyer and

117

Methodist Church lay preacher so feared? Why was he deemed by the apartheid government as so much more radical and difficult an opponent than the regular political prisoners?

Today, Sobukwe is best remembered for initiating and leading the anti-pass law protests of 21 March 1960, and for agitating for a United States of Africa. He was the only liberation leader in South Africa's history to be imprisoned on Robben Island without even a mock trial – he was held in solitary confinement for six years – and banned from praying in public for fear that he would conscientise black people about the struggle. At the end of his sentence, the apartheid Parliament enacted the General Law Amendment Act, which allowed the minister of justice to detain any political prisoner indefinitely; the so-called Sobukwe Clause was renewed every year and never used to detain anyone except Sobukwe. Eventually, in 1969, he was released from prison and immediately placed under strict house arrest in Kimberley. Rumour had it that Sobukwe was fed pieces of broken glass in his food and poisoned in secret. Even after his death, in apartheid South Africa Sobukwe's voice could not be quoted nor heard.

Sobukwe, like nature, is a wonderful metaphor for business. Please allow me to use the self-selecting sacrifice and indomitable spirit of his lifelong struggle as an emblem for the gigantic battle that still faces us in South Africa. 'Strategy' means the plan you develop to win a war; when applied to business, it simply means how to compete. Fixing a broken economy is like nothing else. It is not just a career or a job. It demands everything and will often take it all. It is selflessness personified. It is about living a life that few imagine but many know so well – marked deeply by a lifetime of sacrifice. It is about opening up a world foreign to few, now that the struggle for liberation is almost over and our forebears' war for justice is a distant memory. It is about grief, opening up a nation that often finds it hard to express the values that drive those who have selflessly served with an ethos and heroism, often beyond the point of reason, that sets them head and shoulders above others, revealing many truths essential to understanding Sobukwe's struggle.

Even though he was the founding president of the Pan Africanist Congress (PAC) for only a year before his incarceration, Sobukwe worked within an ethos of teamwork, integrity and duty, making the struggle essentially democratic, listening and communicating carefully to get the best out of the liberation team. This attitude came from Sobukwe's own confidence and intelligence, how he thought, and how ready he was to express his opinion within the framework of the liberation struggle's discipline.

Exposing plans and ideas to robust challenge is vital at a time when arrogance, bluff and half-truths cost lives. It demonstrates how the trust underpinning this openness is built on a tradition of the toughest and most arduous training. Like all rites of passage, challenge bonds recruits together so that each knows that s/he can trust the other and her/himself. Most of all, it proves that a comrade has the integrity to go beyond their own safety, to put the mission and other comrades first. Where selfishness is the worst sin, in that it undermines trust and cohesion, generosity and care make units stronger.

Comrades know one another well, and they care for each other because it matters! Beyond fear there is a romance and faith that are required to fight. Like a church, the struggle transforms this ethos from the ordinary into a badge of honour. Faith in the struggle, its tenets listed as struggle honours, makes dishonour more terrifying than any enemy.

Having achieved democracy, belief in the struggle is not enough. Most of all, you really have to believe in your country to risk everything to defend it. It is never about you; it is about the country we serve! President Matamela Cyril Ramaphosa ended his State of the Nation Address in February 2018 with an invocation that must find both resonance and expression in every one of us:

Thuma Mina
I wanna be there when the people start to turn it around
When they triumph over poverty
I wanna be there when the people win the battle against AIDS
I wanna lend a hand
I wanna be there for the alcoholic
I wanna be there for the drug addict
I wanna be there for the victim of violence and abuse
I wanna lend a hand
Send me.

– words by the late Bra Hugh Masekela

There is an urgent need for all of us to be seized with the task of rebuilding in the post-state-capture era. In the same way that in modern-day Japan they speak of 'after Hiroshima and Nagasaki', or in Russia of the 'post-1917 Revolution', or in Angola of 'after Savimbi died', I have absolutely no doubt that South Africans will look back and talk about 'after 19 December 2017', which ultimately ushered in the 'New Dawn' of February 2018.

So, how do we begin to pick up the pieces after the brazen, industrial-scale looting known as state capture? We are in a critical situation. We are very vulnerable. This is a crisis of epic proportions in the context of a developmental state ideology, which finds expression in our economic vision, specifically the National Development Plan (NDP) 2030. This plan gave us a legitimate right to expect both transformation and performance, equality and justice. And yet the reality is still witnessed through the tearful eyes of the 90 per cent of students at the University of Fort Hare who are totally dependent on the National Student Financial Aid Scheme (NSFAS), not only for their tuition and accommodation but also for their survival. Every day, more children risk their lives for an education in schools that crumble around them. The year 2017 will be remembered for the unparalleled, gruesome images of the painful deaths of Life Esidimeni patients, and the harrowing testimonies of their relatives about trying to locate their loved ones. Key state institutions, state-owned enterprises (SOEs) and state-owned companies (SoCs) were systematically stuffed with hurriedly promoted, often untested, largely incompetent and corrupt 'cadre deployments' with no consideration given to performance.

It requires all social partners to approach the resolution of this, not so much looking at 'what's in it for me?', but rather, like Sobukwe, prepared to make sacrifices. Therefore, to emerge from this self-inflicted, home-grown own goal, may I submit that our institutions, SoEs and SoCs – which were the target of repurposing for the sole intent of ferocious state capture and are now on the way to being transformed, strategically managed and judiciously governed – offer South Africans not only our second but also our real last chance. It took a mere decade to destroy them, but it will take much more than ten years to fix them.

The African narrative of coups, wars, famine and drought, of sick and dying children of people who need saving, who are poor, desperate, hopeless and lost and defined by corruption and HIV/AIDS, must now give way to a new narrative. An Africa that, in the language of poets, is the cradle of mankind, the root of civilisation, where we see ourselves as heroines and heroes, owning the strength in our name, where the sense of joy is an inhibitor of fear, where proud people are worthy of the pursuit of happiness, enveloped by beautiful, mighty images that connect us, where the offspring of brave women warriors live, where happy revolutionaries filled with hope dwell and where achieving our own entrusted dreams can serve as a positive inspirational reference point, steeped in rich cultural heritage, mythology, and symbolism of both science and fiction. Where all are comfortable to play both objects and subjects, where communication is not only verbal and where understanding is more important than love purely because we experience, feel and see love everywhere.

An Africa that, like the rest of the world, has a full appreciation that liberal democracy still means a free press, an independent civil society, constitutional democracy and respect for the rule of law. An Africa where contrition remains an ongoing process in which you have to continue asking for forgiveness and remain grateful for the mercy shown; a complex place, where our children's idiosyncratic upbringing wears away their innocence; where righteousness is deeply powerful and naively abstract; sobering, where apartheid scars are raw, open wounds; a life that few imagine but many taste and know so well; an enigma where articulate, cosmopolitan young women have the means and education of the oppressors but the skin colour of the oppressed; where we can rid ourselves of the discomfort that deeply pains us and be able to shine a light on the class divide and the power imbalance that has torn away the post-apartheid optimism of the rainbow nation – now a sharply divided country, an echo chamber of the identity politics of the country's deeply torn youth and oblivious white compatriots.

An Africa where a racist no longer believes that certain ethnic groups are inferior and is instead given to acceptance. As the economist Amartya Sen put it, 'Appreciating that we all have multiple identities: one can be black, Christian, Sowetan, a mother, a sister, a niece, etc.,' or, as George Orwell says, 'To think clearly, we need to speak clearly.' For as long as colour affects life chances, being colour-blind means not seeing reality. We may draw inspiration from by former president Rolihlahla Nelson Mandela's epiphany upon his release from prison: 'As I walked out the door towards the gate that would lead to my freedom, I knew that if I didn't leave my bitterness and hatred behind, I would still be in prison.'

An Africa of Mangaliso Robert Sobukwe that takes full advantage of its place in history, whose time has finally arrived, propelled by factors necessary for consumer opportunities, such as the rise of the middle class, exponential population growth, the dominance of the youth, rapid urbanisation and the continued fast adoption of digital technologies. An Africa whose millennials and Generation Z implore us to favour ethical consumerism and reject gender stereotyping. A new Africa affirming that it is a growing imperative that corporate responsibility and positive social impact should be at the heart of a business strategy and the driving force behind decision making. Accelerating the achievement and realisation of 'The High Five Agenda for African Development': to light up and power, feed, industrialise, integrate and improve the quality of life for the people of Africa.

For we must never rest until and unless the entire bottom half has been lifted into the middle class. Because our Constitution does not only implore us to acknowledge the injustices of the past but also mandates us all to correct them.

The 'political spirituality' of Sobukwe's leadership

Kwandiwe Kondlo

Kwandiwe Kondlo is a professor in the Department of Politics and International Relations at the University of Johannesburg. He was previously professor and director of the Centre for Africa Studies at the University of the Free State. He holds an MA from the University of Cape Town and a PhD from the University of Johannesburg. The author of two books, his training is in historical studies, with a focus on liberation movements and political economy.

MY VIEW OF ROBERT MANGALISO SOBUKWE's leadership is a positive one. This is not out of feeling sorry for him or trying to proselytise his pan-Africanist political project. He was a leader of note and in reality he was in a class of his own. But I want to argue that the critical ingredients that constituted the calibre and quality of his leadership are yet to be carefully studied. To capture the corporeal essence of Sobukwe's leadership, I invoke in this chapter the notion of 'political spirituality'. By 'political spirituality' of leadership, one is seeking to infer the possibility of 'another kind of leadership' and 'another kind of politics' – a shift from 'a politics of precarity', of a precarious existence, to a politics of devotion, a desire-less politics of sacrifice, which was at the heart of Sobukwe's leadership example.

Sobukwe bestowed on South Africa's pan-Africanism a symbolic weight and example that the Pan Africanist Congress (PAC), the organisation he founded, has failed to emulate. A fearless leadership that leads from the front in the face of life-threatening adversity, an ethically grounded leadership that embraces the possibility of an unending suffering, are leadership virtues that Sobukwe left as a distinguishing mark of South Africa's pan-Africanism. The content and character of leadership is very important. As Hellicy Ngambi argues, 'the major challenge facing Africa is not the absence of leaders, but the absence of appropriate and effective leadership for its diversity of people and resources'.[1] The situation of leadership – especially, political leadership that can be trusted – is becoming dire in South Africa, and as a result democracy in the country is likely to be hit by a legitimacy crisis. This is in spite of the wonderful Constitution and regular elections. This chapter argues that the character of leadership exemplified by Robert Sobukwe is what South Africa doesn't have today. Unfortunately, South Africa has neither spent enough time nor given enough attention to understanding what the strong points were in Sobukwe's political leadership and how these should be cultivated in our society to inform leadership development in a democratic South Africa.

It is a pity that the attempts to paint the entire history of the liberation struggle in South Africa with the colours of one organisation have predominated. This has once again made victims of the country's heroes, heroines and intellectual giants, such as Robert Mangaliso Sobukwe, who suffered exclusion during colonialism and apartheid. They are now the victims of an exclusionary post-apartheid memory, which is largely an invention of today's victors. In cases where Sobukwe features, he is very often contained and represented by the dominating frameworks of a triumphalist narrative of ruling elites.

In my view, the intention, even though not explicit, is to disrupt the epistemological boundaries and internal coherence of Sobukwe's ideas. Hence, there have been attempts to locate Sobukwe's leadership and ideas within the trajectory of the intellectual discourse of the African National Congress (ANC). This is probably correct, but the way it is done in some instances is such that his pan-African thoughts and ideas are appropriated without acknowledgement. His intellectual treasure is thus placed at the disposal of those who made him their enemy.

There was a brief flowering of pan-Africanist ideas during the presidency of Thabo Mbeki, and many in the divided PAC actually felt Mbeki was speaking the language of Robert Sobukwe, hence the debates that dominated PAC circles in 1999, exploring the possibilities of a merger with the ANC. But the subtext of Mbeki's Africanism, one may argue, was to appropriate pan-Africanism in such a way that the PAC itself was without ideological robes. In that way it would have had to fold back into the ANC.

The period also witnessed breakaways and floor-crossings by a few PAC stalwarts, such as Patricia de Lille, who formed the Independent Democrats, as well as Gora Ebrahim, Malcom Dyani and, at a later stage, Thami ka Plaatjie, who joined the ANC. This period, 1999–2008, was lit up by Mbeki's 'I am an African' speech, which touched on pan-African issues and themes and laid the basis for the African Renaissance championed during the Mbeki presidency. One still regards this as a brilliant phase of South Africa's democracy, despite all its challenges. The resurgent pan-Africanism of the Mbeki period, even though intellectually sound, lacked 'political spirituality' of the Sobukwe type. It also lacked grassroots appeal, and one doubts if it in fact reached the 'souls of the black folk'.[2] When Jacob Zuma became president, the pan-African orientation again fizzled out.

But the name and memory of Robert Sobukwe refuses to disappear. He is never forgotten. This is despite the fact that, besides the speeches he wrote and delivered, there exist neither sound recordings of his voice nor footage of him speaking. During the #FeesMustFall protests in 2015, some students raised the issue of finding 'the voice of Sobukwe' in terms not only of ideas but also of literally hearing him speak. It is unfortunate that in his time media recordings of speeches and appearances by leading political personalities were much less common than today. I have read numerous works that discuss or mention, even if hurriedly, the life and leadership of Robert Mangaliso Sobukwe. But I never met him, I never saw footage of him speaking. In spite of this, he continues to have a presence that is both inspiring and edifying. Sobukwe's story underscores the need to 'reverse the historical marginalisation of "other" heroes and heroines and "other" liberation movements whose stories sit on the sidelines of history'.[3]

The story of Sobukwe's leadership and his ideas continues to inspire many South Africans, young and old. Based on the narratives one has heard and the numerous books, journal articles and newspaper commentaries one has read, what I find intriguing is the source, the foundations and the overall character of Sobukwe's leadership. What is it about Sobukwe's political leadership that really made him a cut above others, or what exactly puts Sobukwe in a class of his own? This has led me to evoke the notion of 'political spirituality', a concept others may deem too much a part of Western epistemology, and therefore very much out of line with the trend of decolonisation that is sweeping through African scholarship. The term 'political spirituality' is used here as a 'situational linguistic aid' rather than a binding hermetic category.[4]

The first part of this chapter engages with the conceptual meaning and relevance of 'political spirituality' and relates it to issues of leadership. This is intended only to frame the context of Robert Sobukwe's political spirituality. The final part will discuss leadership lessons we forget to learn from Robert Mangaliso Sobukwe.

The meaning of 'political spirituality' in political leadership

The work of Michel Foucault, especially *The Hermeneutics of the Subject: Lectures at the Collège de France, 1981–1982*, grounds the meaning of spirituality in a manner that is different from conventional religious and theological approaches. Foucault posits spirituality as resulting from an interpenetration of opposites: the subject and truth: '[T]he subject is not capable of the truth … the truth can transfigure and save the subject.'[5] The interpenetration, in other words, is not a simple relation but rather is the 'rebound' effect of the truth on the subject. As Foucault puts it, 'the truth enlightens the subject; the truth gives beatitude to the subject; the truth gives the subject tranquillity of the soul'.[6] What emerges, therefore, is that spirituality is a 'form of 'practice' that originates from the transfiguration of the subject, which occurs due to 'subject–truth relations'.

One could argue that 'political spirituality' occurs in actual fact when the 'political' becomes the sphere of the 'spiritual', that is, when the ethical character of politics as duty to fellow human beings is restored. The meaning of political spirituality is eloquently explained in Václav Havel's *Summer Meditations*, in which he argues that 'one thing is sure: although some may find it ridiculous or quixotic, it is my duty to continue emphasising the moral basis of all true politics, as well as the value of moral rules in all areas of public life, including the economic. It is also my duty to explain that unless we all try to discover in ourselves, to rediscover and cultivate, what I will call a superior responsibility, it will go ill with our country.'[7]

I find that Robert Sobukwe's leadership fits the description of 'political spirituality' constructed in Foucault's thesis and illuminated in Havel's *Summer Meditations*. Sobukwe's involvement in politics and his leadership of the PAC provides the raw material to argue the point about his political spirituality. If you analyse the life of Robert Sobukwe, which is well covered in Benjamin

Pogrund's biography, *How Can Man Die Better*, one of the things you will notice is a reflective life of principle and sacrifice. It also appears that, as an individual, Sobukwe would have preferred to pursue a quiet life of the mind; he was more of an intellectual. But his feeling for the downtrodden, and his awareness of the cares and sorrows of ordinary folk, pushed him in a direction he would not have taken had the situation not been as dire as it was during his time. His awareness of a 'superior responsibility' and the 'moral basis of true politics' forced him to support the split from the ANC, which in his view had abandoned the 1949 Programme of Action. The pain, struggle and strife he endured also came at a personal cost, but his spirit was never defeated.

Robert Sobukwe: the political spirituality of leadership

Robert Sobukwe's emergence as a political leader occurred in a difficult context in South African politics. But, from the very beginning, he showed signs of being a solid and principled leader who had a vision of a much higher cause. Hence, one is tempted to use the notion of political spirituality or integral spirituality to capture the corporeal essence of who he was as a person and as a political leader. The broader political context in South Africa was characterised, on the one hand, by the rise of the National Party, which had won the election in 1948, and, on the other hand, by a bitter and drawn-out political struggle within the ANC – a movement in opposition to apartheid:

> The debate was more about the strategies to be used in the struggle against white supremacy and apartheid than about the character of a liberated South Africa. At the centre of the debate was the long-standing and much older ANC Christian liberal tradition, which emphasised non-violence, multiracialism and universal suffrage along the lines of British democracy. It was

challenged by an emerging youth who espoused a tendency towards radical Pan-Africanism. The role of whites, especially communists, in the struggle for liberation, was among the issues debated.[8]

The debate and internal struggle in the ANC consumed the better part of the period after the 1952 Defiance Campaign. 'Between the years 1957 and 1958, just before the final Africanist split, the debate had assumed the character of an ideological "civil war" within the ANC.'[9] It was at this point that Robert Sobukwe was drawn into the leadership of the Africanist faction of the ANC.

The interview that Sobukwe gave to Gail Gerhart, in Kimberley on 8 and 9 August 1970, is very interesting and revealing, first of how Sobukwe thought of himself, how he viewed and understood the liberation struggle, and, most importantly, how he dealt with the contradictions and controversial issues that emanated from the struggle itself. As Sobukwe explained during the interview:

At the time I first came to Johannesburg, I still didn't see myself as an activist particularly, not of the Leballo type anyway. I saw myself more as an intellectual who could help back up this movement and give it some theoretical strength. PK and his group were 'mainly emotional' in their nationalism; they needed firmer theory, more 'academic' grounding. The articles that were appearing in the *Africanist* [magazine] were a bit wild and diffuse, without much educational value. I felt that in at least every issue there should be one educational article, explaining the nature of the struggle to our people. So I was offered the editorship by PK and I was glad to take it up. I saw this as a way I could make my contribution, and also stay behind the scenes. But as soon as I became the editor, naturally the critics singled me out for attack. I became openly identified as an Africanist.

I was never hesitant to take part, but unlike PK, I believed we should build our strength before inviting such open attack. I wasn't hesitant to participate. I was so very critical of the ANC, and believed so strongly in what we stood for.[10]

In this extract one notices Sobukwe's reluctance to come to the fore and lead the 'Africanists'. He was clearly worried about leading something formed hastily and without wider support, and it also seems he had no intention of leading a breakaway from the ANC. But he could not quell the fires and, in addition, the mark of his intellectual contributions in the *Africanist* automatically placed him in the spotlight. From 1956 to 1958, Sobukwe was involved in a lot of work behind the scenes with the aim of consolidating the establishment and influence of the Africanist faction within the ANC. This he did until the major split occurred at the Transvaal ANC Congress on 2 November 1958, when Selby Ngendane, one of the leading Africanists, submitted a document to the ANC with a list of resignations.

Sobukwe, even though a backbencher (up to the time of the split) was in fact part of the inner circle of the Africanist group that launched the Bureau of African Nationalism. The Bureau operated in all four provinces of South Africa, but was more active in the eastern Cape. The Bureau was, in essence, a secret watchdog of ANC policy. In November 1954, the Africanists founded the *Africanist*, which became their mouthpiece. When the founding conference of the PAC was held, Dr DD Mantshontsho indicated that the name of Sobukwe could not be doubted but he had to be convinced to stand for the position.[11] From existing archival records it does appear that Sobukwe's name, even though not doubted, was in fact contested at the founding conference of the PAC. 'Serious divisions dominated the conference during the elections of National Executive Committee members. The division was between the "party intelligentsia" and the "non–intellectuals". The former faction was embodied in the charismatic personality of Mangaliso Sobukwe and the latter was represented by Josias Madzunya, from Alexandra Township in Johannesburg. The former faction triumphed and therefore the leadership of the PAC became dominated by the educated elite.'[12]

Sobukwe had little time to lead the PAC. This is despite the fact that the PAC needed him so much, as it was in its formative stage. He was the key brain behind the formation and development of its philosophy but was separated from it at an early stage. This perhaps explains, to a large extent, the leadership challenges that have rocked the PAC from the time of Potlako Leballo's leadership in exile in 1962 up until today. Nyathi John Pokela, who led the exiled PAC from 1981 to 1985, brought some stability, but this did not last. One can even argue that when the PAC was unbanned in 1990, it was already a dispensable force, except for the power of its ideas. The public spats and fights between contending factions of the PAC at the funeral of Zondeni Sobukwe, the wife of Robert Sobukwe, on 25 August 2018, were a disgrace. They demonstrated that in as much as Robert Sobukwe left behind a memorable example of the calibre and standard of leadership that the PAC and Africa at large really need, he also took away with him 'the prodigal paradox of an ethical political revolution'.[13]

Sobukwe was arrested and spent part of his jail term on Robben Island and was later kept under house arrest until he died in 1978. During this period, the organisation fell into the reckless hands of people unable to channel its radical ideological energy into carefully selected strategic initiatives in exile and inside South Africa. But, during his short time as PAC president, Sobukwe's leadership was immediately felt in his organisation. Those who worked with him, especially Elliot Mfaxa, did not fail to remark on Sobukwe's personal demeanour, trustworthiness, sharp intellect and common touch. His intellectual leadership is clear when you examine the principles and strategies enshrined in the new organisation's basic documents. These documents include the Pan-Africanist Manifesto, the Constitution of the PAC, the Disciplinary Code and the Oath of Allegiance. Sobukwe's inaugural address at the launch of the PAC is also counted among the PAC's basic documents. It provides a body of thought that constituted the fundamental character of the ideology of the PAC. These ideas were further inscribed in the PAC Manifesto.[14] Over the entire exile period, the organisation was sustained by documents developed by its founder. Key among these was the Pan-Africanist Manifesto, developed by Robert Sobukwe and AP Mda.

It is the power and strength of Robert Sobukwe's soul, and his neglect in the political and intellectual spaces of post-apartheid South Africa, that makes him even more interesting as a research subject. The issue of the ethical self, determination and unwavering conviction are all signs of deep spiritual strength. During the interview with Gail Gerhart, when asked about his role in the 1960 anti-pass campaign, Sobukwe indicated that 'we believed that if we followed our plan, with the leaders in front, with sincerity, conviction, and strength, that the power of our example would be enough to mobilise the masses to action, to non-collaboration'.[15] The unwavering conviction in the integrity of a higher cause (the liberation struggle), something one may even call the 'truth' (using Foucault's words) had such an impact on him (the subject) that it brought about a transfiguration of the self – the spirituality of the self in politics.

Sobukwe admits during the interview to having formulated the PAC's definition of an African. It is a definition that shows the inclusive approach the PAC used in constructing a non-racial identity of a South African. He defined an African as 'anyone who owe[s] his first loyalty to Africa and accept[s] the rule of an African majority'.[16]

I recall the conversation I had with the late Dini Sobukwe, the son of Robert Mangaliso Sobukwe, when I visited Graaff-Reinet in 2011. I was particularly touched by his recollection of the kind of person his father was. He indicated that Robert Sobukwe was a prayerful person and that in his prayers he would even pray for his enemies, his political competitors; he would even pray for the ANC and for Nelson Mandela. Dini also indicated, in my recollection, that his father never wanted to be hero-worshipped, and that 'it would hurt him in his grave if people start hero-worshipping him'. In his lifetime, Sobukwe 'did what he had to do and never expected songs of praise' – 'Yes, we can praise him, we can admire him, we can learn from him but we should never think we are doing him or the Sobukwe family a favour.'

The discussion with Dini Sobukwe, a courtesy call at Mrs Sobukwe's house and a drive around the township where the young Robert Sobukwe had lived with his family, as well as a visit to the gravesite, gave me an impression of the kind of person Robert Sobukwe was. I gained more ideas about his personal, political and spiritual life. At the gravesite, I was touched by the words inscribed on his tombstone: 'True leadership demands complete subjugation of self, absolute honesty, integrity and uprightness of character and fearlessness, and above all, a consuming love of one's people.' To me, it disclosed elements of a 'political spirituality' that characterised Sobukwe's political leadership. He merged a strong spiritual life, a principled personal life and a commitment to the liberation struggle of South Africans. His ideas, and especially his enunciation of the land question, have not been fully examined – something that has come to haunt South Africa a quarter of a century into democracy.

This is the man whom even pro-apartheid government columnists such as Aida Parker described with respect: 'When you enter, as you talk to him, you gain much the same impression of power, of leadership, as you do when with South Africa's Prime Minister Verwoerd.'[17] Anthony Lewis of *The New York Times* said that 'a few times in his life a reporter meets a political figure and senses authentic greatness: a magnetic external presence combined with a sense of inner serenity.'[18] Barry Streek summed it up when he said, 'When Sobukwe spoke, Africanism made sense.'[19]

The leadership lessons we forget to learn from Robert Mangaliso Sobukwe

Why does South Africa need leadership of Sobukwe's stature and character? In other words, how does one describe the essence of the challenge facing South Africa today? Again I wish to invoke the notion of a 'politics of precarity', which emerges from the work of intellectuals such as Ching Kwan Lee and Yelizavetta Kofman (2012),[20] as well as African writers such as Ben Okri. A 'politics of precarity' infers to a large extent the 'multidimensional weight of the world', which embodies social suffering through degradation of work, 'a fractured and racialising citizenship, excessive human vulnerability and unequal burdening of toxic risk'.[21] In our situation and context in South Africa, I want to argue that the 'precarity of our politics' is more about the rent-seeking behaviour of political elites leading government and business entities, and that this is threatening the overall legitimacy of the democratic state. Patronage networks are so pervasive in our political space. The political party, rather than being a tool of the people to keep elected leaders accountable, is instead a conduit between the government and private capital, and is used to facilitate private access to public resources. This is eroding the legitimacy of the state. Without state legitimacy, we cannot realise the South African dream. It requires leadership of integrity to condition and ensure the legitimacy of the state. Getting us out of the 'politics of precarity' requires, first and foremost, an organised and non-partisan civil society, and second, a political leadership that has moral authority. It is in this context that the leadership of Robert Sobukwe becomes critical.

The intention here is not to eulogise Sobukwe or turn him into an angel, which he was not. He never claimed a monopoly of truth regarding the ideas that his organisation espoused. In fact, in the interview with Gerhart, Sobukwe concedes the vagueness of some ideas in the PAC and how they were open to misinterpretation. When asked about the PAC slogan, 'Africa for Africans', Sobukwe responded:

> Yes. It was so funny, because by this time Benjie [Pogrund] and I were already friends, and he used to really get after me about this one. Also the late Patrick Duncan. They argued that you couldn't promote exclusivism then hope that tomorrow the people you had organised exclusively would turn around and begin recognising these other non-Africans as Africans. I could see this argument, but I still felt that history would bear us out and that we were choosing the correct course.
>
> We knew many people agreed with us … But regardless of what our strength was, we had to stand on our principles.
>
> I know it is true that there were times when we simply were not clear in our own minds of how to deal with the situation. [These are not the exact words; but the idea was definitely expressed.] This is why sometimes our slogans were misunderstood or ambiguous. This perhaps reflected confusion in my own thinking, but I was always certain of certain basic principles.[22]

This showed leadership, as it is not easy to be critical of one's own ideological position and ideas. But it also shows the importance of principle in leadership as well as of being prepared to take leaps of faith based on principle. What we don't find in our political leaders today is that rare ability to reflect critically on the party's ideas, self-reflection on whether a person really deserves to lead, and the honesty to serve without advancing self-interest.

What I find complex about Sobukwe is how his 'self' constituted 'itself' into the kind of subject/person he was. Whatever his 'self-fashioning', it made out of him one of the outstanding leaders in South Africa's political history. Foucault explains self-fashioning as 'practices whereby individuals, by their own means or with the help of others, [act] on their own bodies, souls, thoughts, conduct and way of being in order to transform themselves and attain a certain state of perfection'.[23] Sobukwe's leadership had an amazing depth and wiring, which connected the 'self', the purpose, politics, unyielding perseverance and acceptance of pain as part of 'a self-surrendering self'. Some of the poems he loved, and are quoted in Benjamin Pogrund's biography,[24] are also revealing of the amazing depth and single-minded commitment Sobukwe had. One of these poems is Vladimir Mayakovsky's 'A Cloud in Trousers':

Wherever pain is – there am I:
On every single tear that's shed
I myself have crucified.

The poem carries a deep meaning when one reflects on the suffering, humiliation and pain that Sobukwe endured in his lifetime. Would he have remained the same person were he to have tasted the juice of power and comfort? This is a question that is difficult to answer, as it involves a lot of speculation. But what is clear about Sobukwe is that he was a leader who owned himself; he owned his own soul and was not compromised by any deal or possible deals.

The words on his tombstone, especially 'subjugation of self', are significant in terms of insight into his leadership, and especially during the time we are in as a country. To overcome yourself is not easy, yet it marks the very essence of true greatness. The greatest of great leaders is the one who has struggled with and eventually conquered himself. That leader has the ability to lead and live up to the challenge of personal example. This is what Robert Sobukwe did.

Why is freedom such a bitter fruit?

Anele Nzimande

Anele Nzimande graduated with a law degree from Wits University. She was active in the Law Students' Council and a leader in the #FeesMustFall movement. She has been a legal researcher at the Centre for Applied Legal Studies. She has created an online company offering custom-made clothing, and is the founder of Alunamda Media, a content marketing agency.

I AM CONFRONTED by black indignity everywhere I turn in South Africa. I wish I could disappear behind the high walls of the Northern Suburbs of Johannesburg the way our political and business leaders do. The indignity of black people offends me. It is troubling and distressing. The calloused begging hands, the dark and hollow eyes, and the volatile voices of despair are enough to make me want to disavow my blackness.

Recently, I was in Pick n Pay to buy myself a meal during my lunch hour. As I waited for someone to attend to me, I noticed the gentleman standing next to me counting his coins to make sure that he had enough money for the fried chips he had just ordered. The woman serving him had just announced how much they would be – R20. He had that familiar dusty, worn-out look of black men who do onerous work that pays very little. This was a man who no longer dreamt about the future; he used his energy sparingly and focused only on getting through 'today'. I approached him, '*Sawubona bhuti.* Do you mind if I help you with that?' I said, handing him a R20 note. 'Ah, thank you, my sister,' he said, and I smiled in acknowledgement.

It is true that colonialism and apartheid have dealt a huge blow to black history (and possibly even to the future of black people). At some point, we must be willing to draw a line in the sand. We have to take full responsibility for our future as black South Africans, and it's time for black elites, the 'sort-of elites' and 'almost-elites' to do some serious introspection and soul-searching. We are overdue for an honest collective self-analysis as black South Africans.

Why have we failed to build a country where black people don't need sympathy and compassion in order to survive? The desperation is palpable and nauseating. We remain synonymous with the denigrating experience of begging. Even with a black government in the stead of vicious white minority rule, we beg.

'If only our government could just build schools for us.'
'We are just asking that the government pave the roads so the ambulances can drive into our village.'
'Our children don't have jobs.'

We are suffocating under the tyranny of mediocrity and greed; they have wounded the democratic project. We are dealing with a sluggish economy, a limping healthcare and education system, and rising disillusionment. Nigerian-born author Chigozie Obioma argues that though many African nations were sabotaged by self-seeking white imperialists who engendered their failure from the beginning, this is only a part of the cause. Speaking of his home country, Nigeria, he elucidates that a culture of incompetence, endemic corruption, dignified ineptitude, destructive selfishness and greed play a major role in the unravelling of a nation. This seems to have been the fate of our country – where opportunity and prospects fall only into the laps of the connected. It turns out that it is *not* enough just to have a black president. You need a president who advocates for his people. We need leaders who will empower black people so that we are fully independent and able to support ourselves.

I doubt that black people want to be beholden to their leaders forever. There is, even in the youngest child, a strong, defiant sense of independence. My son is two and a half years old and one of his favourite things to do is to remind me that he can do things himself. When I offer to tie his shoelaces, he will remind me, with a stern look on his face, that *he* can do it. When I offer to remove the plastic wrapper from the straw and stick it into the juice box for him, he will remind me (in a high voice) that he is *very* capable of doing this himself. Alone. Without my help. And sometimes he does succeed, but my job is to be there to provide support in the event that he needs me. It is not my job to make sure that he is perpetually dependent on me. And so, our leaders thrive on our neediness and we thrive on their benevolence.

Our politics has become a bedlam of ambitions and despair as we contend with a fierce, overarching and prevailing ideology of 'It's our turn to eat.' In South Africa today, politics has been reduced to nothing more than strategy and spectacle. Political leaders seem more concerned with maintaining power by pretending to care than by actually caring. The leaders who *are* moral at best suffer alienation and intimidation, and at worst meet their end through assassination.

I am told, and would like to believe, that there was a time when leaders called themselves selfless and actually meant it. We have no way of knowing this. When leaders have opportunities presented to them to be selfless, and then fail to demonstrate this characteristic, it can only lead us to wonder if they were ever what they claimed to be. Perhaps the signs were always there, but there was a wilful blindness in the face of a more powerful, stark evil to overcome.

But, in the wake of 1994, it began to stir and heave and throw off its grave clothes; our hidden agendas and ulterior motives came out to play. The stage was set for a new era of politics.

Black people are good at navigating the familiar terrain of 'collective struggle'. We can relate to struggle. We lived it for so long. Black pain is shared, and common to all. For years, we forged the ties of our shared misery and collective sorrow, but we never learned how to cultivate love that leads from a place of triumph. We stoked each other's anger and believed that all of us black people, as the ones who were oppressed, had an innate goodness that was incorruptible. Oh, but how wrong we were.

The days of people being prepared to listen and being treated simply as loyal subjects are over. The people are unhappy with their leaders. Politicians often say they care about 'their people'. Indeed, they constantly refer to the poor as 'our people' in a way that infantilises the poor as objects who must always be available to feed their credentials as revolutionaries. Why is freedom such a bitter fruit?

How will we know if our leaders love us? In the words of Robert Sobukwe, they will display integrity and uprightness of character.

The lonely prisoner
was a man of letters

Derek Hook

*Derek Hook is Associate Professor of Psychology at Duquesne University in
Pittsburgh, USA, and Extraordinary Professor of Psychology at the University
of Pretoria. He is the author of* A Critical Psychology of the Post-colonial
and Voices of Liberation: Steve Biko, *in addition to articles on Frantz
Fanon and the psychology of racism. He is the editor of Robert Sobukwe's
letters from Robben Island, published in 2019 by Wits University Press as* Lie
on Your Wounds: The Prison Correspondence of Robert Sobukwe.

THERE ARE SEVERAL WAYS in which Robert Mangaliso Sobukwe is
typically remembered in South Africa today. We tend to think of
him as: a hero of the anti-apartheid struggle; the inspirational first
leader of the Pan Africanist Congress (PAC); a political prisoner
unjustly consigned to years of solitary confinement on Robben
Island; Wits University lecturer and proud Africanist intellectual; etc.
As vital as each of these aspects of his identity is, together with his
ongoing legacy, they leave out something crucial.

Sobukwe was not only a man of courage and an astute political
thinker, he was also a literary intellectual, someone who devoured
newspapers and journals, who loved novels, and who read widely
in history, drama and poetry. A folklorist and translator, always
ready with an African proverb, biblical verse or witty turn of phrase,
Sobukwe was a storyteller. Indeed, he was a writer, and not merely

a writer of letters – as his lengthy period of confinement forced him to become – but a man *of* letters. We have, in other words, for too long neglected this aspect of Sobukwe's life: his literary life as both reader and writer. By the same token, we have neglected his letters. These are not only important historical documents in their own right, but also provide us with engaging accounts of Sobukwe's own life.

This chapter emerges from a larger project – the publication of Sobukwe's surviving Robben Island prison letters.[1] It was during this research that I first came to appreciate Sobukwe's literary talents, his wit – he is, as we shall see, often very funny – and his distinctive storytelling voice. It is precisely this storytelling voice that I wish to foreground in this chapter.

I do so by focusing on fragments of his correspondence with Nell Marquard, a white liberal and retired academic who had struck up a friendship-by-correspondence with Sobukwe by writing to him while he was on Robben Island. Unlike Sobukwe's writings to Benjamin Pogrund – many of which appeared in Pogrund's biography, *How Can Man Die Better*[2] – these letters relied on no previous personal contact. Therein lies much of their charm. Sobukwe was obliged to rehearse – and often very entertainingly at that – a good deal of his own personal history, particularly that pertaining to his Graaff-Reinet upbringing. (We do not, sadly, have access to Marquard's letters to Sobukwe.) We are thus afforded a rare opportunity: to have Sobukwe himself narrate aspects of his childhood and upbringing, sprinkled with jokes and literary and political allusions, in his own distinctive voice.

Establishing an 'African' friendship

In a letter dated 11 October 1963 – the first of his letters to Marquard that I have been able to find – Sobukwe thanks his new correspondent for the various subscriptions she'd signed him up to (*The New Yorker, Life, The Listener*) before moving on to two of the topics that would feature in much of their subsequent correspondence – literature and gardening:

> I have quite a busy day. Besides studying and reading (I have quite a range of reading matter). At the moment I am reading [George] Orwell's *1984*. I have just finished *The Ugly American*). I also do some gardening. I have a fairly large garden, larger than my Mofolo one. But the soil in this part of the country is – I am sure you'll agree, patriotic Cape Townian though you are – the despair of the amateur gardener. The vegetables (carrots, beetroot, beans) have somehow germinated but the flowers have not yet announced their arrival. Should both flowers and vegetables bear fruit, however, I'll undertake to make the Sahara blossom.

In such early letters, it was important for both parties to establish a series of common interests that would bridge their different backgrounds and political standpoints. Although Marquard was clearly a progressive, she was also almost a generation older than Sobukwe (she was in her sixties when they started corresponding, he had only recently turned 40). Her comfortable middle-class existence in suburban Cape Town, while geographically close to Robben Island, was simultaneously a world away. As politically informed and progressive as Marquard was, she would no doubt have stopped short of the radicalism of the pan-Africanist cause that Sobukwe had sacrificed so much for. Sobukwe, gracious, polite, 'gentlemanly' throughout their correspondence, no doubt sensed this, but nevertheless found a way to make their friendship work, largely by reference to South African history, African current affairs, British political events and literature.

A remark Sobukwe makes in his next letter to Marquard, in

January 1964, makes it apparent just how little he had known about her:

> I must say that I was not a little surprised to learn that you were in your sixties ... I haven't met you, of course, but whenever I read your letters I have a picture of a tall lady with nothing to suggest that she was a day older than thirty-five.

He goes on to speak of his family's recent visit to Robben Island:

> I had quite a pleasant time with my wife and the children. I had quite a few tales to tell them – in spite of the African taboo against relating folk tales during the day: the guilty party, it is said, will sprout horns. It is but a sign of the times that my kids laughed such ideas to scorn. The twins (boys) were a year and a half old when I left home and have now attained the manly age of five. Fortunately for me they were satisfied, at first sight, that I was the fellow their mother told them so much about.

Understated as these lines are, they would have conveyed to Marquard something of the bitterness of Sobukwe's situation – a father who, because of his political convictions, was barely recognisable to his youngest children. Importantly also, Sobukwe finds a way, modest at first, of broaching a topic dear to his heart – African culture and values. This becomes increasingly central in the letters and eventually becomes a mainstay of their correspondence: Sobukwe providing his thoughts on African intellectuals (Akweke Orizu, Wole Soyinka), leaders (Nnamdi Azikiwe, Kenneth Kaunda, Kwame Nkrumah), history and current events (the volatile Nigerian situation in the mid-1960s). As much as he was an erudite and engaging conversationalist on a wide range of issues – debates on British parliamentarians, on the US and the global political scene, on the Western literary canon and South African history – Sobukwe would not have been true to himself if he had not been able to foreground Africa in their friendship, indeed to make their friendship in some way 'African'. We see Sobukwe doing this in a May 1964 letter, in which the formality of his early correspondence gives way to a more openly affectionate tone:

> Thank you for [your] … letter. It was so AFRICAN! … [W]hen you ask an African how he is, you're in for it. You'll get a report on the weather and the state of the crops, the state of health of his family … friends, recent deaths and births and finally the assurance – with which, incidentally, the report was prefaced – that by and large things are not bad. A carry-over, most probably, from [older] days … Common, perhaps, to all peasant populations so that, strictly speaking, I have no right to make the chauvinistic claim that it is TYPICALLY AFRICAN!

Despite this, he is at pains to correct any impression of chauvinism – his comment here being both light-hearted and yet also, one presumes, somewhat serious. The relationship between Marquard and Sobukwe now becomes viable, centered on a commitment not only to progressive values, but also, in some way, to Africa itself.

In April 1967, Marquard suggested to Sobukwe that they drop the formality of addressing each other as Mr and Mrs, and instead refer to one another on a first-name basis. The salutation of Sobukwe's 1 May 1967 letter to Marquard ('My dear Nell') reflects this change, which Sobukwe appears to have felt rather self-conscious about:

My dear Nell

First of all, regarding the salutation: I am not feeling as confident as the grammatical 'possessive' might suggest. And I have traced the reason for my uneasiness back to Graaff-Reinet.

They are a lot that is very status-conscious those Graaff-Reineters. And status is determined, by and large, by the years of the calendar, so that anybody who is a mere five years older than one will remark, when addressed by name: 'Jy moet 'n draai maak'! [You have to come around] – They would tell me 'ek vat sleg kanse' [I am taking chances] in addressing you by name but I shall make the draai [come around] when we meet.

Thank you indeed for suggesting that the formality come to an end:

Something there is that doesn't love a wall,
That wants it down,
says Robert Frost.

This speaks volumes about Sobukwe. Not only is he affectionate, but he also shares a piece of his own boyhood history – drawing on a location ('township') context that Marquard was probably unfamiliar with – while still reaching out to her by including a (touching) poetic reference that she would recognise. (The lines that Sobukwe cites come from Robert Frost's poem 'Mending Wall', which contests the proverbial idea that good fences make good neighbours.)

Oblique strategies: Sobukwe's understated political views
In a May 1964 letter, Sobukwe responds to a series of questions that Marquard had previously asked:

No, I did not know Prof MacMillan. He was at Wits before my time. I have read his books though, including 'The Cape Color Question'. That was when I did 'Native Administration' for my degree. Nor is Governor [Henry] Barkly a complete stranger to me. I met him in that involved series of '[Xhosa] Wars'.

Much is being left unsaid here. It was while studying Native Administration at Fort Hare that the full extent of the structural injustices of apartheid became evident to Sobukwe. This was a clear turning point in his political commitment to the struggle. So, while Sobukwe would often discuss South African history with Marquard, we can assume he was being not only polite but also restrained in many instances. In the above comments, for example, Sobukwe acknowledges Marquard's evident interest in the history of the Cape liberal tradition without expanding on the topic. This was doubtless because such liberal pioneers – such as Henry Barkly, a former governor of the Cape Colony who supported the Cape's non-racial constitution of the time – would not have been heroes to him but proponents rather of the process of European colonisation that he wished to see vanquished (hence the association he makes between Governor Barkly and the Xhosa Wars between 1779 and 1879).

One should not mistake Sobukwe's tact, nor his willingness to engage in conversation about thoroughly white middle-class interests, for any diminishment of his own pan-Africanist political views. Given that these letters were being read by the security police and needed as such to avoid explicit political content, one might mistakenly draw the conclusion that Sobukwe's political beliefs had softened or mellowed. This was not the case. Take, for example, a remark Sobukwe made to his wife, Veronica (in a letter of 20 October 1964), in respect of another white liberal correspondent:

> Mrs … has written. She says she was sorry to read that refugees in Basutoland were all singing my praises as their leader. She hopes I'll denounce them all and tell them I am now 'a disciple of the Lord Jesus Christ'. I suppose I'll have to take up ministry after that and be a good little Christian Kaffir. I don't think I'll answer the letter. I'll hurt her if I do.

Some historical context is necessary here. Sobukwe's correspondent probably had in mind Poqo, a military offshoot of the PAC.[3] Potlako Leballo, Sobukwe's ally in the PAC, had called a press conference in Basutoland (now Lesotho) in March 1963 to announce that Poqo and the PAC were one and the same. He went on to assert the inevitability of African revolution in 1963, an event that would doubtless involve the loss of white lives. As Benjamin Pogrund argues, there is no evidence to suggest that Sobukwe was in any way involved with Poqo (he was, after all, imprisoned at the time of these events). This being said, Sobukwe was clearly reticent to denounce any of his Basutoland followers – seemingly inclusive of Poqo members – in the way seemingly demanded in the letter.

I should note that Sobukwe's above remarks are, in many respects, uncharacteristic (they are the only unguardedly acerbic comments I have found in reviewing all of Sobukwe's archived letters). These comments remind us that Sobukwe's evident love of the Western literary canon, his interest in global political affairs and even his engagement with liberal ideas did not in any way negate his commitment to the pan-Africanist cause. How he could be true to these views, even in the context of censored prison letters with a white liberal correspondent he didn't really know, tells us about both Sobukwe's magnanimity and his rhetorical finesse.

Sobukwe frequently used humour as a way of alluding to his political concerns in a self-deprecating, even self-ironising way. Consider the opening of his 19 June 1964 letter to Marquard:

Thank you very much for your letter, the books and the edibles. I noticed, incidentally, that the chocolates were labelled 'dark' and wondered whether you had made the choice in reference to my colour prejudices! They were a real and rare treat for my palate ... but I would hesitate ... to say that their palatal success was primarily due to their colour.

A not dissimilar strategy is evident in his 14 September 1966 letter to Marquard:

My birthday occurs on the 5th December, on the same day as that of Mr CR Swart, the State President! I am rather upset to learn that he will be retiring soon because I have always felt flattered to think that the SABC and numerous other institutions and person[s] who probably loathe me were nonetheless celebrating my birthday.

The irony on display here – particularly Sobukwe's claim to be feeling upset at the State President's retirement – was evidently lost on his security police censors. These comments are subversive in a subtle way; the implicit comparison between the two men leaves us in little doubt as to who Sobukwe thinks should actually be ruling the country.

On 22 July 1964, Sobukwe speaks again of his wife, and his political views are again obliquely present:

I read that she has applied for my release. Well, she told me nothing about it ... I have not made any personal (non–personal even) request to the cabinet for my release. The only letters I have written are friendly ones, like this to my friends.

While this is all conveyed in a perfectly convivial tone, Sobukwe is alluding to a political principle of the utmost importance to him. He would not in any way petition the apartheid government for release or any form of preferential treatment, a view he stuck to throughout (and before) his incarceration. To do so, he felt, would be to cede the apartheid state a degree of legitimacy it did not possess. These political values were remarked upon by Nelson Mandela, who in *Long Walk to Freedom* commented:

> I have always respected Sobukwe, and found him a balanced and reasonable man. But we differed markedly about … prison conditions. Sobukwe believed that to fight poor conditions would be to acknowledge the state's right to have him in prison in the first place. I responded that it was always unacceptable to live in degrading conditions … Sobukwe responded that prison conditions would not change until the country changed.[4]

A Graaff-Reinet boyhood

Having previously established that Marquard herself had family links to Graaff-Reinet – a topic clearly close to his heart – Sobukwe notes, as a way of closing a July 1964 letter:

> I haven't heard from Graaff-Reinet yet – my home town, unfortunately! The place has always bred rebels it appears. I'm expecting my brother to tell me of the stock losses they have suffered. He thinks Graaff-Reinet to be the Capital of the Republic.

This topic is revisited in Sobukwe's next letter to Marquard (of 17 September 1964):

> Yes I was born and bred at Graaff-Reinet. And what memories I have of the place, still covered with thick bush and with the

loveliest prickly pears imaginable. I saw the bush disappear and houses rise and streams run dry …

Although these recollections may have struck the security police censors as rather innocuous childhood memories, Sobukwe's political sentiments are, once again, not far below the surface. Sobukwe offers his thoughts on the various languages spoken by his family, and the mixed form of Graaff-Reinet isiXhosa:

> I spoke Afrikaans fluently as a child though never so well as either my brother or my eldest brother both of whom, up to this day, can deliver an impromptu sermon in that language. My father, on the contrary, never learnt to speak Afrikaans but was recognised locally as an authority on Xhosa which he loved and spoke with a rare beauty …

> Graaff-Reinet Xhosa, of course, is a species on its own, spoken in an area covering Hanover in the North and Aberdeen, Jansenville in the South West. It bristles with 'maars' and 'dans' and 'togs', 'assebliefs' ['buts', 'thens' and 'after alls', 'pleases'] even having 'ronanti' (goeie naand) [good night] and 'rondara' (goeie dag) [good day] as forms of greeting in place of the traditional 'bhota'. You'll excuse my spelling. I never *studied* Afrikaans.

Sobukwe has evidently found his métier here, combining several of his favourite themes (Graaff-Reinet, languages and translation, 'multi-ethnic' African identity) in his own inimitable storytelling voice. These themes are continued in a letter of November of the same year, in which Sobukwe brings to life not just the familiar accents but also the mannerisms of his fellow 'Graaff-Reineters':

> Forgive me if I indulge in my usual reminiscences. But I can't help remarking that while the English pedantically wish one

another a 'Merry' Christmas and a happy New Year, we Graaff-Reineters – the location population – wish one another a 'happy' Christmas and a 'happy' new year and we say it loudly, person to person. We aren't mercenary in outlook – far from it – but we do, all things considered, expect those on whom we confer the blessings of the Gods to show their appreciation – a piece of cake … a bottle of beer, shall we say?

However, it often happens that our friends have nothing but good wishes to give us in return. The formula is: 'Same to you', said indifferently or warmly, depending on our feelings toward our well-wishers. There are characters at Graaff-Reinet, however, who are known to hate having their good-wishes reciprocated, preferring a solid, tangible token of good-will. They are quick to follow their 'happy Christmas' with 'en moet my nie "seventy-you" gee nie!' [and don't give me 'seventy-you'!] – in the idiom of our location.

This is very funny. But Sobukwe has by no means exhausted his interest in the multilingual accents and idiomatic stylings of those he grew up with. On 16 March 1966, Sobukwe wrote to Marquard that

There was a time at Graaff-Reinet when it was fashionable for the ladies of our location – the less inhibited ladies – to declare: 'Of course, ja, dit pak op my bors ja' [Of course, yes, it's rising in my chest, or the bile is rising[5]] whenever they intended 'om iemand te skree' or 'om iemand to shout' [to shout at someone], both expressions referring to a deplorable practice whereby the deformities and deficiencies of the 'iemand' [someone], real and imaginary, mental, physical and spiritual were loudly and eloquently enumerated, to the delight and/or embarrassment of the ever-present crowd.

We had experts, of course, poetic geniuses with amazing powers of observation and description. In those days, ladies were on the plumpish side and small waists and foundation garments were, by the class I am dealing with, looked upon with scorn. Men were terrified of such women, oh but terrified! And who wouldn't be, of people who on the spur of the moment could describe the physiognomy of a rival as an 'afdrant gevreet' [sloping face] simply because the individual concerned had a rather broadish and flattish nose![6]

I could write pages about them, the darlings who brought me up.

Sobukwe evidently found common ground with Marquard over the fact that their multilingual heritage (Marquard was from an Afrikaans family) had seen many 'amendments' being made to English. On 28 June 1967, he commented to Marquard:

We don't have to apologise to each other for the amendments our people make to English. You'll remember my references to Western 'syphilisation'. At Healdtown it was the accepted thing for fellows from Basutoland (as it then was) to tell the girls 'I laugh you' for 'I love you'. And then there is your Afrikaner's difficulty with the aspirates [t] and [p]. These are our 'separate development' peculiarities!

One can only wish, given Sobukwe's ear for accents and verbal interplay, that he had written more, made these observations the basis of a piece of dramatic art. In his letter to Marquard of 20 November 1964, Sobukwe pokes fun at his former Graaff-Reinet Methodist congregation, noting how apartheid divisions (of coloured as opposed to African identities) inevitably broke down (not without humorous consequences):

Your references to the snobbery that attached to Nederlands [early Afrikaans language and culture] in the olden days reminded me of our coloured preachers at Graaff-Reinet. The African and coloured people constitute one congregation, in all denominations, so that services are conducted in both Xhosa and Afrikaans. In those days, the thirties, the Methodist Church seemed to believe that a preacher was a more reliable agent of God if he was uneducated. The emphasis was on the 'indwelling spirit'. The result was that most of our preachers, African and coloured, were barely literate. However, it was an unquestioned convention in those days that a preacher just could not see a word if he did not have his glasses on. And as most of them were labourers who had to change into their Sunday bests, it wasn't unusual for them to find they had left their glasses behind.

But, and this is what all this nonsense is leading up to, they had to create the impression that they *could* read. It was very important in those days to be thought able to read. Those of our coloured preachers who could read, enjoyed their 'zechenen tot hem' [blessing to him].

One old man, who couldn't read, would invariably ask his congregation to sing 'gesang 256 in maXhosa taal en 46 in Hollands' [hymn 256 in Xhosa and 46 in Dutch]:

Dag des wonderen, dag des oordeel en al wat daar op volg: [Day of miracles, day of judgement and everything that follows] And they would bring the roof down. For God was understood to be very indulgent. Some sinners had been known to go to heaven because they had used their musical talents for the glory of God. And musical talent meant lung-power, that's all.

Oh, but they were an imaginative lot! Here's one preaching on the 'Fall of Man', painting a picture of God calling 'Adam! Adam!' and Adam replying from the black recesses of some thick bush, 'here am I'. God then asks him if he has eaten of the fruit and he replies 'It is this woman *You* gave me. God ignores the implied accusation, passes on to Eve and she blames the snake. God looked it up and down as it stood there in arrogant defiance. 'It's these blinking legs that gave you ideas,' said God, and with that 'whish', he cut off the legs and flat on its belly fell the snake. This, mind you, is given in onomatopoeic language, with appropriate gestures – faithfully reproduced by the interpreter – and when the snake falls 'bhaxa', explosive consonants and clicks and gestures convey most vividly the precipitate prostration of the original snake.

In a September 1966 letter, Sobukwe takes yet another opportunity to refute the mutually exclusive ethnic designations that the apartheid government hoped to extend and enforce (especially in the form of separate ethnic 'homelands'). Even while referring back to his clan totem and thereby his historical identity, Sobukwe nonetheless rejects an exclusive Xhosa identity:

I call my clan 'Baboons' because that is the totem of my clan. There are thus crocodiles, baboons, monkeys, lions, etc. You'll, therefore, realise that those who claim to know me do not in fact know me because, if I am not mistaken, I have been described as a Xhosa: I am not, as you can see.

This is followed by a typically humorous – and no doubt apocryphal – historical anecdote:

Thank you for the interesting stories about the Bushmen. They are called '*abathwa*' in Xhosa and Zulu and a phonological variant in Sotho. One common story about them is that whenever they met a Xhosa hunter they would pose the question 'when did you see me?' and since they were very touchy about their size one had to be careful to have seen them a long distance away. Unfortunately, one did not always know from what direction they had come and it was quite a risky job answering the question. The Xhosa being experienced liars lied their way out. One of them is said to have replied: 'I saw you when you were still over there on that mountain over the...re!' He pointed to a mountain in the South only to be told by the um-thwa that in fact he had approached from the North. 'Then it was your shadow I saw,' was the reply.

On liberalism

An obvious drawback of remembering Sobukwe only in certain ways – and of the limited number of biographical explorations of his life – is that we lose a sense of how Sobukwe has the capacity to surprise us. On 5 June 1968, after sharing his thoughts on the assassination attempt on Robert Kennedy, Sobukwe offers his views on the immigration restrictions Britain had recently placed on Indian Kenyans:

> You do have a way of putting things, Nell. You say Britain is the most civilised country [in the world] 'and that in spite of her restricting the entry of Kenya Indians'. I laughed when I read that. It's such a gentle rebuke! But aren't we being unfair to Britain? She has enormous economic difficulties. And this is not a steady immigration flow: It is a flood. And contrary to economic laws it is not moving towards an area of economic expansion. The *timing* has been bad. The workers feel very insecure with over 500 000 already unemployed. Unfortunately the immigrants happened to have a high melanin content [brown skin pigmentation] and in our colour-sensitive world this fact was over-emphasised.

Obviously, we need to take into account who Sobukwe is writing to, and under what conditions, and not generalise too widely on the basis of these written remarks. Nevertheless, it is notable that Sobukwe does not censure Marquard's claim (that 'Britain is the most civilised country') and in fact suggests we take a realist's perspective when considering the issue of immigration into Britain ('enormous economic difficulties ... immigration [as] a flood'). Sobukwe is not ignoring the issue of racism (hence the reference to melanin content), yet he adopts a more pragmatic – and indeed tolerant – political stance than one might have assumed. In the same letter he goes on to add:

> It was with pride that I read of the Liberal Party's decision to disband. To have argued, in the circumstances, as liberals have tended to do throughout the years, that 'half a loaf is better than no bread', would have been tragically despicable.

This seems a puzzling comment. The PAC's political stance – like that of the Black Consciousness movement to follow – was, for the most part to be suspicious of the influence of white liberals.[7] Not only was it invariably the case for stalwarts of the PAC that liberals wanted to take a dominant role in the anti-apartheid struggle, such liberals also stood in the way of a pan-Africanist agenda of returning '*Izwe Lethu!*' ('Our Land!') to the African peoples from whom it had been stolen. Indeed, for many within the PAC, pan-Africanist politics – which squarely foregrounded the needs of the oppressed African majority – took clear precedence over an assimilationist liberal vision of equality. (Hence the PAC's opposition to the multiracialism of the ANC's Freedom Charter, a type of multiracialism which, as Sobukwe put it, 'simply means transfer of the prejudices and bigotry that applies to in the present [apartheid] society to a new society'.)[8]

One can thus appreciate why Sobukwe may have been gratified to hear of the Liberal Party's decision to disband. There are several instances in subsequent letters where Sobukwe decries what he calls the political instability of liberals. '[A] liberal cannot be consistent,' he says in a letter to Marquard (9 May 1972), before going on to add: '[I]f Alan Paton, in all sincerity is to be heard to say that there might be some good in apartheid ... [then] to the oppressed he has ranged himself on the side of the oppressor.' It is then all the more surprising that in the extended extract cited above, Sobukwe notes that it was '*with pride*' that he heard of the decision, an indication of an identification with that same Liberal Party. Such an assertion possesses, once again, the ability to confound us in our expectations of Sobukwe, certainly so if we have assumed that all of Sobukwe's values and political thinking are determined by a radical commitment to Africa and Africa alone.

In retrospect, however, these comments are perhaps not so surprising. Despite the more strident anti-liberal interpretations of Sobukwe's Africanism, Pogrund asserts that by mid-1960, Sobukwe's men (that is, the PAC leaders) 'would have been willing to accept the amalgamation of the PAC and the Liberal Party, had the situation arisen'.[9] Sobukwe as liberal? This seems as difficult to imagine for hardline pan-Africanists as it is for many white liberals who insisted that 'Black Power' was tantamount to reverse racism. Such a characterisation is seemingly supported by the title of Tom Lodge's review of Pogrund's biography of Sobukwe, which was titled, tellingly, 'A liberal of a different colour'.[10] My point here is not to endorse such a view but simply to stress how Sobukwe's letters call us to consider the complexity of Sobukwe's personal and political views, which were seldom if ever one-dimensional.

Pain

Responding to Marquard's question whether he had started reading a CP Snow novel that she had sent him earlier that year, Sobukwe responded:

> I have not yet started on Snow's *The Masters*: not because I do not have time or am not interested, but because I am afraid. There is a thin, choking pain that runs through Snow's novels – a kind of primeval, community pain, unaccountable and incurable – that I find difficult to bear. Roy Calvert and Sheila Knight [characters in Snow's fiction] leave me limp with pain. They seem to suffer purely and simply because they are themselves; their suffering is written into the code of their personality. There is nothing they can do to avoid it and there is nothing their friends can do to contain their pain. I am intellectually unprepared at the moment to expose myself to similar suffering.
>
> When we were boys at Graaff-Reinet we used to hunt snakes, lizards, butterflies … Whenever a snake entered a hole our leader, older and bolder than the rest of us, would smoke it out after placing a blade in the ground. I never saw this happen, but I was assured by the others that when the snake left in that direction, the blade would cut into its soft belly and as it felt the pain it would push forward more firmly, hoping to escape the pain but merely succeeding to disembowel itself. That is how I feel Snow's tragic characters behave.

Nell Marquard reflected on this passage, some twenty years after receiving Sobukwe's letter cited above, observing – accurately, I believe – that 'Suffering in others hurt him deeply … he found Snow's *The Masters* [1950] almost insupportable because of [the] pain that runs through [it]'.[11] Of course, there was the considerable suffering that Sobukwe was himself going through at the time –

loneliness, estrangement, the denial of human contact, etc – and yet Marquard's implication rings true: the suffering of others was, to him, more intolerable than his own pain.

If we skip ahead a few years to 1974, after Sobukwe had been released from Robben Island and was living in Kimberley, we begin to appreciate how pain itself was something that provided a bond between Marquard and himself:

> I learnt some time ago that one cannot put oneself in another's position. We may express sympathy, feel it and even imagine the pain. But we cannot feel it as the one who suffers it. They have a saying in Xhosa that the toothache is felt by the one whose tooth is aching.

Sobukwe was writing just after the death of Marquard's husband, the noted Cape liberal, author and historian, Leo Marquard. Touching as this acknowledgement of Leo Marquard's passing would have been for Nell Marquard, the real poignancy of Sobukwe's letter comes a little further on, when he starts speaking of the myriad difficulties he has faced since leaving Robben Island:

> It has not been a good year for me. I had planned to leave [from Kimberley] … by car on the 31st May and make straight for Cape Town. But these boys beat me to it. They came on the 30th May, 1974 to serve the fresh lot of bureaucratic output. Well it's good to know that our security is entrusted to such alert people.

Although he makes light of it, one senses in Sobukwe's letter that the constant surveillance and harassment by the security police was taking its toll. He continues:

Veronica has had a major operation as you probably read in the papers. She should have had this operation last year, but did not and the condition got worse.

She has made a remarkable recovery, thanks to my very efficient and tender nursing, and has now gone back to Joh'burg for a check-up. From there she will be to Durban to spend a week or so with her sister before proceeding to Swaziland to see the children.

These understated lines could only have masked Sobukwe's sadness and anger at being alone once again after his ordeal of six years of near-complete solitary confinement on Robben Island, and indeed, at not being able to accompany his wife in her time of need. It is only on the last page of the letter that Sobukwe seemed finally to find the words that suited both his emotions and the note of commiseration that he wished to convey to Nell:

> The Xhosa have standard words of condolence. They say
> Akuhlanga lungehlanga hala ngenxeba
> (There has not occurred what has not occurred before … LIE
> ON YOUR WOUND).
> God bless you
>   Affectionately
>   Robert

This resonant phrase – which also appears in Sobukwe's letters to his friend Benjamin Pogrund – applies equally, if not more so, to Sobukwe himself. 'Lie on your wound(s)' is a call to bide one's time, to heal, and to reconstitute oneself despite evident suffering. It is a call to have courage, to bear the moral burden of pain. This phrase perhaps contains a clue as to why letter-writing was so important to Sobukwe. To write was, perhaps, a means through which he could express his hopes and thoughts, the stories, jokes, the African historical anecdotes, which despite defining him were never his alone. More than this, to write of such shared ideas and experiences would also have been to reiterate how he could not be unburdened of the suffering associated with those hopes and thoughts, that there was a suffering that he needed to endure alone.

Blacks and whites in building a just South Africa

Bobby Godsell

Bobby Godsell was senior labour-relations adviser at Anglo American Corporation for 20 years, from 1974. From 1995 to 2007 he was CEO of Anglo's gold-mining interests, which were later restructured into AngloGold Ashanti. Since then, he has been a member of South Africa's first National Planning Commission, and briefly chair of the national electricity utility, Eskom. He is a director of the Industrial Development Corporation and co-chairs Citizens South Africa, which advocates for active citizenship.

I WANT TO REFLECT on three powerful South Africans from the 1960s and 1970s. I seek to understand what their lives, deeds and words said about justice and race relations. I will then reflect on what these ideas suggest as our country prepares to enter the third decade of the 21st century.

Robert Mangaliso Sobukwe was born in Graaff-Reinet in 1924 and completed his secondary schooling in the Methodist Church school at Healdtown before completing a Bachelor of Arts degree at the University College of Fort Hare. After teaching at a township high school in Standerton, he joined Wits University as a language assistant. Sobukwe was active in student politics at Fort Hare; in the Youth League of the African National Congress (ANC) he helped to bring about the Programme of Action in 1949. This programme, together with the 'African Claims' document adopted by the ANC in 1943, confirmed Sobukwe's identity as an Africanist.

Disputes both about strategies of resistance and the role of non-blacks in the framing and execution of these strategies led Sobukwe to join other Africanists in forming the Pan Africanist Congress (PAC) in 1959. In the next year, on 21 March 1960, this organisation called on black South Africans to leave their passes – which they were required to carry by laws governing influx control – at home and present themselves at police stations for arrest. Initially, a small group did this at the police station in Sharpeville. After some hours, the group had grown into a large crowd. The police response was to open fire on both protesters and spectators, killing 69 people.

Sobukwe was found guilty of incitement and sentenced to three years' imprisonment. Shortly before this sentence ended, he was moved, in a very unusual pattern of imprisonment, to a former warder's house on Robben Island, and was separated from all other prisoners. This detention continued for six years, being renewed each year by a clause that had to be approved by the all-white South African Parliament. It became known as the Sobukwe Clause, as he was the only person ever imprisoned under its terms. In 1969, Sobukwe was moved to Kimberley, under house arrest, where he spent the rest of his life until his death from cancer in 1978.

Bantu Stephen Biko was born in Tarkastad in 1946. He completed his schooling at the Anglican and Catholic church schools of Lovedale and Mariannhill before commencing medical studies at the all-black medical school at the otherwise almost all-white University of Natal. Biko, together with a group of black and Indian students, broke away from the multiracial and broadly liberal National Union of South African Students (Nusas) to form the blacks-only South African Students' Organisation (Saso) in 1968. Central to the new student body were the ideas loosely described by the name Black Consciousness, seeking both positive and black-defined meanings for the way black South Africans experienced being in apartheid society. Biko and seven other Saso leaders were placed under banning orders in 1973. In 1977, Biko was detained for breaking his banning order and was brutally assaulted. He died of his injuries after days without appropriate medical attention, and after being transferred in a small truck from Port Elizabeth to Pretoria.

Rick Turner was born in Cape Town in 1941. He finished his schooling and undergraduate university education there before undertaking a study on existential phenomenology at the Sorbonne in Paris. After a short interlude back in Cape Town, he took up a lecturing position in political philosophy at the University of Natal, where he played a critical leadership role in both student politics and the renascence of black unionism in the early 1970s. He was served with a banning order in 1973, at the same time as Steve Biko and other Saso and Nusas leaders. In 1978 he was assassinated, almost certainly at the behest of the South African government's security services.

What were the critical ideas that linked these three lives and helped shape their times?

Turner and Biko were close friends and clearly shared many beliefs and values about their society. Biko had some contact with Sobukwe during the latter's house arrest in Kimberley.

A shared sense of a just society

In 1972, Rick Turner wrote a utopian essay titled 'The Eye of the Needle: A Guide to Participatory Democracy in South Africa'.[1] This set out an ideal future society that has removed race barriers and included all citizens in full and meaningful participation in the country's political, economic and social life. This vision of an inclusive, participatory and just society fully resonates with everything that both Sobukwe and Biko wrote about the South Africa they sought to build.

In a postscript to this essay, penned just one year later and titled 'The Present as History', Turner speculated on how such a participatory democracy might come about. He explored the need and the possibility of building a powerful mass black political organisation. This would require an alliance between the fledgling organisations of black workers that were already appearing. This alliance between black workers, the ideas of the Black Consciousness movement and the 'space' created by some black leaders who had assumed leadership roles within institutions created by the separate-development ideology of Afrikaner nationalism offered a chance to escape the vice-like grip the white minority regime had on South Africa in the early 1970s.

Both the Africanist PAC and Black Consciousness Saso deliberately avoided either advocating or endorsing armed struggle. The PAC, like Turner, was keenly interested in collaborating with black workers, Saso much less so.

Turner's strategies for building a participatory democracy were diverse and varied, and included an energetic engagement with critical centres of white liberal power, especially the English-language universities, press and churches. He appeared less optimistic about engaging with Afrikaner intellectuals, although just a decade later the Afrikaner-controlled Human Sciences Research Council published a report on what was coyly titled 'Intergroup Relations', the substance of which echoed in many parts the English churches' Study Project on Christianity in an Apartheid Society, for which Turner wrote 'The Eye of the Needle'.

Much of the debate provoked by the creation of first the PAC and then Saso and other formations of the Black Consciousness movement focused on their blacks-only character. This was often perceived as anti-white. Even more, it was described as a negation of the idea of a non-racial future South Africa. But any thoughtful reading of the writings of both Sobukwe and Biko will quickly indicate how wrong both these reactions were and are.

Both the Africanism of the PAC and the Black Consciousness of Saso sought to define and defend the role of black South Africans in their own organisations, determining their own strategies and speaking in their own voices. This declaration of agency was clearly needed as an alternative to the often-suffocating role played by leaders drawn from the white community who sought to act in those organisations on behalf of black South Africans. In the case of the ANC, these whites were often communists. Leaders from the Natal and Transvaal Indian congresses also played prominent roles.

Both Sobukwe and Biko recognised situations in which they shared values with communists, socialists and liberals. They could also see the value of strategic alliances with other organisations. They were, however, determined to create spaces where black South Africans could plan positively and creatively for themselves and think, speak and act freely.

Not the slightest indication can be found that either Sobukwe or Biko envisaged or wanted a future South Africa shorn of its white citizenry. They were deeply committed to a common humanity shared by South Africans of all races. Unfortunately, the negative response by some whites to Africanism and Black Consciousness confused their determination to give blacks space and a voice with the end goal of the society the black organisations wanted to create.

It was a tragic misunderstanding. It was surely responsible for the absence of effective alliances and coalitions with many org-anisations that shared an opposition to the apartheid state and a determination to replace it with a non-racial democracy.

Even sadder was the failure of the white ruling elite to engage Sobukwe and Biko and Turner in dialogue. After Sobukwe's initial three-year prison sentence for incitement, he was effectively re-moved from society and political action. Yet his seclusion offered opportunities to read, study and interact with his family and visitors, greater than those available to many other political prisoners. Why did the architects of Afrikaner nationalism not use his presence in their custody to engage with him about his views and hopes for the future?

A similar pattern was present in the state's reaction to Biko. Though banned, Biko was never charged in court. Instead, at the Saso trial of 1974–1976 he was a key, even a star witness for the defence. The court record of his interaction with Judge Boshoff in this trial is a comical and also tragic Rorschach test of the way in which the young man and the elderly judge lived in a country they both called South Africa. Here is an example:

> *Judge Boshoff:* Mr Biko, why do you people then pick on the word black? I mean black is really an innocent reference which has been arrived at over the years the same as white; snow is regarded as white, and snow is regarded as the purest form of water and so it symbolises purity, so white there has got nothing to do with the white man?
>
> *Biko:* Right.
>
> *Judge Boshoff:* But now why do you refer to you people as blacks? Why not brown people? I mean you people are more brown than black.
>
> *Biko:* In the same way as I think white people are more pink and yellow and pale than white.

When Biko was detained, the assault on him was savage, and the treatment by an array of senior police and police-appointed medical officers was inhuman and an example of state terrorism at its very worst. It is hard to reconcile the state's ambivalence towards Biko during his banning, which at least in some respects allowed for continuing activities, including travel, with the brutality of his murder.

Race relations

As South Africa prepares to enter this third decade of the 21st century, signs abound of black South Africans asserting positive identities. This positive consciousness is evident in as quotidian things as names, hairstyles and dress codes. It is evident in the growth of black African publishing. It is evident in the creation of black-designed and black-led institutions and cultural spaces across our society.

White South Africans should delight in this positive con-sciousness. It is an assertion of both the identity and agency of the majority of our citizenry. Precisely as Sobukwe and Biko urged, this is black South Africans defining their own space, in their own voices. It is about the nature and role of black South Africans as citizens. Indigenous hair and dress do not deny white people their role in this shared and non-racial society.

As with Sobukwe and Biko, there are some important lessons.

At the heart of Sobukwe and Biko's struggle was the desire for black South Africans to speak for themselves, in organisations of their own design, and with interests, values and beliefs of their own definition. The conscious and unconscious way in which white communists, socialists and liberals appropriated this space and spoke for their fellow citizens quite naturally, was rejected – as it should be rejected today.

Then and now, this emphasis on agency for black citizens does not in any way preclude shared organisations and agendas. Sobukwe in the early 1960s is on the record as contemplating cooperation with liberals. The key learning from Sobukwe and Biko is perhaps agency and positive identity first, and cooperation second.

There are other lessons for white South Africans in the Africanism and Black Consciousness of past decades.

The first is to see, recognise and respect black-defined spaces, agendas and actions. The desire of whites has often been to incorporate their fellow citizens into spaces and institutions deeply shaped by whiteness. This often renders the incorporated as second-class participants in a reality they have no room to substantially shape.

Increasingly, spaces exist that are designed, or indeed directed and shaped, by black South Africans. Whites need to do the travelling. They need to leave their ghettoes, and venture into both black and shared spaces. This travelling may well involve physical trips to unfamiliar venues. They will certainly involve an ordering of events, agendas and discourses that will be unfamiliar, at least in part. It will involve the literal experience of being a minority. This is what whites are in South Africa (and indeed in the world). These experiences will often be uncomfortable – but also deeply rewarding in terms of new insights and of a new identity for the newcomer. Sometimes the newcomers will be clumsy, ignorant. They must step back and listen. And even apologise.

A second vital learning is to share the oxygen. An analysis of much of our social discourse reveals an over-representation of white South Africans. If we had verbatim transcripts of these discourses, they would reveal an even greater predominance of the minority voice. Reduced to an aphorism, I guess the advice is: show up (in your neighbour's space) as often as you can. And once there, shut up at least some of the time. Learn to listen actively before you engage.

None of this is to suggest in any way that whites (and members of other minority groups) are second-class citizens. No one is here on sufferance. No one is a visitor or a guest. Nor is it to suggest that race defines everything. Overwhelmingly, national concerns transcend race. Aversion to corruption and the desire for an inclusive prosperity are two important contemporary examples. Indeed, the opportunities now exist for building new shared institutions and agendas. These opportunities are greater and stronger than they have ever been.

Shared prosperity

Though a just society may be hard to define, it is, like beauty, not difficult to recognise. This is equally true of its opposite, an unjust society. From Turner, we can learn the importance of having a clear end goal, ideal state or specific sense of what we wish to create.

The core elements of a just society are the foundational injunctions of all world religions. Closer to home they have been clearly articulated in documents such as 'African Claims', the Programme of Action, the Freedom Charter and 'The Eye of the Needle'. Of direct application to our times are the aspirations set out in the Preamble to our country's 1996 Constitution, as well as in the Bill of Rights contained in this Constitution. The content and character of a just society are again well described at the start and end of the long poem, 'Our future – make it work', in the 2011 National Development Plan's vision for South Africa 2030:

> … we live in a country which we have remade.
> We have created a home where everybody feels free yet bonded
> to others; where everyone embraces their full potential …
> … South Africa belongs to all its peoples.
> We, the people, belong to one another.
> We live the rainbow.
> Our homes, neighbourhoods, villages, towns, and cities are safe
> and filled with laughter.
> Through our institutions, we order our lives.
> The faces of our children tell of the future we have crafted.

Another vital learning from Turner is the need to pair a clear sense of future vision with a well-articulated and realistic sense of strategy, or how we might get there. Perhaps the central idea I take from Turner is that strategy and hope are in fact essential fellow travellers.

What do these insights tell us about present struggles for a just society? To answer, we must move from the abstract to more concrete elements of justice. Two burning issues dominate much of the contemporary discourse: land and jobs.

Land

Any consideration of land must begin with a sober recognition of our country's history. The control and ownership of land today is the product of colonial conquest. Land was taken by armed conquest. The consequence of both colonial settlement and in particular the 1913 and 1936 Land Acts was to reserve effectively 87 per cent of South Africa's land for white ownership and use. The remaining 13 per cent is held communally and controlled by traditional authorities. What makes South Africa unique as an African country is that the colonialists stayed. This makes the unravelling of past conflicts about land that much more difficult.

The 1996 Constitution, in its now well-read Section 25, makes three promises about land. The first is that where land was taken by a specific race-defined action it shall be returned to its original owners. The second is that all South African citizens should have 'just and equitable access' to land. The third is that all citizens should enjoy a meaningful security of tenure.

These seem only promises. How do we ensure their achievement?

Some restitution has taken place, though it has been slow and thousands of claims lodged remain to be dealt with. Thus far, the government has elected to use a pattern of expropriation based solely on market value, and the 'willing buyer, willing seller' principle. In fact, the Constitution requires only that compensation for land restitution be 'just and equitable'. The Bill of Rights identifies market value as one of five measures to determine what is just and equitable. The other four are: the current use of the property; its history of acquisition and use; the extent of state investment and subsidy; and the purpose of acquisition.

The slow pace of restitution appears to be largely a product of bureaucratic failure and corruption, as identified in 2017 by the High Level Report, chaired by former president Kgalema Motlanthe, on Parliament and accelerating fundamental change.[2] There seems no reason why the remaining claims for restitution of land should not be expeditiously, transparently and fairly completed.

With regard to the second promise, of equitable access, it is necessary to inquire into the purpose for which citizens may seek land. Two broad purposes suggest themselves. The first is for economic activity, especially food production. Here we need to heed Turner. Over the last few decades, markets for food production have been fundamentally transformed. For most of the post–Second World War decades, food production was producer-controlled. Governments and farmers decided what should be grown. Governments subsidised farmers and food production. They often funded the stockpiling of food. The continuing evidence of this practice is to be seen in the large grain silos that guard rural landscapes all over 'white' farming areas.

In recent decades, food production has become consumption-controlled, with the retail networks deciding not only what gets grown, but also how this gets to the supermarket shelf, hence determining the economics of food production.

This shift is already evident in the patterns of commercial agriculture in South Africa. Natural-person, single-owner or family farming have all declined. Increasingly, food is produced by large agribusinesses capable not only of producing food, but also of managing both the logistics and economics of getting food to market. A large part of this process is negotiating off-take agreements with retail chains. Producing food is a very risky business without assured access to markets.

Policies that seek to increase black South African involvement in food production need to take account of global food markets.

These are characterised by low tariffs, declining government support and the dominant role of retail food chains. The contours of contemporary global food markets create both obstacles and opportunities for just and equitable citizen access to land for food production. The new opportunities for food production are well described in the 2011 National Development Plan. A number of pilot projects are exploring the role of black citizens in the economic activities and institutions created around farming that seek to ensure that food produced results in sustainable wealth creation.

The hunger for land for secure residence may well be present among the majority of our citizenry. To address this hunger, we will need to ensure not only equitable access but also secure tenure. Here, urban and peri-urban land is crucial. In fact, land for residence is critical in every part of the country.

To address this need, we will have to grapple not only with the ownership of land but also its control. Sectional-title ownership and condominium complexes have already come to dominate commercial housing in urban areas. Ensuring both equitable access and security of tenure in those areas that have a history of townships or locations raises a quite different set of challenges, as does security of tenure in informal settlements. Perhaps the most policy-complex set of issues revolves around ownership of, access to and regulation of communal land.

Making good on the land-related promises of the 1996 Constitution will require more than a chorus of slogans. A careful consideration of the problems experienced in the first 25 years of our democracy, as identified, inter alia, in the High Level Report, is a good place to start, such as the evidence it heard that 'land reform policy has drifted from its initial pro-poor focus to one marked by signs of elite capture'.

Jobs

If the hunger for land is one intense centre of the national discourse, the search for jobs is another.

In any ideal contemporary economy, citizens should be able to be economically active, using their labour, skills and experiences to provide goods and services to others in exchange for fair reward. It is just this ideal that has been at the heart of the social compact that was the foundation not only for economic progress but also political stability and social cohesion in so many countries after the Second World War.

This was the ideal that inspired Franklin Roosevelt's New Deal in the 1930s, and Lyndon Johnson's War on Poverty in the 1960s. It inspired the establishment of Britain's National Health Service in 1948. Across Europe, Asia and Latin America, countries pursued not only economic growth but also full employment.

Employment is the second objective of the US central bank, with price stability its first target. High levels of unemployment have everywhere been seen as a social ill, as dangerous as high levels of inflation. There are growing indications, however, that the goal of full employment is rapidly becoming unachievable. At least two forces are at work to make employment maintenance, let alone growth, difficult.

The first is the rise of fund-manager capitalism. In the 1980s, Margaret Thatcher and Ronald Reagan lifted the regulation on pension funds and life insurance – the main sources of contractual savings. Previously, most savings had to be held in low-risk bond instruments, which require no active management. Allowing these massive streams of capital formation to flow into much more volatile equity investments created a new control structure for capitalism. These funds are managed by fund managers, who are most often active traders in equities, perhaps buying and selling a single equity several times in the typical 90-day period over which the fund manager's wealth-creation performance is measured.

These new captains of capitalism have reshaped the nature of the firm through the pattern of their actions. The single important metric for a publicly listed company is its market capitalisation. This metric is calculated by multiplying the last trade in its shares in a trading day by the full amount of shares in issue. This metric encourages fund managers to engage in short-term trading. To create wealth using this measure they have only to replicate short-term price movements over the 90-day period.

Creating wealth has come to be measured by this rather arbitrary metric. In a similar way, the purpose of the firm has been narrowed to only achieving maximum returns for its shareholders, normally now represented by the fund managers who trade in its shares. In this context, employment is clearly a cost that reduces profits, and therefore the share price.

During the 12 years I spent reporting every three months to the 20 or so mainly American fund managers who traded in AngloGold shares, two questions were my constant companions. The first was about South Africa's politics. Despite the at least formal ending of the racist political and constitution regimes, many fund managers expressed concern about the continuing levels of poverty and economic exclusion. Could political stability be sustained in this context? The most common question about the firm was what were we doing to reduce costs and increase the margins between costs and revenue. If we had reduced employment in the three months under review, this produced a positive response from fund managers. My attempts to connect the dots between poverty and unemployment failed miserably.

The second force undermining the expansion of employment is the advance of the digital revolution, one that has been in the making from before the last world war. These advances are to be seen in the militarisation of computing devices, increased storage, more rapid digital processing and the increasing application of digital capacities to what were previously mechanical devices, perhaps most vividly illustrated by 3D printing. Finally, there are the advances in both big data and artificial intelligence.

Taken together, these advances have been given the benign-sounding label of the 'fourth industrial revolution'. All the changes in technology are reshaping the global economy. All are alive and well in the South African economy. All are making it harder to tackle the disturbingly high levels of structural unemployment in our economy.

This is the context in which the promises of political elites with regard to jobs must be measured. For some years now, there has been a kind of job-creation bazaar evident in our political discourse. As the leader of one political party promises to create five million jobs over ten years, so another will promise more jobs over a shorter period.

Yet the same technological advances that have reshaped the production of both goods and services are now also reshaping the architecture of work. In this they have been supported by what are often labelled neoliberal economic policies. It has become easier to fire workers. Indeed, the conventional promise of continued employment has now reverted to piece-work employment. Many service workers operate on a zero-hours contract. The defined pension benefit was meant to ensure a worker's financially secure retirement after several decades of employment. This has been almost universally replaced by a defined contribution concept, which makes the pension or provident fund simply a savings fund.

As first-time job seekers can seldom expect several decades of secure employment, the idea of a home mortgage, with a 10-, 20- or even 30-year repayment period becomes high-risk. This risk became evident in the 2008/2009 global financial crisis. In this climate, it may well be that in five or ten years' time the top 40 companies trading on the Johannesburg Stock Exchange will all employ fewer people than they do today.

This is the hostile environment in which job hunger in South Africa must be addressed. The ideal of full economic inclusion must of course remain. But it will have to be pursued in the light of contemporary realities.

It seems to me fundamentally irresponsible to promise young people jobs. They will have to use what they have to get what they want. This will be transactional, and in only a minority of cases at best is it likely to result in employment that is long-term and secure, and supports a pension fund, home mortgage and medical aid.

The goal of economic inclusion will have to be pursued, together with a fundamental review of the structure of our economy. We will need 21st-century housing ideas. The provision and funding of healthcare will have to change. The balance of taxation as between income and consumption will need to be reviewed. State-provided support through grants and subsidies will also need to be reviewed, including the concept of a basic income grant.

This is the agenda for those who seek (as we all must) the equitable inclusion of all in an economy that both accommodates and fairly meets the needs of all.

If we are to address these challenges with integrity in this new century of low growth and growing global divisions between defensive insiders and angry outsiders, we will need both courage and wisdom. We will need to draw on the courage and wisdom of Sobukwe, Biko and Turner.

In his grave, still paying a price for his integrity

Joel Mbhele

Joel Mbhele is a co-founder of MANJ Neuro and Forensic Psych Company, which provides psychological services to law firms in Gauteng, Limpopo and North West. He is a clinical psychologist with the Zimbabwe Truth Forum, providing healing for traumatised Zimbabweans in South Africa. He is a resident psychologist for the Ethics and Governance Think Tank at the Gordon Institute of Business Science (GIBS). He worked for the South African Department of Correctional Services as a clinical psychologist. His job entailed providing psychotherapy to convicted offenders.

THE GOVERNMENT that came to power in South Africa in 1994 inherited the economic and social legacies of apartheid. It was faced with a large pool of unskilled and unemployed labour, acute and widespread poverty, and poor access to education, health and other basic public amenities for a large majority of the population.[1]

The government promised to address these challenges. Moeletsi Mbeki, in *Advocates for Change: How to Overcome Africa's Challenges*, argues that not much has been done to address these challenges. He says that South Africa has what it takes to be an economically independent nation but something seems to be hindering its progress.

Mbeki raises these questions about South Africa and Africa: what is lacking in a land that has the most minerals on earth, that has a huge tourism potential based on its enormous cultural, ecological and geographical diversity, on a continent that has the world's largest reserves of the platinum-group metals, as well as chromium, gold, manganese and large reserves of other minerals, a continent that is rich in history and heritage, a continent that has great world icons?[2]

Africa needs a renewed sense of moral and purposeful leadership, as Shields, Edwards and Sayani argue in *Inspiring Practice: Spirituality & Educational Leadership*.[3] To substantiate their call, they say that Africa needs the kind of leadership that takes into account the need for social inclusion, for new and heterogeneous school communities, and for democratic citizenship.

In an earlier book, *Architects of Poverty: Why African Capitalism Needs Changing*, Moeletsi Mbeki argues that there is a generally expressed consensus that Africa lacks dynamic and innovative political and economic leadership.[4] In regard to South Africa, how do we restore leadership in a country that has to spend hundreds of millions investigating corruption while millions of people live in abject poverty? A society that seems to have chosen charisma over character, politics over people, slogans over truth, and government officials who succumb to corruption because they don't want to lose their jobs. The fear of poverty and the deceitfulness of wealth seems to have captured our integrity.

In reading Benjamin Pogrund's biography of Robert Sobukwe, *How Can Man Die Better*, I found myself inspired and astonished by the level of integrity with which Sobukwe lived his life. As a psychologist, I wanted to write about his intelligence, upbringing and interactional style. I wanted to comment on the psychological impact of imprisonment on Robert Sobukwe, but I just couldn't help but be drawn more to his personality trait of integrity. This chapter is about Robert Sobukwe's integrity and the price that he paid for it.

Defining integrity

I define integrity as consistently upholding a certain level of moral standards and values regardless of context or circumstances. Lack of integrity manifests itself in inconsistencies, for example male politicians who speak for gender equality in public but abuse women in their homes; priests who preach from the pulpit against sexual immorality but sodomise children in their houses; ministers who publicly insist on the quality of education in public schools but still send their children to private schools. Inconsistency!

One cannot talk about Sobukwe's leadership without talking about integrity. My view is that integrity finds its expression in the African philosophy of Ubuntu.

Ubuntu

At the centre of Sobukwe's hard work, excellence, boldness and sacrifice was his conviction about human dignity. In most instances, Sobukwe's servanthood was inspired by the conviction that every human deserves respect. Archbishop Desmond Tutu described Sobukwe as utterly selfless and dedicated to people. It is reported that Sobukwe used to remain behind at school to give extra classes to students. On several occasions he left his comfort zone for the benefit of others. With his intelligence and level of education, Sobukwe could easily have lived comfortably with his family and not become involved in the struggle for freedom. However, he believed in the protection and respect of fellow human beings, regardless of race, language or social status, and he fought for freedom because he believed it was the right thing to do. Ubuntu was at the centre of his politics.

The word 'Ubuntu' is the combination of two Zulu words, *ntu* (human) and *ubu-ntu* (human-ness). The direct translation of Ubuntu is 'humanness'. The definition of the concept of Ubuntu is highly influenced by Africans' conception of a human being.

According to businessman and thought leader Reuel Khoza, Africans define a person as a being whose nature is determined by his or her relationship to the community.[5] Johann Broodryk describes Ubuntu as 'an ancient African worldview based on the primary values of intense humanness, caring, sharing, respect, compassion and associated values, ensuring a happy and qualitative human community life in the spirit of family',[6] while Mfuniselwa John Bhengu calls it 'the art of being a human being'.[7] For philosopher Dirk Louw, 'Ubuntu is an African concept advocating for the sharing of what one has, or use what you have for the wellbeing, prosperity or advancement of others'.[8] We can conclude that these various definitions conjure up images of supportiveness, collaboration, cooperation, solidarity, sharing, caring and sympathy.

Khoza argues that Ubuntu is a South African version of African concepts like pan-Africanism. According to him, pan-Africanism was coined by a West Indian philosopher named Edward Blyden, who insisted that Africans have their own sense of God, their own moral codes and their own spiritual life. Khoza says it was the poet Aimé Césaire (1982) who coined the term *négritude*, which he said is an essence of being an African. Both Blyden and Césaire believe that Africans have a sense of universal brotherhood. As Khoza puts it: 'Africans sharing, treating and respecting other people are values that are deeply embedded in the spirit of each and every African person.'

This is reinforced by Broodryk, who states that Ubuntu is an ancient philosophy or worldview that has its roots deeply anchored in traditional African life. According to Khoza, in other parts of Africa they use the concept of African humanism to refer to an African personality that leads to collective existence and intersubjectivity. In South Africa, the term Ubuntu was coined to refer to this African humanism. Other advocates of Ubuntu, such as Professor Geoff Moore, an expert in business ethics, say that the concept of Ubuntu was frequently used by Desmond Tutu.[9] According to Broodryk, Ubuntu is based on an African aphorism that embraces that which is morally good, and which brings dignity, respect, contentment and prosperity to others, the self and the community at large. He says that Ubuntu encompasses two main principles. First, it promotes a sense of brotherhood: people should seek to give emotional and physical support to each other. As Students' Representative Council (SRC) president at Fort Hare, Sobukwe was moved by the plight of nursing students who had been expelled from Victoria Hospital. It is reported that these students spent two weeks sleeping on the open hospital lawn. He played a crucial role in ensuring that they received blankets and food. His compassion for fellow students inspired him to attend to issues that were beyond his mandate as SRC president. His family background, as part of a Christian family of seven children, might have helped to teach Sobukwe the principle of sharing.

Second, Ubuntu teaches that all people should be respected and treated with dignity, regardless of who they are. Sobukwe's commitment to serving humanity with dignity is well captured in the speech that he gave at Fort Hare:

> Education to us means service to Africa. You have a mission; we all have a mission. A nation to build we have, a God to glorify, a contribution clear towards the blessing of human kind. We must be the embodiment of our people's aspirations, and a doctrine of hate can never take people anywhere. It is too exacting. It warps the mind. That is why we preach the doctrine of love, love for Africa.[10]

Sobukwe's integrity was built on the conviction that all humans deserve respect and love. He stood for this conviction to the point of death. In addition to his commitment to humanity, his integrity was shown by his work ethic. His leadership and influence was a result of his genuine love for people, hard work and self-development.

Diligence

> Work hard, and you will be a leader; be lazy, and you will end up a slave. Hard work will give you power; being lazy will make you a slave.[11]

One of the benefits of hard work is influence: when we look around and try to find what is common to all the influential people in politics, religion, sports, business and other fields – whether their influence is bad or good – it all comes as a result of hard work.

Robert Mangaliso Sobukwe was born on 5 December 1924 in Graaff-Reinet. From an early age, his mind was filled with new and exciting ideas about the world. He was always a diligent learner. It was his knowledge and eloquence that gave him such a great influence among his peers.

This is the man who founded the Pan Africanist Congress and led the anti-pass campaign that so frightened the apartheid government. We might not like some of his political ideas, but the truth remains: Robert Mangaliso Sobukwe was one of the most influential politicians of the struggle. His diligence in studying and his eloquence in public speaking are what history remembers him for. Today, South Africa lacks leaders who rise to power through hard work. We have leaders who are appointed to run ministries about which they know nothing, and about which they have no interest in learning. The culture of working your way up has been replaced by political affiliations and bribery.

If you invest your time in a particular subject, you naturally become an authority in that area. Sobukwe invested time in learning about African politics and economics. This is what gave him influence among his peers.

Integrity teaches us that leadership is learned through humility and not manipulation. From the life of Robert Sobukwe one can extract a lesson of leadership that is concomitant with the philosophy of Ubuntu: leadership is earned, and as an individual you serve your way up. Sobukwe was from a poor family when he started at Healdtown. He had no knowledge of politics, but through his humility and teachability he learnt politics, history and leadership to such an extent that his peers regarded him as an informed individual worthy of their trust. It was not by accident that he was elected SRC president. Sobukwe's integrity is also demonstrated by his willingness to pay a price for what he believed in.

The cost of integrity

South Africa has taken a stand against corruption. Millions of rands have been spent on establishing commissions to investigate corruption. Those who resist the temptation of corruption are often hailed as heroes. Every opposition party promises to fight corruption and to lead the country with integrity. The need for integrity is preached by media houses, politicians and civil society, but this does not bring an end to corruption. The question is: why do we increasingly see the rise of corrupt officials in politics, corporates and religious institutions, etc.?

Sobukwe's commitment to serve humanity is shown by the challenges that he had to endure in his lifetime. He faced a number of painful experiences in his student life, political career, personal life and professional career. His ideas often attracted controversy and punishment. Already in high school he started paying the cost of integrity. He was appointed as a school prefect and one of his responsibilities was to look out for students who urinated in the school corridors. Pogrund reports that Sobukwe was so committed to the task that he would climb on top of a classroom roof to catch offenders. He was able to trap a number of students by using this strategy. This made him unpopular among the students and even earned him the title of sellout. Sobukwe was not bothered; instead, he insisted that he would act in the same way if he had to track down offenders.[12]

In December 1946, as a first-year student, Sobukwe gave a speech at Fort Hare's Wesley House residence. According to Pogrund, the speech was on parochialism and the frivolous attitude of students in the hostel. The speech offended senior students and they decided not to speak to Sobukwe for a month.[13] This did not change Sobukwe's convictions about student life.

As SRC president, Sobukwe told his fellow students never to fear victimisation: 'I said last year we should not fear victimisation. I still say so today. We must fight for freedom for the right to call our souls our own. And we must pay the price.'[14]

Sobukwe understood that standing up for what you believe in will cost you. This was shown not only in his speeches but also in the life he lived. He risked losing financial support and facing victimisation as a student. He was always prepared to pay the price. This is what I call integrity. Integrity is not cheap, which is why few of us can live and lead with integrity. It is a rare commodity in politics and business. Big companies fall by the wayside because of a lack of integrity. Many individuals have decided to keep quiet about corrupt activities in government and corporate life because they are not ready to pay the price.

Sobukwe was sidelined and punished by the authorities because he would not compromise his integrity. He was imprisoned for nine years under very harsh prison conditions. Having worked in prison myself, I witnessed the psychological trauma of being separated from family, friends and the community at large. According to deprivation theory, when inmates enter prison, they are faced with major social and psychological challenges that result from the loss of freedom, status, dignity, possessions, autonomy, security and personal relationships. Institutionalisation creates anger and bitterness in some inmates, hence some of them leave prison more violent than before. The unfair, inhuman and traumatic conditions that Sobukwe had to endure in prison would have easily led an average inmate to anger and bitterness. Sobukwe understood the intention of his enemy.

The conditions enforced on him were designed to cause Sobukwe to desire personal freedom and forget about the freedom of all oppressed communities. Sobukwe refused to play into the enemy's hands. He understood that by doing so he would compromise his integrity. Viktor Frankl says that 'everything can be taken from a man but one thing: the last of the human freedoms – to choose one's attitude in any given set of circumstances, to choose one's own way'.[15] Sobukwe chose to keep an attitude of respect towards his enemy. He refused to be angry and bitter, and instead chose to ask the priest to pray for his enemy. Sobukwe refused to lower his morals to the level of his enemy. He kept his integrity to the point of death.

It is sad to note that not only did Sobukwe pay the price in his lifetime, but also that, in his grave, he is still paying for his commitment to freedom. His legacy suffers the same isolation that he suffered under the apartheid government. Very little is taught about him in our history curriculum. I was surprised to hear from a Grade 12 learner that she had not read anything about Robert Sobukwe in her history textbook. When his wife, Veronica, died in August 2018, I spent the whole day listening to popular radio stations in the hope that they would talk about her. To my surprise, little was mentioned about her and the role that she played in the struggle. The sweat, tears and blood of the Sobukwe family remain untold, unknown and uncelebrated. This is a tragedy.

As a high-school student, Sobukwe was called a sellout for doing his work properly. As a tertiary student, he was sidelined for speaking his mind. As an adult politician, he was detained for fighting an oppressive system. His legacy as a political icon remains chained, isolated and uncelebrated. Many young people do not know much about the life, politics and leadership of Robert Sobukwe. It is sad to note that the isolating of his legacy did not end with the apartheid government. In his grave, Simangaliso Sobukwe is still paying a price for his integrity. Integrity is costly. Today, South Africa has talented, intelligent and passionate young people who want to take this country forward. The question is: how many of them can pass the test of integrity?

Farmers: Common ground is needed for land reform

Willem Pretorius

Dr Willem Abraham Pretorius was born and grew up on a farm close to Modimolle, in Limpopo province. He inherited the farm, lives there, and raises cattle, sheep and grows vegetables. He is president of the farmers' organisation Agri Gauteng. He is also an ordained pastor in the Dutch Reformed Church, serving in the Kameeldrift congregation in Pretoria.

THE MORE I READ about Robert Sobukwe, the more fascinated I become with his story and life, but most of all the values he stands for. The reason for this is that I, as a white male, have grown up in a certain culture, which includes capitalism. As I write this chapter, looking at someone who differs totally from myself, questions about my own values come to the fore.

Sobukwe and his supporters, calling themselves Africanists, broke away from the African National Congress (ANC) and in April 1959 created the Pan Africanist Congress (PAC), with Sobukwe elected unanimously as its president. He set out the aim of the PAC: white supremacy must be destroyed. The African people could be organised to do this only under the banner of African nationalism in an all-African organisation.

Sobukwe aimed to unite blacks in South Africa against a common enemy, the white people, and with that, the government. The government feared Sobukwe because of his personal strength and courage, his commitment to fighting for freedom, his eloquence, his quiet charisma and his enunciation of African nationalism. Clearly, he was watched during his initial three years in jail, and the security authorities concluded that this was an enemy too dangerous to be let loose. The same happened on Robben Island, this time to the extent that within the first year, the government really took away the key and decided to let him rot in virtual solitary confinement; only the deterioration of his health led to his banishment to Kimberley, where he was ceaselessly watched and his visitors followed.

Sobukwe rejected the 'multiracialism' of the ANC, which allowed only blacks as members while working with separate racial movements for whites, coloureds and Asians in the Congress Alliance. He spoke instead of the 'human race' and sought the government of Africans, by Africans, with everyone who owes his or her only loyalty to Africa and who is prepared to accept the democratic rule of an African majority being regarded as [...] African.

Sobukwe was a black intellectual who, through 'Service, Sacrifice and Suffering', believed he could unite black people against the white enemy. His characteristics – a hardworking intellectual with a worthwhile dream (uniting black people) – also became his downfall: his dream was not bought by everyone and he struggled to sell it to blacks.

In any evaluation of the life of Robert Sobukwe, one can focus on different aspects. Being part of the conversation on land expropriation without compensation that is under way in South Africa, I want to focus on Sobukwe's policy of Black Consciousness in this regard, and how it differs from the policy of the predominantly white agricultural sector.

It is now 2019, and the ANC-led government has governed South Africa for the last 25 years. For them, the Freedom Charter is the document that guides them. The government has also put forward the National Development Plan to apply the Charter in the daily lives of South Africans. The purpose is to help South Africa become an equal and just society in which wealth and happiness are shared by all the citizens of our country.

The difference between Sobukwe's and my understanding of today's ANC is in the belief that, for Sobukwe, the core of a successful South Africa is in a Black Consciousness Movement, a black movement by blacks for blacks, whereas for the ANC it is a just and equal society for all races. The focus in the ANC is to develop the country as a rainbow nation.

White politics has been spiralling downwards since 1994. There is one small Afrikaner white political party, and even this now has members of the coloured community. They share the Afrikaans language and certain values as the glue for the party. It's a slow shift to the left.

Comparisons

The Black Consciousness Movement, of which Robert Sobukwe was a leader, holds that you cannot own land. Land is part of the essence of mankind. The land, the water and the air you breathe – you cannot say it is yours and put a value on it. It is not a commodity. When God created the world, He created it for His pleasure and commanded man to work the earth, to fill it, and give names to animals. All land belongs to God.

For black people, the land is not only something on which they live, but it also has a spiritual component. The land is a place where the spirits of the ancestors live and meet with them. They can consult the spirits regarding their problems; they can also celebrate life with them.

Land that belongs to all people is also the place where their cattle can graze. Cattle are also part of black culture. You slaughter a cow when people die; you slaughter one when your child is getting married. When you slaughter, you celebrate life and death by singing.

The above are the conclusions I reached during my conversations with people who today still live by the dreams of Robert Sobukwe.

On the other hand, for white South Africans, land is a commodity. We, as white Christians, interpret the Genesis text as a command that the human race must till the earth for the benefit of those who live on it. But, when we turn to using the Bible for an argument, we start with the New Testament. In the New Testament, land and economic well-being are not that important any more. Even the understanding of family has changed: family are no longer your brothers and sisters and slaves, but rather those who believe in Christ.

White people live by a capitalist economic model in which everything has a monetary value. For us, land is not only where we live but it also has a value that we can use to trade with. In our Western philosophy, there is no place for a piece of land that has no value. The same goes for water: you pay for the water you use.

Capitalism also values labour as an economic output: it is productivity. We measure the worker's output and pay accordingly. In South Africa, the context has been that black people have worked for white people. The economic system that we as white South Africans have used is focused on maximum profit. Capitalism in its naked form is also consumerism. We consume everything. If we take land as an example, we will work the land to get maximum profits, which sometimes means we will pump all the water, take out all the trees, and plant and reap until we get enough money.

To begin talking about land we have to sit around a table and find common ground between these two different views.

Land debate

I am going to use the land debate as an example of the challenges that we South Africans are experiencing today.

The ANC decided that expropriation of land without compensation will take place. The party wants to change section 25 of the Constitution, amending it so that it allows expropriation without compensation. The government decided on a process whereby all role-players could have a say. One of the processes was oral submission at hearings held in different towns and cities throughout South Africa. The other process was the handing-in of written submissions to the parliamentary portfolio committee that is guiding the process. There was also a third process by which certain organisations – including Agri Gauteng, the organisation that I represent – were invited to present submissions to the committee.

Agri Gauteng is a federation of farming organisations and communities within Gauteng province. Our aim is to help the agricultural community to develop agriculture, make farming profitable, and provide stability. Agri Gauteng also provides help with sustainability in the province through taking part in decision-making at provincial and national levels. We are one of the provincial bodies that form part of Agri SA, the national association representing the agricultural industry.

Below is a selection from the written submission made by Agri Gauteng. In reading it, bear in mind the principles of Robert Sobukwe described above. The basic principles of the submission are as follows:

- Food security must be secured and enhanced at all costs.
- The way forward: The National Development Plan 2030 gives important direction and provides indicators that can be helpful to fast-track land reform.
- In our submission, we use the following as premises:
  - In this debate, it is not only the land that is important but the people as well.
  - We acknowledge the inhumanity of the past. People were not treated fairly and were not seen as human beings.

- Communities – *it takes a village to raise a child*. People in communities need one another to rebuild the rural areas.
- We reaffirm the responsibilities of the state and the organised agricultural community.
- In compiling this document, we also make use of the High Level Report, chaired by South Africa's former president Kgalema Motlanthe and issued in 2017, on legislation and fundamental change.
- As farmers, we experience the importance of *the healing of the soul of our people*.

Agri Gauteng and land reform

In his first State of the Nation Address, on 16 February 2018, President Cyril Ramaphosa quoted Hugh Masekela's song, 'Send Me (*Thuma Mina*)'. He said that Masekela anticipated a day of renewal, of new beginnings:

> *I wanna be there when the people start to turn it around*
> *When they triumph over poverty*
> *I wanna be there when the people win the battle against AIDS*
> *I wanna lend a hand*
> *I wanna be there for the alcoholic*
> *I wanna be there for the drug addict.*
> *I wanna be there for the victims of violence and abuse.*
> *I wanna lend a hand.*
> *Send me.*

We answer to our calling as farmers and also to the call of our president when we say: send us. We want to be there when the people of our country will have access to land in a fair, equal and sustainable way. We want to be there to participate in a process of land restitution and the reformation of policies pertaining to the redistribution of land. We want to be there when the dignity of the people of our land is restored, when people have access to land, food and jobs. We want to be there when foreign countries and companies invest in our economy and help to create the wealth and prosperity deserving of people who are committed to an unwavering work ethic and dedication to create access to opportunities for their children. *Thuma Mina, Somandla.*

We believe that farmers and labourers form the backbone of rural areas. They are the people who spend their money in our small towns. If we can help them to be strong, we help the whole community. We serve the nation regardless of creed, race, sexuality, background or gender.

The services and support that we deliver to our broader communities, in particular the needy and marginalised, are countless. We are also becoming more and more multiracial in our membership and we are committed to expanding the unity that we are beginning to experience to all the citizens of South Africa.

According to the 2017 state audit, the surveyed land in South Africa amounts to 114 223 276 hectares – 93 per cent – of the country's total surface area. The total area of agricultural land, according to the 1993 census, was 97 036 986 hectares, of which commercial farmers owned 82 557 220 hectares and previously disadvantaged persons 14.5 million hectares, or 14.9 per cent. Since 1994, more than 3.6 million hectares (4 per cent) of agricultural land has been lost to other uses, such as mining and residential and industrial development. The total area of land used for agriculture in 2016 was 93 453 558 hectares: 73.3 per cent of this is in the hands of white commercial farmers and 26.7 per cent in the hands of previously disadvantaged persons (including land held by the government on behalf of black beneficiaries).

Equitable compensation

Section 25 of the Constitution goes on to say that property may be expropriated for a public purpose or public benefit subject to just and equitable compensation. Public interest specifically includes land reform and the nation's commitment to achieving equitable access to natural resources. Section 25 also includes factors to be considered in the calculation of compensation, such as the history of the acquisition of the property, the purpose of expropriation and the market value. Historically, the government decided to use the principle of 'willing buyer, willing seller', which was contrary to section 25.

Access to land is not necessarily ownership, it must be noted. Access to land may mean leasehold and/or being able to use the land. This aspect also protects the security of tenure of historically disadvantaged communities and those dispossessed of property after 19 June 1913 through the racially discriminatory laws of that time and later.

The key phrase in the resolution is probably as follows (taken during the ANC's Nasrec conference, December 2017): 'Expropriation of land without compensation should be among the key mechanisms available to government to give effect to land reform and redistribution.' Then come the famous caveats: '[W]e must ensure that we do not undermine future investment in the economy, or damage agricultural production of food security. Furthermore, our interventions must not cause harm to other sectors of the economy.' [1]

These caveats are indeed of the utmost importance. Note the use of the word 'should' in the resolution. We would like to argue that expropriation without compensation should be a last resort and must take place according to the guidelines set out in the Constitution.

To reduce the risk when a farmer cannot repay his loan, banks often couple a loan to the value of the land by registering a bond that allows it to sell the land as a last resort. If the Constitution were to be amended to allow expropriation without compensation, it could endanger the faith that banks place in the land as security and set in motion a chain reaction that would eventually lead to the ordinary consumer losing out. If the state can take land without paying for it, then the integrity of the land market will be compromised and banks will not be able to recover depositors' money loaned to farmers. No bank has sufficient liquid assets to pay out all of depositors' money in one go, as funds are locked up in long-term investments.

As much as economic transformation and/or inclusive economic participation are needed in South Africa, expropriating agricultural land without compensation will seriously damage the sustainability of the agricultural sector, its commercial viability and national food security, which will only deepen poverty.

Expropriation without compensation erodes property rights. And once this happens, land can no longer serve as collateral. Any deprivation of property without compensation constitutes a very serious breach of an individual's rights.

A policy of expropriation without compensation will discourage investment in farming technology and innovation, which drives agricultural productivity. The sector will regress, productivity will be compromised, and further job losses will follow. This may well throw the country deeper into recession in the coming years. South Africa will face international disinvestment and the risk of losing the benefits it currently enjoys from the African Growth and Opportunity Act (Agoa), which gives sub-Saharan nations, including South African farmers, duty-free access to the lucrative US market.

In addition, agriculture is critical to the development of the economy as the sector that has strong backward and forward link-ages with the rest of the economy. Through backward linkages, agriculture purchases goods such as fertilisers, chemicals and implements from the manufacturing sector. On the forward linkages side, agriculture supplies raw materials to industry and the food supply chain in general.

The amount of compensation paid must be 'just and equitable', reflecting a balance between the public interest and the interests of the landowner. What the amendment seeks to do is to remove the phrase 'subject to compensation'. But what the government has never done is develop a land-reform policy that considers 'just and equitable compensation'. Under the current Constitution, the governing party could still craft legislation with its own definition of 'just and equitable compensation'.

We are in favour of compensation for landowners who are deprived of their land for land-reform purposes. Compensation must be determined based on considerations of fairness and equitability.

Food security at all costs

Sections 27(1) and (2) of the Constitution guarantee every citizen the right to sufficient food, whereby the state must take reasonable measures to ensure the realisation of this right. To ensure fulfilment of this constitutional imperative, the cabinet approved the National Policy on Food and Nutrition Security in 2013.

South Africa's population has increased quite rapidly in the past ten years, and is projected to reach more than 80 million in 2035. This means that food supply must be greatly increased to sustain the growing population. Land is one critical factor of production in the agricultural sector, and its ownership is critical for the sustainability of the sector. Since it is the responsibility of the agricultural sector to produce food, its productive capacity will need to be enhanced to avoid food demand surpassing domestic supply, and to ensure that the sector remains adequately competitive. This can only be possible if commercial farmers remain on the farms.

The difficulty that all stakeholders face – claimants, landowners and the state – is the absence of clear guidelines to determine 'just and equitable' compensation in any particular case. The budget for land redistribution is contained within the budget vote for Rural Development and Land Reform and appears as a line item titled 'Land Reform' alongside 'Restitution' and 'Rural Development'. Here our focus is on the 'Land Reform' budget line only. The fact that, in many instances, beneficiaries do not receive title to the land that is allocated to them is, in our experience, a huge impediment to the successful establishment of new black commercial farmers. These farmers have no security of tenure and cannot access production finance.

An RDP of the soul

In his address to Parliament in February 1999, President Nelson Mandela said that our nation needs an RDP of the soul. In his eulogy at Winnie Madikizela-Mandela's funeral, President Cyril Ramaphosa said: 'We must also recognise our own wounds as a nation. We must acknowledge that we are a society that is hurting, damaged by our past, numbed by our present and hesitant about our future. This may explain why we are easily prone to anger and violence.'

We urgently need an RDP of the soul. There are too many signs of untended wounds, hurt, anguish and emotional suffering that have not been dealt with. If we don't address them now, they will haunt us forever.

Reconciliation and restoration will not happen as a result of legislative transformation and measures only. It will happen because good people share their stories and needs, and find a way forward in which all benefit. I want to be part of the RDP of South Africa's soul by bringing the well-meaning people of all races together in safe spaces so that we may enjoy and witness and marvel at the miracles of reciprocal insight, reconciliation and restitution.

We have to restore the moral convictions of our people. Too many ethical bottom lines have been abandoned for the sake of short-term gain. The land debate provides us with a golden opportunity to redress our ethics and regain our dignity.

We have to believe in the beauty of our dreams. We have to believe that the world and our country can become a place where everybody's dignity is safe and guarded by a common commitment to respect, listening, embracing and loving. But we will only be able to maintain our hope through faith in the grace and truth of God. We will have to be witnesses to His presence and of His hope-sustaining love. The RDP of the soul will not happen without our nation's profound understanding and experience of God's truth and love.

Conclusion

When considering a country as economically unequal as ours, it is obvious that economic transformation must occur. It is among the issues that matter most. One thing is clear: until poor South Africans own their homes, be they in cities or rural areas, development will remain stalled.

In the conversation on the topic of land expropriation without compensation, the ANC middle ground is slowly making a stand that the model we must develop can allow expropriation without compensation, but that this cannot be the norm. In more and more conversations, the common ground is that it is not necessary to amend section 25 of the Constitution. This opens the road to a dialogue between black and white on expropriation without compensation.

Using Robert Sobukwe's model that all land belongs to black

people will only spill over in dividing a frail nation. It will not help to rectify the atrocities of the past and will also not help in creating wealth and stability for the new South Africa. Legal land distribution and rural development are crucial economic growth tools for poverty reduction.

Shallow non-racialism
destroys our people

Ishmael Mkhabela

Ishmael Mkhabela is a community organiser who builds and regenerates communities and grassroots institutions in health, policing, housing and education. He is chairperson of the Steve Biko Foundation and the Johannesburg Inner City Partnership, and deputy president of the Institute of Race Relations. A former schoolteacher, he was founding chairperson and later president of the Azanian People's Organisation (Azapo). He has served as chairperson of the National Housing Board, National People's Housing Trust and Johannesburg Social Housing Company.

HOW SHOULD ONE REASSESS public representatives in a situation where their history and their contribution to society are deemed to be the sole property of political parties? I am convinced that Robert Mangaliso Sobukwe is larger than party, country or continent or single ideology. His legacy speaks to our common humanity, challenges the world we live in, and is still relevant to oppressed and liberated people everywhere.

In situations where people are oppressed, exploited, dispossessed, humiliated, stripped of their freedom, and their dignity undermined, one or a group among them will surely rise and risk their own person and livelihood and show the way out of tyranny and slavery. It could be Moses, Martin Luther King Jr, Malcolm X or Mahatma Gandhi. In South Africa, we have had, among others, Nelson

Mandela, Steve Biko and Robert Sobukwe. In their own way, each led their followers and paid the price. More than forty years after the death of Robert Sobukwe, South Africans have not forgotten that he was one of the relentless nonconformists and rebels who lived and died in the cause of freedom for the country and Africa.

The ideals, values and truth that he stood for are alive and relevant among the youth and older persons alike. Amazingly, he burst into the public eye only for a brief, tumultuous moment: in that dangerously eventful moment he articulated his views and outlined bold resistance strategies. These fundamentally changed how South African black people saw themselves, and reassessed the strategic and tactical options for resistance and change. After a period of less than two years, he led the Pan Africanist Congress (PAC) and its campaign of passive action against the imposition of passes in March 1960. The campaign served to reveal the true nature of the violence and brutality that the apartheid architects relied on in order to maintain white domination and racist rule. The campaign was a last-ditch effort to defeat the planned total control over black people's freedom of movement and denial of the exercise of choice over where they could stay, work, trade or visit.

Sobukwe exposed and revealed for all to see the lie, theft and fraud of apartheid and colonialism. The passive-action campaign provoked an extreme response from the apartheid establishment. Their murderous actions changed overnight the misguided views of world leaders about apartheid's criminal rule. New approaches to struggle, including isolation of the apartheid government and its tribal Bantustan creations, were adopted by black people, sympathetic supporters and governments. The campaign, led and conducted in a spirit of absolute non-violence, was indeed an important turning point for South Africa. *The national liberation movement was thereafter intensified and supporters and social activists adopted a multifaceted programme of action* (author's emphasis). It is accurate to conclude that the impact of the campaign resulted in a growing and more visible black liberation movement during the late 1960s, 1970s and 1980s. During this period, strong waves of community, worker and student upheavals inside the country hastened the collapse of the ruling white-supremacist National Party government.

Student and community activists took note of the kind of leadership that was required to break the back of white rule. They drew their lessons and inspiration from the exemplary lives of Sobukwe and Biko, here at home, and from Frantz Fanon and others further afield. South Africa was then fertile ground for planting new thinking, and for the adoption of a more militant response to ever-present police violence as well as to the entrenched system of apartheid and colonialism. At that time, I was old enough to be both an active observer and participant in the unfolding struggle, first within the youth Christian clubs and the University Christian Movement (UCM), and later at the University of the North (now University of Limpopo) where I developed social and community organising skills. More importantly, I took an interest in engaging in sophisticated and robust ideological and power analyses of society — an excruciating theological and intellectual exercise. Unprecedented morale- and awareness-raising activities exposed us to, and deepened our understanding of, the source and nature of our exploitation, dispossession and oppression. All these were very important. Imprisonment, detention without trial, torture and other repressive and violent measures adopted by the white authorities were rendered ineffective. The administration ultimately gave in to unyielding, organised people's power.

I became increasingly convinced that oppressors and those who abuse power always achieve unintended outcomes. Their excesses helped to strengthen community organising, black solidarity and the inevitable escalation and radicalisation of resistance. As noted, imprisonment, banishment and the silencing or killing of leaders only raise their stature and further deepen the commitment of the affected people to their just cause. The names or the memory of imprisoned leaders such as Sobukwe were invaluable to the struggle. The names of prisoners and those murdered by the police were always read and lionised during commemorative events.

Talks during events and prayers reminded the nation of their unwarranted suffering, sacrifice, key pronouncements, vision for society, leadership styles, positive attitudes and other distinctive personality traits. I still believe that the practice should be continued for the benefit of current and emerging leaders. A strong perception has been created that Sobukwe was quintessentially a people's leader and that he suffered with them, stayed among them, and led by example. His assertions that black people needed to wean themselves from dependency on white political, academic, media, financial, cultural and religious elites had, and continue to have, strong appeal and resonance for later generations of black leaders.

The rejection of the uncritical, childlike reliance on the mercy and charity of the compromised and self-serving elites was truly a liberating, motivating force among black people, especially the youth. It encouraged us to take responsibility for achieving our freedom and development. It fostered radical and profound social and spiritual change. Nothing was to remain the same and unaffected. We reflected and saw ourselves differently and in a positive light. The means and end of the struggle were also seen in a new light. People's power, black power, became a menace and an immediate threat to entrenched white interests.

These developments were, in many respects, associated with Sobukwe's leadership and the burgeoning pan-Africanist and related Black Consciousness movements. The emergence of the Azania movement posed a real threat to the old, uncontested, hegemonic leadership of the black liberation struggle. The movement was a necessary precedent to the recovery of people's power, a prerequisite for victory over apartheid's despotic rule and its unsophisticated psychological and mental warfare against the people. The movement was eminently relevant for forging one united nation. Azania, I thought, would rise above a collection of ethnic, racial, regional and ideological entitlements, tendencies and greedy factions.

Factions thrive and flourish by deliberately failing to recognise, coexist with, and accept or tolerate different people or communities who do not think or act in a prescribed manner. It is hard to be a nonconformist, a misfit or one who is difficult to pigeonhole. Powerful interests to the left and right have hopelessly failed to understand the values, principles, concerns and aspirations that were the driving force that made Sobukwe a unique gift to the then-benighted beloved country. I have reached out to friends, some of whom were imprisoned with Sobukwe, to understand the kind of person he was. I gained a sense that he was more than a conventional freedom fighter. My wife, Bongi, explains that he was no seeker of personal position, privilege or power. The man was grounded and anchored and lived for a higher vision for society and Africans. Bongi and our daughters, Ntsako and Hlawulani, point out that Sobukwe was a liberator of the people and, therefore, did not take part in struggle to achieve the trappings of political power.

Yes, he held a lofty vision for Africa and Africans. He was of service to that end and nothing else. I also think that the system or establishment, his political opponents and powerful elites on both the left and right believed that he was inherently a disruptor of their anti-black and self-serving interests. Any initiative hatched among black people on their own was suspect. The establishment remained convinced that it was erroneous to accept that Africans had any inclination or will to chart an egalitarian future for South Africa. I will return to this point later in this chapter.

We must recall that by the end of his student days, Sobukwe had decided to dedicate his life to opposing any institutionalised or legalised diabolical systems. He urged his fellow students to aim to serve Africa with love and to defend it against systems that benefited from denigrating, humiliating and plundering it. To him, Africa and its offspring had been robbed of their birthright to dignity, freedom, land and ownership of anything, including life and soul. He also read widely and diligently studied all the available literature written by African leaders and other authorities. This inevitably led him to accept the burden of a specific kind of leadership. He had to lead the resistance movement and guide it to power and the right to act, speak or think freely in building an inclusive egalitarian society. He trusted his mind and intuition and was comfortable and confident in applying his acquired knowledge.

Responsible action and independence of thought seemed to define Sobukwe's life. This was to be his inimitable contribution within and outside the African National Congress (ANC) and South Africa. Mathatha Tsedu, one of the leading national scribes, is of the opinion that Sobukwe was 'steadfast, unflinching and always dignified in the way he resisted oppression. His immense intellect explains why those who understood his potency feared him.' Christine Qunta adds that he was 'one of South Africa's most outstanding intellectuals whose writings and ethical leadership remains relevant today. We do not honour his legacy sufficiently.' There is sufficient evidence that 'he was ahead of his time'. He anticipated the nature of future national struggle for land restoration and self-rule. Africans were to independently lead their people and be ready to confront the might of local and foreign powers. This required the rise of a dynamic and forceful movement.

The movement was open to the threat of being railroaded and weakened. One of the primary objectives of the movement was to reveal and expose all the forms of deceit and trickery that underpinned the system. These shielded, strengthened and sustained the undeserved privileges and influence enjoyed by socially connected black groups, as well as by white political, religious, academic, media, and financial elites, both right and left.

The development of the movement made Sobukwe a target of sustained slander and repression. This has continued despite the fact that Sobukwe, within the time and resources available, publicly corrected the misconceptions about him and the movement he led. It must be stressed that he strove for the achievement of a dream and a vision of society characterised by the enjoyment of true and real freedom and equality for all, irrespective of race, origin or culture. The fate or well-being of human beings was for him of more significance than racial affiliation. He went on to preach the efficacy of non-collaboration with oppressors and their schemes. This was the hallmark of his unbending principles, and led to the illegitimate government itself being totally scorned, isolated and shunned inside and beyond South Africa. The government was stripped of all semblance of legitimacy. Apartheid laws, government institutions and its selected leaders were not tolerated.

None of this won Sobukwe any public acclaim or sympathy. He remained white South Africa's arch-enemy. His detractors were the prime or potential beneficiaries of white privilege and power. The majority of white opposition, inside and outside Parliament, was no less hostile. Communists, as the self-proclaimed vanguard of the liberation movement, were equally incensed. He was, therefore, roundly condemned as an incorrigible extremist and a virulent instigator of racial hatred, primarily against white and vulnerable minority groups. He was portrayed as racist, unappreciative, disloyal, extreme, demonic and dangerous.

Obviously, that did not deter Sobukwe. We, like him, also had difficulty with those who propagated or unreservedly accepted and promoted the racist notions of multiracialism/multiculturalism or flimsy non-racialism in society. This matter has not been settled and continues to be an endless nightmare that bedevils the lives of significant sections of South Africans, especially the disadvantaged, marginalised, under-served and destitute.

South Africa's business and government leaders are generally corrupt, unscrupulous and self-serving, and often they stand for nothing else but party-political and financial interests. We must not forget, however, that this country has always boasted of its abundance of principled and selfless leaders. We are grateful that we have had Sobukwe among this exceptional and outstanding crop.

I understand the value of education and the formative influence of university life. While at the University College of Fort Hare, Sobukwe participated in student and youth politics. Like many students from poor backgrounds, he did it regardless of the threat of losing future promised privileges and a rosy professional career, as well as the danger of having his university studies abruptly terminated. Many relate that later in adult life, he was confronted by his employers and asked to choose between advancing the black cause and pursuing a thriving academic career and its comforts. He chose Africa and a precarious future. The choice he made was part of the development of a rare leader who came to be celebrated and even worshipped.

It must always be recalled that in those days the apartheid government did everything in its power to co-opt influential black people. They were often enticed to serve its wicked interests and assist in butchering and fragmenting the country and people. The preferred means to win over black leaders was through bribery, blackmail or the threat (and use) of force and violence. There is no testimony that Sobukwe ever succumbed to any of these. He has never been accused or suspected of being a sellout. He never betrayed the cause for private gain or advantage. Love of money was not in his character. He was incorruptible, and it was unthinkable that he would compromise his basic core values for honey, money or position. In fact, there is a strong consensus among those who marched and were tried and imprisoned with him that he was always ready to stand for the truth, to suffer and to expose his life to danger for the advancement of fellow human beings. I think that he would always stand on the side of people rather than position, privilege and power. He would defend, feed and shelter the weak and the wounded.

The leader who exposes himself to inevitable danger in order to advance the freedom and well-being of his people deserves to be emulated. Such a leader helps people and his followers to overcome the fear of loss, death, repression, imprisonment or other hardship. We have had many exemplary leaders who fully understood what it took to overcome fear, and to intentionally confront it. As a young activist and a firm adherent of black theology, I was, during reflection and in Bible studies, constantly exhorted to be fearless when confronted by evil forces. I strongly held the view that those who opposed and oppressed us were victims and feared the inevitable and necessary change. Thus, I got involved in politics in search of public morality and freedom. The outcome, I believed – then and now – would be material, spiritual and political gain for all. Fighting for liberation and freedom was to me a collective obligation and a responsibility of citizens. It was a humane act that would result in personal and collective redemption based on truth and justice for people and communities.

In this regard, I remember the particular words of admonition by Father Buti Tlhagale of the Roman Catholic Church, who was later appointed Archbishop of Johannesburg. It was early in 1978 and we faced incessant police intimidation and widespread arrest of young activists. It was common for the police to violently disrupt legitimate political meetings. Father Tlhagale counselled against fear of the illegitimate, vicious prime minister, John Vorster, and his lackeys. He added that our resolve and capacity to challenge oppressive systems would diminish if we were to harbour fear. We, just like Sobukwe, also elected not to afford any unwarranted respect to government-approved local and national representatives.

We have recently heard loud calls for the state to continue to honour the memory of the departed leaders of the struggle. Such calls are necessary and timely. Reflecting on what made leaders tick in their private and public lives might serve to advance social cohesion and a nation-building agenda. The omission and failure to recognise the important contributions of credible leaders leaves many poorer. No one wins. We lose our way as well as the wisdom and experience of ages. The practice of not honouring all deserving leaders renders all of us intellectually malnourished and morally bankrupt. This results in a shameless display of public inconsideration and a failure to account to country and people. It is therefore timely for South Africa to hear Sobukwe again speak frankly to the nation from the grave. We ignore at our peril his sane voice and patriotic contributions to our national conversations and debates. He must again speak about the conquest of our people, land dispossession and love for Africa, and provide appropriate light and solutions to current deadly African migrations, endemic poverty and increasing inequality between the rich north and the poor south. He must sound a stern warning about the entrenched divisions, factions, racism and xenophobia that leave Africa sick and polarised.

Mercifully of late, some writers and academics, rising from their self-imposed slumber, acknowledge that the wisdom of Sobukwe must be applied to our dire situation. It is acknowledged that he remains silenced and that the erasure of his memory deprives society of constructive guidance and insights. It is our national duty to raise his voice of reason and continue with his unfinished work of compassion for the savaged and abused people of Africa.

The south is still to deal with the uncomfortable consequences of many untruths about itself. These untruths must be dealt with once and for all. We have not forgotten that most of the positions that were close to Sobukwe's heart continue not to receive due consideration from the establishment, both old and new. In its long history, and for an extended period, the current governing party and its allies have meekly been able to countenance the disdain and disrespect that was shamelessly shown to toiling and suffering black people. Its practice was to ignore some of the concerns that were raised by black militant leadership. The importance of organising and leading people for self-defence and self-realisation was lost. Sobukwe, on the rough long road, actually embodied some of the unfulfilled demands for black people to be recognised as equals then and always.

I have given myself the space to dwell upon missed opportunities, and have allowed some measure of digression in this discussion. The aim is to seek answers to how best to critically assess the contribution and appreciate the character of our past leaders for the benefit of the aspiring ones. The answers might serve to help society make informed choices and objective judgements. It is worth understanding why Sobukwe has always occupied such a special and revered place in our national discourse. The electoral fortunes of the movement he led, and remains associated with, are not a true reflection of the kind of leader and person that he was. We also may argue that a person's political affiliations should not necessarily diminish his or her stature and significance in society. Leadership style, skills, values, character, personality, reputation and demonstrated public moral decency should be the considered standards.

In this regard, we have already noted that Sobukwe was an influential and charismatic figure who never lost the common touch. In addition, he was an excellent communicator who was comfortable with sharing his ideas openly and frankly with individuals and

crowds. This has worked in his favour. Generally, he was highly
esteemed by acquaintances, peers and associates. These are the
assertions and observations of both friend and foe. Sobukwe was
a remarkable leader. He gave us a renewed sense of purpose and
pride. He also made us believe in, and now encourages us to bring
about, long-delayed fundamental change and genuine freedom.

———————

Unsubstantiated charges continue to be made that the pan-
Africanists were a bunch of opportunists. We cannot here ad-
judicate and settle the accusations levelled against the PAC by its
old political rivals, in particular the Congress Alliance. It is recorded
that the PAC was quick to take the initiative and clumsily went
ahead of the Alliance. I am inclined to believe that Sobukwe had
excellent tactical reflexes and a sense of strategic opportunity.
I do not think that it is wise to negotiate strategic battle plans with
rivals or opponents. One of the lingering questions in my mind
is: what would have happened to South Africa if he had not taken
the responsibility and led the campaign of 21 March 1960? In my
mind, from that day onwards, truth and justice started to prevail
although at an unavoidably heavy price.

It could be claimed that Sobukwe was in the same league as
Mahatma Gandhi and Martin Luther King Jr, and that the world
has much to learn from these great 20th-century leaders. They
confronted the violent forces in their countries, armed with truth
and a reliance on people's power. We dare not ignore their legacy,
exemplary lives and teachings.

These individuals have demonstrated the importance of striving
for justice while being responsible for our actions in relation to
our interests and those of others in the country or communities.
We cannot ignore that our well-being lies in ensuring that we

recognise, protect and promote our common or shared national values. They were mindful that, ultimately, we need to draw together our people and to build nations. History, place of origin, race, gender, class, tribe, caste and religious differences are all part of our existence. In all political and economic situations and contexts where these coexist, what moral alternatives are open to us? What must change? We should learn to work better and more creatively and to deal with the unacceptable wealth distribution and hopeless sense of powerlessness that only breeds conflict and violence among the haves, have-lesses and have-nots. We must find appropriate solutions to problems and address genuine contending interests and legitimate concerns. The liberals, radicals, conservatives and progressives in our midst cannot be wished away, and they must, therefore, be required to play their respective constructive roles. We need to recognise each other while we strive to protect and promote the ideal conditions that sustain life, human dignity, freedom and progress.

I think that these leaders have ably shown that change demands hard work and a good fight. A fight can express itself as bargaining, a contest, a managed controversy, conflict or confrontation that leads to discussion, negotiation and settlement. It is commonly held that solutions that avoid confrontation are not possible during social crises. We need to warn, however, that strategies must not be mistaken for principles. Some leaders among us never believed that a change of power and the end of white domination could best be achieved by working together with people who had previously painfully and silently experienced humiliation and disgrace at their hands. Sobukwe's call against the representatives and agents of institutionalised terror did not require the blessing of the white establishment or black elites that privileged their stake in the status quo. When those who experience the hardship of oppression demand change, they need not ask for permission, be polite, or adopt pleasant means of struggle. The reality is that they yearn for freedom and need to shake off their shackles to gain it and to enhance life.

Black leaders who have shown deep love for Africa and their long-suffering people are seemingly a perpetual abomination and an affront to the establishment. In fact, it was deemed inappropriate and not in line for black people to love themselves first before they could extend love to other people. Black leaders who openly and with no qualms embraced themselves and the cause of black folks have often been isolated, punished or exterminated. Why was a historic fact affirming that Africa belongs to Africans an unmitigated criminal act? It was indeed also a crime to declare to all that 'black is beautiful'. That black people were expected to accept non-racialism uncritically and unconditionally was one of the scandals of our age. It was in fact naive to expect black people to deny that they were black as well as African. How were they expected to confront the painful fact that popular national leaders of the past were grudgingly accommodating and tolerating of white supremacist tendencies and practices? They had wrongly held to a warped belief that through negotiations, discussions and appeals they would ultimately be accommodated as part of the system.

Progressive ideological developments within the ANC in the 1940s, more than thirty years after its inception, were the outcome of the work of, and the adoption of, an Africanist-inspired 1949 Programme of Action of the Congress Youth League. These ideas, not the ANC, deeply resonated with Sobukwe's ideas and were in sync with his ingrained political inclinations. It is not far-fetched to claim that if the ANC had pursued the Programme of Action and the objectives it spelt out, the split that resulted in the formation of the PAC could have been avoided. The Programme also enjoyed an acknowledged special appeal among some key leaders within the Black Consciousness Movement that later surfaced with the formation of the UCM, the African Students' Organisation and Black People's Convention, as well as the Azanian People's Organisation.

All these organisations were understandably hostile to white-led organisations and the undue influence of their leaders regarding the pace, priorities and direction of the national liberation movement. It soon became clear that white leaders sought to create national political and student organisations that they could control intellectually and materially. In that battle for ideas there were some who preferred the less taxing and seemingly more expedient approach of executing their resistance against racism. They were openly welcomed into existing ideological frames offered by communists, liberals or tired conservative leaders. The boat was not to be rocked. Sobukwe, therefore, was never to be forgiven for actively dissociating himself from such organisations. Instead, he continued to build self-organised militant capacity and refused to be co-opted into feeble and meek political arrangements.

In the late 1950s, black people were no longer prepared to further explore or entertain apologetic and defeatist ways and means to fight white power. The realisation of self-rule and self-determination was the primary issue. There was no doubt that a fresh reorientation to life was required, together with the rejection of any forms of assimilation or integration into white structures or political programmes. Africans were then exercising extreme caution. What became exciting to me about all this was that Africans were increasingly refusing to react to external plans or initiatives. New values, attitudes, loyalty and love for Africa were to be prioritised and infused into society. The overriding concern was support for social, economic and political liberation of Africa and Africans. I bought into that development.

I believe that mistrust of white leaders, both liberals and communists, had merit. It was not going to be easy to wean black

South Africans from dependence. Be that as it may, one of the urgent tasks that faced the emerging African leaders was, on the one hand, to foster the development of their own confident black leadership and to build black solidarity and power, while, on the other, systematically destroying the divisive, entrenched walls of the urban–rural divide, tribalist tension and ethnicity. Black power and radical non-racialism were to be perceived as an effective antidote against white supremacy. The establishment had to reckon with black power rather than powerlessness. The days of toying with the efficacy of white or colonial trusteeship were over and completely discarded. So was the acceptance of gradual change that was the preserve of deferential reformist and conservative leaders. The adoption of an assertive and contested approach to change also saw a growing hatred for perceived double standards, hypocrisy and inconsistent practices that were associated with white voters and some elites, as well as high-profile proponents of the anti-apartheid struggle.

We need also to be reminded that black members of various missionary churches were always unhappy with the dominant influence of the minority white members. In 1884, 1892 and 1896 they walked out of the Methodist Church of Southern Africa in protest against the disproportionate representation of whites in leadership positions. Nor was this withdrawal confined only to this denomination. Other denominations have, and continue to deal with the scourge of racism and persistent white control. Some whites have recently opted to start their independent private congregations where they continue to worship without any interference or challenge from black members.

––––––––

It is now appropriate to examine the influence of Christian moral teachings on African leaders such as Sobukwe and how they conducted themselves in public life in a segregated society. Was the struggle more of a political response, without any moral imperatives and ethics? Dr Mokgethi Motlhabi, one of South Africa's leading theologians, reminds us of the significance and marriage between secular (philosophical) and religious (theological) ethics in struggle. Drawing on Walter G Muelder's *Moral Law in Christian Social Ethics*, he asserts that we cannot ignore that human beings are expected to examine and prioritise their self-willed values and strive for responsible action based on moral deliberations, thus making consistently good choices and decisions. One was, therefore, called to be just or to love one's neighbour. It is taken for granted and advisable in this regard that one should adopt an intervention or pastoral formula or model: 'see – judge – act'. This model was to some extent related to the black-theology practice and reflection that was deliberately relevant to the dehumanised, oppressed and exploited of humankind. I found this model to be apt in the de-velopment of social and power analyses, which guides my work in communities and within religious congregations.

Theology inspired the rise and vibrancy of Black Consciousness and also involved a broad spectrum of those who were historically exploited and oppressed by law or practice. We have already noted that many fighters and champions for justice and pursuit of truth were bound and obedient to their faith or lofty ideals. They were expected, to a greater extent than others, to be more consistent with what they projected as their set of life ideals and standards. Ethical reflection and responsible action were imperative in the conduct of their private and public affairs. God, to them, was viewed as the embodiment of the moral ideal, and it is therefore not absurd to claim that those who strongly believe in this see their life as a cooperation between themselves and God in life's battle of ideas and justice.

Rather than it simply being a political question, liberation was a more comprehensive approach to life. To the theologically influenced leaders, their primary role in life was to change or improve relevant situations, and to engage in self-criticism while learning to love themselves as they showed love to others. It was a question of respect or acknowledgement of all other persons, of cooperating with others in pursuit of shared values, and of acknowledging that enlightened self-interest is directly served through the promotion of public service. A public representative or a leader of the people should be accountable, open, transparent and able to hold followers and other leaders to account.

I think that Muelder's moral law, which specifically deals with one's conduct in community and in public or business associations, requires special mention: 'All persons ought to form and choose all their ideals (in harmony with other [moral] Laws) of what the whole community ought to become; and to participate responsibly in groups to help them similarly choose and form all their ideals and choices.'[1]

The intention here is not to further elevate Sobukwe, but I would be failing in my task if I were not to declare my belief that leaders forged in the fury of the African liberation struggle found strength in their faith as much as in their political ideology. A spirituality and faith in fundamental truths is not limited to Christianity or religion. I would like to believe that it was through faith, based on examined black theology, that many of those who may one day be forgotten committed themselves to live and die for a cause. In fact, there was no distinction between embracing faith and fighting the good fight of the people, by the people and for the people. These black men and women did not shy away from confrontation politics and standing up for the truth. They blew away the myth that genuine and authentic leadership and serious political activism were the exclusive preserve of white students, their societal institutions and other vested economic and political interests. Self-direction and self-organising, as well as critical reflection, helped me and others to become radicalised while developing confidence and character, and while planning militant actions for justice and change for the better.

To combat white supremacy and white dominance, leaders like Sobukwe did not advocate the mindless discrimination, prejudice, racialising of public life and rampant racism that have recently been allowed to define life in South Africa. These leaders demanded that South Africans should appreciate and know more about themselves, love Africa, and be active, informed agents for positive change and meaningful contributors to the world. Shallow, caricatured non-racialism destroys and divides our people. It undermines and tarnishes the unfinished work and the noble contribution of Africanists and Black Consciousness. South Africa must not again adopt the diabolical hymnbook and profane Bible that guided and ordered the life of exploitative and oppressive colonialists and racists. We must find out: what made Robert Sobukwe so feared by the arch-architects of apartheid, and made them so determined to quash his existence and his stamp on our politics?

The indomitable spirit of Sobukwe is testament to our African agenda

Nkosazana Dlamini-Zuma

Nkosazana Dlamini-Zuma is Minister in the Presidency for Planning, Monitoring and Evaluation. A longtime African National Congress anti-apartheid activist, she served in the cabinet from 1994 until 2012, successively as minister of health, foreign affairs and home affairs. From 2012 to 2017 she headed the African Union. This essay was first published in The Star *(Johannesburg) on 4 July 2018.*

BARRING PEOPLE from attending a funeral or memorial service was recently [in August 2018] a discussion in South Africa. Yet, testifying in front of the Truth and Reconciliation Commission about the life and death of her husband, Mrs Sobukwe suggested that 'a funeral is a funeral'.

Asked about the presence of Mangosuthu Buthelezi at her husband's funeral, she said even a witch should be allowed to attend a funeral. She went on: 'It is not good to chase anybody away from a funeral. It is not a good thing. There is no dignity in that, no honour. No matter how cruel you are, you should not be chased away from a funeral.'

Such was the African legacy of Robert Mangaliso Sobukwe.

In this one answer, Mrs Sobukwe described the life and legacy of her husband. This year, 2018, commemorates the 40th anniversary of his untimely death.

While Ntate Sobukwe might have died from unnatural causes, there was no doubt that his rapid deterioration in health within a span of a few years could be laid squarely at the feet of the apartheid security police.

The man whom apartheid police kept in custody under the Sobukwe Clause, even after his official release was supposed to occur, would not be surprised that the recent South African Reconciliation Barometer, conducted by the Institute for Justice and Reconciliation, identified that the majority of South Africans believed that access to land was integral to addressing inequality. Only 8 per cent of South Africans denied that access to land would address inequality.

Significantly, half of whites and Indians – 49 per cent and 51 per cent, respectively – believed that resolving the question of land would address inequality in South Africa. The figures were 67 per cent and 59 per cent for Africans and coloureds, respectively.

Yet Sobukwe is also best known for his articulation of the Africanist agenda. As a member of the ANC Youth League, Sobukwe was elected president of the Students' Representative Council at the University College of Fort Hare, and would a year later end his term with a speech recalling the importance of Africanism within the movement.

In that speech, he said: 'Let me plead with you, lovers of my Africa, to carry with you into the world the vision of a new Africa, an Africa reborn, an Africa rejuvenated, an Africa recreated, a young Africa. We are the first glimmers of a new dawn.

'And if we are persecuted for our views, we should remember, as the African saying goes, that "it is darkest before dawn", and that the dying beast kicks most violently when it is giving up the ghost.'

These words of Sobukwe, coming in this, the 55th year of the founding of the Organization of African Unity, the precursor to the African Union, must entreat us as Africans and South Africans to refocus our attention once again on the peace and prosperity of the African continent.

We must, as Sobukwe declared, ensure that we hold a 'vision of a new Africa, an Africa reborn, an Africa rejuvenated, an Africa recreated, a young Africa'.

Yet the question that must assist our consciences as Africans must be whether Sobukwe would be pleased with the state that Africa and Africans in particular find themselves in today.

If we were to look at the UN Human Development Index (HDI), for example, we would see that much more work needs to be done in order to pay particular attention to the development of Africans on the continent.

This particular international index measures, annually, life expectancy, education and per-capita income. These, according to the Pakistani economist Mahbub ul Haq, who established the index, would allow people to explore their capabilities and take advantage of opportunities.

Yet in 2016, two years ago, only five countries on the continent reported a 'high human development'. These were the Seychelles – coming in on the top for African countries but ranking at 63rd place in the world – Mauritius, Algeria, Tunisia and Libya.

Indeed, the last one may be a surprise, given that it has been embattled in a civil war since the fall of Muammar Gaddafi, but this human development ranking proved just how effective the Gaddafi administration was in providing development for ordinary Libyans. In 2017, according to International Monetary Fund (IMF) estimates, Libya recorded the highest percentage in gross domestic product (GDP) growth on the continent, with 55 per cent.

Thirteen African countries follow in the 'medium human development' category on the HDI, among them South Africa, Botswana, Gabon, Egypt, Morocco, Namibia, Ghana, Kenya and Zambia.

The rest of the African countries, 35 of them, find themselves in the 'low human development' category. The country at the bottom is the Central African Republic (CAR), while others, including Ethiopia, Djibouti and Ivory Coast, also find themselves in this category.

These last three are specifically pointed out because in 2017 their GDP growth rate was over 7 per cent, according to the IMF. This growth must mean development for the people of those countries, or else it was just benefiting the few on top.

The three worst-performing African countries on the HDI were the CAR, Niger and Chad. However, in 2017, both the CAR and Niger could boast a GDP growth rate of over 4 per cent.

These figures, from the World Economic Outlook of the IMF, show that the CAR, Niger and Chad host three of the most unequal societies in the world in terms of the 2016 inequality-adjusted HDI.

Equatorial Guinea, which in 2017 boasted the highest GDP per capita at over $34 000 (R466 000) per annum, was only ranked a medium human development country.

In the aftermath of the global economic recession in 2008/2009, many countries, especially in Africa, lost the focus that they had in the previous decade, to develop the continent. Yet African leaders must pay attention to establishing thorough redistribution policies within their countries.

Indeed, as the IMF data suggests, only three countries experienced negative growth in their GDP rate in 2017: Equatorial Guinea, the Democratic Republic of Congo and South Sudan.

In other words, this indeed is proving to be the African century, where African economies are growing, but this growth must translate into yielding better lives for Africans. As Sobukwe prophesied, Africa is being reborn, rejuvenated and recreated in this new dawn.

We must not be surprised that, sadly, the only three countries where growth did not occur are the three countries where Africans are fighting each other. Even more so, we must learn from the life of Sobukwe that Africans cannot afford to be fighting each other at all, even to the extent of barring others from funerals.

We must learn to respect and work with each other, putting cheap political points and egos aside, in order to realise a better human life for all on our continent.

'Speaking as one African to another':[1] The letters of two men in unfriendly times

EF Daitz

EF Daitz is a doctoral candidate at the University of Cape Town. Her dissertation concerns the personal correspondence of Robert Sobukwe and Benjamin Pogrund between 1960 and 1977.

BETWEEN 1960 AND 1977, Benjamin Pogrund, then a journalist at the *Rand Daily Mail*, and Robert Sobukwe, the founder of the Pan Africanist Congress (PAC), exchanged a remarkable correspondence, providing us today with a finely textured portrait of friendship between two men in unfriendly times.[2]

Robert Sobukwe was among a group of Africanists who broke away from the African National Congress (ANC) in 1958 to form the PAC in 1959. In 1960, he was arrested and sentenced to three years' hard labour for inciting Africans to break the pass laws as part of the PAC's anti-pass campaign. In 1963, Parliament passed the General Law Amendment Act, which amended the Suppression of Communism Act, among other laws, giving the minister of justice the prerogative to prolong the detention of political prisoners indefinitely. Under this clause, Sobukwe was transferred to Robben Island and spent a further six years in solitary confinement without charge or trial. In 1967, he was banished to the mining town of Kimberley, his movements and speech severely proscribed by a banning order. In 1978, he died of lung cancer.

Pogrund was a liberal journalist who spent much of his time in South Africa's townships among the locally organised opposition to apartheid, reporting on politics. He met Sobukwe in the mid-1950s, not through his activities as a journalist or Sobukwe's activities as a leader of the PAC, but by happenstance through Pogrund's fiancée, Astrid, who was studying isiZulu with Sobukwe at the Wits University in Johannesburg. A deep and abiding friendship blossomed.

Pogrund regarded himself as a liberal and was actively involved in various circles of liberal and African-nationalist opposition to apartheid. In 1990, he published a biography of Sobukwe titled *How Can Man Die Better: The Life of Robert Sobukwe.* In 1997, he presented his correspondence with Sobukwe, upon which the biography was based, together with other correspondence and research materials written by Sobukwe and concerning him, to the Wits Historical Papers Research Archive. This collection is known as the Robert Sobukwe Papers.

Here I am interested in three ways in which the letters might invite the interest of a contemporary readership.[3] First, the letters bring together the voices of two men with apparently irrecon- cilable ideological commitments − one a liberal, the other a pan- Africanist − in an intimate and amicable exchange. In doing so, they invite us not to take for granted the enmities between various political formations during the liberation struggle and to avoid the assumption that what activists said publicly had an uncomplicated relationship to the nature of their personal lives. Far from ruining our heroes, their more unruly affinities − such as that between Pogrund as a liberal, and Sobukwe as a pan-Africanist − serve to humanise them. Like us, they had to live out certain contradictions as a condition of their humanity. For this reason, friendship was possible even among those who, on paper at least, were foes.

Second, the letters provide us with a picture of friendship that is at odds with the way in which relationships across 'race' during apartheid are commonly represented. This is not because the trend toward brutality is an inaccurate characterisation of relationships across racial difference under apartheid so much as it is because we do not yet have a fully developed literature that explores the emotional ambiguities of life under the regime.

Third, as an intimate exchange between two men who had no business consorting with one another and even less carrying on a warm friendship, the letters surface a kind of ambiguity that I think is productive for the state of public conversation in South Africa today, which is, much like public conversation globally at present, starkly intolerant of the messiness and lack of ideological clarity that any human life entails.

Writing of their friendship in 1967, Sobukwe would say that he found the term 'friend' inadequate and incongruous to describe Pogrund:

> Helen Suzman visited me in here too, as you know, and she greeted me with the words 'I was with your friend, Benjie, yesterday.' I was forcibly struck by the inadequacy if not the incongruity of the term. I *have* friends, of course, of whom I am very fond. And high on the list are Mrs Marquard and Prof Wellington. But I have long passed the stage of even thinking of you as a friend. I don't want to be sentimental about that. So I suggest that you and I stick to a simple Bob and Benjie in our dealings with each other, in the same way as my biological brother, Charles, and I stick to our nicknames.[4]

To which Pogrund replied:

Both your letters moved me very deeply, particularly your second one. There is no shame – there cannot be any – in my telling you that I cried when I read it. I feel so very close to you, Bob. I recall constantly the last times we were able to see each other, of the many hours when we ranged in our chats over every conceivable subject as though we had never not been seeing each other. I have said before, and I say again, that it is little that I do for you and your family. You deserve a lot more, and so often I berate myself for not doing more for you, and so often too I pray to G-d [*sic*] that I had the power to act effectively on your behalf. I feel a terrible pain within me about your situation. What more can I say than to agree with you that it should continue to be 'Bob' and 'Benjie'?[5]

It is perhaps precisely because the letters were written and exchanged under the watchful eye of the censors that both Pogrund and Sobukwe engaged in less typically 'masculine' exchanges, often discussing mundane or intimate matters, because they could not write in an openly political register or on topics of a more obviously political nature. Instead they discussed the pleasures of food, fashion, music, gardening and literature, the details of their domestic lives, the gossip about their antagonists, and international politics. Had they been able to discuss politics more openly at home, we might have inherited a less atypical set of letters.

The censors, for their part, appeared to have read the letters with their own coarse sensibilities in mind, confiscating and censoring, for instance, a letter in which Sobukwe referred to his 'enemies', but allowing another, in which he contemplated the difficulties of raising children without racialising their consciousness in what was a deeply racist society, to pass without comment or reproof. Indeed, when Sobukwe referred to Pogrund as an African – 'speaking as one African to another' – in a fashion commensurate with his non-racial convictions, the censors were silent. I suspect this is because they did not recognise their own preoccupations in either Pogrund or Sobukwe's letters precisely because of the register in which the letters were written.

Thus, in 1966, Sobukwe received a warning from the Special Branch not to express any political opinions in his letters. The offending sentence, according to his wife, Veronica, in a letter she wrote to Pogrund at the time, was, 'If I had failed the enemy would have rejoiced and my friends would have been grieved.'[6] On the other hand, a letter that is arguably all about the predicaments of living in a society whose racism one staunchly opposes, but written in a less overtly political vocabulary, passed through the mail unremarked. In this letter, Sobukwe writes:

My dear Benjie,

In your letter of the 5th February you state that you were happy to note that my use of the term 'African', in an earlier letter, had no racist connotation or simplification.

Imagine my joy then when I received a letter from my daughter informing me that on their way to Joh'burg from Cape Town they met someone she calls 'Ausie Mary' ('ausie' being the Sotho equivalent of the Afrikaans 'ou Sis' = elder Sister) who had for some time been employed by 'Ntate Pogrund'. Now 'Ntate' – for the benefit of you Zulus – is the Sotho term for 'father'.

I have been rather strict, Benjie, in bringing up my children. I have stressed that their responses must always be accompanied by a polite 'father' or 'mother'. In other words I want 'yes, father', 'no, mother', 'thank you, father' from them and not just 'yes', 'no' or 'thank you' etc.

I need not tell you, of course, that I have been hard put to it to decide how I can train them to show this politeness to *all* [underlined thrice in the original] people irrespective of colour, without making them colour-conscious. And lo and behold, my child, most naturally, without any self-consciousness writes of 'Ntate Pogrund' as she has written of 'Ntate Mothopeng' before.[7]

It was without doubt not the state's intention to produce such intimate talk between men, but that seems to have been the effect of the restrictions on what they could discuss.

The quotidian nature of much of the correspondence means that the intimacy of the friendship cannot be fully attributed either to resistance to the machinations of the state or to the imperatives of the liberation struggle. For instance, their rapport was not simply a function of the fact that it was useful to Sobukwe to have a white man operating outside prison on his behalf, nor can it be reduced to a shared antagonism towards the communist left, though both factors played a role in their relationship. In these letters, the rapport between the two is located in the particulars of their daily lives instead.

For instance, in a telegram of 5 October 1964, Sobukwe asks Pogrund to buy birthday cards for his twin sons,[8] to which Pogrund responds, in a letter of 12 October of the same year:

Your telegram about the twins' birthday was received and promptly noted upon. I sent out two birthday cards, inscribed 'All my love, your Tata', and I tried to make my handwriting as neat and small as possible to make it look at least something like yours. I also sent them some small presents.[9]

This kind of domestic back-and-forth between Pogrund and Sobukwe is typical of their letters. For instance, on 1 June 1966,

Sobukwe requests that Pogrund make the arrangements for his wife's birthday:

> Finally, Benjie, on the 27th of July is my wife's fortieth birthday. I should like her to know that she is highly appreciated. Do you think you could organise a present from me and the kids? I am writing early so that you may consult me if you wish. I leave the choice of a present to you. I am writing to Miliswa too, to appraise [*sic*] her of the great event.[10]

Pogrund then wrote a letter addressed to the Sister-in-Charge at St Mary's Hostel, where Miliswa Sobukwe was at boarding school, enclosing R8 pocket money for the Sobukwe children, including Dalindyebo and Dinilesizwe, and asking that Miliswa be allowed to use some of the money to send her mother a telegram for her birthday.[11] He then wrote to Sobukwe to confirm that he would see Veronica on 27 July to celebrate with her. On 21 July Sobukwe responded, writing:

> I have just received a letter from Miliswa in which she informs me that their schools reopen on the 18th of July. I realise then that *our* plans for bouquets by the children will have to be dropped. I hope she received my letter before she left so that she should know, at least, that *we* had intended her to play an important part in the festivities.[12]

Sobukwe often included Pogrund grammatically in these schemes as though the two men had taken these decisions together, rather than Sobukwe sending his instructions to Pogrund, and Pogrund faithfully carrying them out. The plans for Mrs Sobukwe's birthday are 'our plans', the intentions are shared, 'we intended …', and so on.

On 28 July 1966, Pogrund replied to Sobukwe:

My dear Bob, I am hastening to write this short letter to you to let you know that all went well on your wife's birthday yesterday. I delivered to her, as a personal gift from you, sweetpeas, and from you and the children, a tea service as we arranged. This is a set of 'Royal Standard' English bone china, and I think your wife liked it a great deal. My own gift was a black leather handbag, while my girlfriend presented a box of toilet soaps. One thing on which you and I slipped up: you should have sent me a little note to include with the tea service. As we had not done this, I had to improvise, and the note I delivered from you and the children read: 'To a wife and mother. For your courage and devotion.'[13]

With the digitisation of the archive of the Robert Sobukwe Papers, and Derek Hook's recent publication of an edited volume of Sobukwe's prison writing, the letters will find a broader audience than has hitherto been the case. Hopefully, this will lead to renewed interest in Sobukwe and the blossoming of a thousand different interpretations of the relevance of his life and work for contemporary South Africa. My view is that in bringing together two voices from apparently disparate ideological camps, in a warm and intimate exchange, the letters present us with an ambiguity in the record of our past. And the task of the contemporary scholar, I think, will be to resist the temptation to resolve that ambiguity and to allow for descriptions of the South African past that are more complex, particularly when it comes to the emotional lives of its protagonists, than we have thus far been able to contemplate.

The letters invite us to rethink the category 'African' as one that might be open, beyond its racially essentialist usage, to all who are committed to a common future on this continent based on justice, equality and freedom for all.

Getting to know his true grace

Andrew Walker

Andrew Walker was raised and educated in the New England region of the United States and attended university at Trinity College in Hartford, Connecticut. He has spent his 30-year career in the field of international human resources, and is presently the global head of remuneration and employee mobility for Ernst & Young, based in New York City.

WHILE ATTENDING UNIVERSITY in the US at a small New England liberal arts college in the late 1980s, I witnessed the increasing activism among students opposing the apartheid regime. Even on my little campus a mock shantytown was erected, with banners calling on US companies to divest from their South African business interests. Nelson Mandela was a household name, and support for ending the separatist policies seemed universal in my part of the world. Nevertheless, the details of what the opposition was doing within South Africa, and what was being done to the opposition, were almost entirely unknown to me.

Many years later, by then married with two small children, I was living in London as an expatriate. Perhaps the greatest perk of those years was access to other countries during holidays and school breaks. We covered a lot of ground in Western Europe and occasionally ventured further afield. I was nearing the end of my five-year secondment when we made our way to South Africa, a place I had for a long time hoped to visit.

For a variety of reasons, the African continent always had a strong pull for me. As children, my cousins spent several summers in Central Africa accompanying their father, a professor of art history, who conducted academic research there. They shared amazing stories of what they saw and did. One cousin returned often to do aid work after finishing his university studies, and still does so today. In my childhood, the work of Jane Goodall, news about the Ethiopian famine, and photos of wildebeest, lion and zebra all filled me with awe and curiosity about Africa. In high school, I wrote a paper on the work of Alan Paton, reading *Cry, the Beloved Country*, which opened my eyes to the injustices of the apartheid government. Later, Mandela's release and ascension to the presidency filled me with respect, joy and hope. So, visiting Africa, and South Africa in particular, was near the top of my bucket list. In late 2008, I embarked for Cape Town with my wife, son and daughter.

We took in many of the famous sights: Table Mountain, the Cape of Good Hope, penguins at Boulders Beach, the V&A Waterfront and a wildlife preserve. I saved a visit to Robben Island for later in our trip. Although I expected it to be a highlight, I was wholly unprepared for the impact it would have on me, and the passion it would ignite.

The Robben Island tour included a guided walk through the prison compound, led by a former prisoner, and an opportunity to stand in Mandela's cell. Afterwards, we boarded a bus to see other buildings on the island, as well as the quarry where the prisoners worked. Our clever bus driver followed the designated route in reverse, to avoid getting caught in the queue of buses forming in the other direction. Near the end (normally the very beginning), he pulled over onto a small side road to avoid blocking oncoming traffic. We stopped in front of a collection of buildings set away from the main prison compound. Almost as an afterthought, while we waited for traffic to clear, our bus tour guide (not the former prisoner who led our walking tour) casually pointed out the housing for the warders, the kennels for the island's guard dogs and the tiny cottage where Robert Sobukwe had been held in isolation far from the other prisoners. This remote spot was like an island within an island.

The name Sobukwe sounded vaguely familiar but I didn't know why. The bus tour guide, who was younger than the prison guide, explained briefly that Sobukwe was considered such a threat to the government that he was separated from all the other prisoners. He inaccurately described Sobukwe as a fierce militant who resorted to violent measures. I wondered how could I know nothing of this man who was considered such a threat to the apartheid regime that he was held away from the main prison. In fact, he was the *only* isolated prisoner on the island. Even Nelson Mandela, the face of the anti-apartheid movement to the world, was held with others, including his friends and associates. 'Who *was* Robert Sobukwe?' I asked myself.

Not much later, with the traffic jam over, we continued on our way. But the curiosity stayed with me. As we awaited the ferry back to the mainland, we browsed the island's gift shop, where I found Benjamin Pogrund's biography of Sobukwe, *How Can Man Die Better*, and brought a copy to the till. The clerk stamped the inside cover with the words, 'Bought at Robben Island Museum', and before long it would become not just one of my favourite *books*, but also one of my favorite possessions.

That night I flipped through it, looking at the photos and acquainting myself with the distinguished-looking gentleman who had so alarmed the South African government. He didn't look violent or even remotely threatening. Rather, he appeared academic and friendly. During the long flight back to London, I leafed through the pages (with frequent interruptions from my children). I continued reading it on the Tube during my commute to and from work, and at night before bed. This was a book to be savoured, not quickly devoured, so I took my time and read it slowly. I was mesmerised by the life, hardship, courage, intellect and superhuman character – and, sadly, the death – of this rarest-of-rare human being. His story and his relationship with Pogrund held me rapt like no other book I've read. At some point midway through the book, the question I had asked myself during that fortuitous bus-tour traffic jam on Robben Island changed from 'How could I not know about this man?' to 'Why doesn't *everyone* know about Robert Sobukwe?'

Even before I finished the book, I felt compelled to talk about it to anyone and everyone. It bothered me that one of the museum's own tour guides so greatly misunderstood Sobukwe, and, what's worse, propagated that misunderstanding to many others who visited the island. Suddenly, it became my mission to make sure people not only knew of Sobukwe, but also knew what he stood for, and appreciated his critical role in the fight against the apartheid regime.

Unable to find the book in any bookshop outside South Africa, I ordered ten copies from the South African publisher. I distributed these to friends, family and other potentially sympathetic contacts, including the very pro-Africa chairman of the board of Reuters (today Thomson Reuters), where I worked at the time. My request to each recipient was twofold: 'Please read this book and *pass it along*.' Copies went to various cities in the US and to several places around London, but I daydreamed of ways to get it even broader attention.

Beyond the book, I also wanted to know more about the author, but there wasn't much information readily available about Benjamin Pogrund. The Wikipedia article was far too brief and I couldn't find him on LinkedIn or Facebook. Facebook did reveal another Pogrund named Jennie. I recalled one photo in the book of Benjamin's daughter sitting with Robert's children. Holding the photo in the book up to the computer screen, I compared the young face to the Facebook profile picture and thought, *this could be her*. I sent her a friend request, asking if indeed she was Benjamin Pogrund's daughter. To my delight, she was, and we began a wonderful correspondence about Sobukwe, her father and her own experiences growing up in South Africa, where she lives today.

Jennie in turn introduced me to Benjamin himself, and to Sobukwe's son Dini, who worked so hard to preserve his father's legacy through the Robert Mangaliso Sobukwe Trust. I have enjoyed an irregular but ongoing correspondence with both, and I was thrilled to learn that Benjamin had told Robert's widow, Veronica, about me and my interest in their story. I often asked Dini how I could help with his Trust efforts and celebrated his successes in arranging exhibits to improve South Africans' awareness of his father, including one held on Robben Island. It was an honour and a privilege to be in contact with both of them.

Jennie and I eventually met when a business trip took me to Pretoria, where she lives, and it was thrilling not only to see my pen pal in person but also to make a physical connection to someone who had known Sobukwe in life. On several occasions, Benjamin and I narrowly missed being in the same city at the same time. Although a resident of Israel, at one point he attended an event *in my office building*, but I was away on a business trip at the time. We finally met in New York, where I am now based, when a book tour brought him to the city in 2016. He presented me with a signed copy of the third edition of *How Can Man Die Better*, which sits next to the original copy I bought on Robben Island, which he also signed for me that day.

At one point several years ago, I saw a comment posted on the Sobukwe group's Facebook page by a girl who wrote that she was Robert's granddaughter. I responded, commenting on how much I admired and respected her grandfather. Sometime later, I mentioned the exchange to Benjamin and he confirmed that he knew her, Otua, the daughter of Robert's own daughter. Some years later, I heard from Otua out of the blue. She remembered me and wanted to tell me she planned to attend university in the US. It was so much fun for me to expand my Sobukwe pen pal group and we have stayed in touch, even meeting at Wellesley College, where she enrolled. Wellesley is one of the top colleges in the US, the alma mater of Hillary Clinton, Madeleine Albright and journalist Diane Sawyer. Otua's acceptance and success there proves that she inherited her grandfather's brilliance. It was Otua who informed me of Veronica's passing, before she herself returned to South Africa for the funeral.

I've read many compelling biographies, and throughout my life I've been inspired by the stories of a number of great people, including some of my own ancestors and relatives, but I have never been so drawn to a figure as I have to Robert Sobukwe. It's hard for me to explain it in a way that helps others understand, and I am certain I've fallen short here, but to me he represents the essence of aspired humanity. Self-made, intelligent, wise, empathetic, strong, principled, articulate, reasoned, disciplined, charismatic and caring, to name perhaps his most striking attributes. Sobukwe led from the front, and his beliefs remained steadfast in the face of the most extreme oppression, in a way that is otherwise unimaginable.

At many times, I was brought to the brink of tears both by the extreme cruelty to which he was subjected and by his most remarkable character, demonstrated time and again in his composed responses. One of the most poignant sections of the book deals with an exchange between Robert and Benjamin during the Robben Island years, when Robert chastised Benjamin for his expression of pride in the wake of a distant political victory. Robert's reply came complete with historical analysis and the summation that one must be magnanimous in victory, not vengeful. If anyone could be forgiven for harbouring sentiments of vengeance, it was

Sobukwe. Yet, as Pogrund wrote, 'I was struck, as I so often was, by the absence of self-pity.'

Robert Sobukwe is my role model, my idol, my hero. I am incredibly grateful to know him through the pages of his biography and through the connections I've formed with several of his family and friends. It saddens me that his legacy was hijacked, at his very funeral no less, by a militant element, but that may help to explain why he is not better known today. The tide seems to be turning, largely through the efforts of many, such as Dini and Benjamin, so that Sobukwe is now better known and appreciated. It remains my hope, however, that *everyone* will come to know the true grace of Robert Sobukwe.

Sharing my grandfather's pains and hopes

Otua Sobukwe

Otua Sobukwe is the granddaughter of Robert Sobukwe. Born in Washington, DC, she grew up in Kampala, Uganda, until the age of six when she moved with her mother, Miliswa, to Cape Town. She did her schooling there. She is a student at Wellesley College, near Boston, Massachusetts, pursuing a double major in economics and political science.

In loving memory of my dearest Uncle Dini who recently passed away. I will love you endlessly, forever and always.

THE FIRST TIME I met my grandfather, I was four years old. At that time, he didn't have a name or a face but existed solely as a man whom my mother would occasionally speak of. It had been almost twenty-three years since his passing, but I was at an age when time, reality and space were convoluted terms that didn't quite make sense to me. And so, not having met this man, nor fully grasping what 'death' signified, my childhood imagination placed him in my private repertoire of mythological creatures: behold Santa Claus, the Easter bunny, the tooth fairy and my grandfather.

Each of them danced in my mind and visited me in my sleep, comforting me in times of loneliness. When I reached out to speak to him, I imagined that my grandfather was tall and had a deep voice, with the same calming presence that my mother had. I imagined that he liked the same things I liked, and sometimes I imagined that he would watch me play in the garden. That he would see me speak to the flowers and butterflies, lost in my imaginary world, and that he would smile from a distance as though he were some sort of angel. As I got older, he developed a face with eyes like mine and a smile like my mother's, but it was not until years later that I remember looking at a picture of him and thinking to myself that this face, with all of its unfamiliarity, looked almost exactly as I had imagined it. From my earliest recollection, my grandfather was a presence in my life that I couldn't yet articulate or fully acknowledge, but I felt it was there.

The second time I met my grandfather was in 2005. I was seven years old and this time I met him only partially. I will explain this a little later. My parents had just separated and so my mother and I moved to South Africa to live on Robben Island with my Uncle Dini. The decision to leave Uganda, where we lived, was fairly abrupt. I remember feeling a deep sense of loss and disorientation when we landed in Cape Town. What was this place? What were the people like? Did they have butterflies here? My mother told me that we were going to live with my Uncle Dini, his partner and her son, and that it wouldn't be the same as Uganda but that I would be just as happy.

I remember the first boat ride to Robben Island and how it all felt so far away and unfamiliar. I remember feeling afraid that the waves were going to swallow us, or that the boat was going to capsize into the mouth of a giant whale. I remember thinking that my new home was going to be surrounded by vast amounts of water, and that I couldn't really swim. What if something happened and I had to swim? But this small island soon became my home, and I forgot about the water and the waves and the whales and I let myself be free. And this freedom created some of the fondest memories of my childhood.

My recollection of Robben Island is at times blurry. I remember it in fragments, without any real chronology. We lived in a peach-coloured house that had a big front yard, with a braai pit in the back where we used to cook most of our dinners. The house had three bedrooms, a dog and two cats that belonged to Auntie Gaby (my uncle's partner). Her son, Tshawe, was a few years older than me and went to the local school on the island. Other than the school, which had maybe just under 40 students, we were a fairly small group of kids.

Even though we were young, I remember immediately feeling like the odd one out. I wasn't fully aware of the different languages that were being spoken but their English accents sounded different from what I was used to, and at the time mine was Ugandan. I remember tweaking my words to sound more 'coloured' and was once teased for saying 'lekker kwaai' (cool), without knowing what it meant. I felt younger too, for some reason, and had to mature very quickly.

Despite our differences, we were all very close and treated each other as siblings. I had two best friends, Bianca and Allison, and we would spend hours walking along the seashore, looking for rabbits or playing with the stray turtles. Sometimes we would go into the forest and collect pine cones for a braai later that night, or we would visit Auntie Ruth. She was an artist who lived on the eastern part of the island, who always gave us small candy treats while teaching us how to make beautiful shapes with paint. If we had any money we would go to the only store on the island and get Simba chips and Chappies chewing gum. And if we had a bit more we would treat ourselves to hot chips at the café, which was always considered a luxury.

But apart from the time we spent together, what bonded us most was the daily commute many of us had to make to attend school on the mainland. I remember waking up at 5 am every morning to take the island shuttle that would drop us off at the harbour. After the hour-long boat ride to the mainland, my mother and I would walk through the Waterfront to the taxi rank. The taxi would then take us to the station in town and from there we would walk up Parliament Street, then St John's Street, and turn into Hope Street, eventually arriving at my school. The commute could take two to three hours in total. After school, my mother and I would do the same trip back, leaving around 2.30 pm and arriving back on the island just before 7 pm, in time for dinner.

Sometimes the boat would be delayed and it would take two hours to make the trip from the island to the mainland; at other times it would stop midway through the journey to allow a whale to pass. By then whales had become fascinating creatures and us kids would all press our faces against the windows, peering into the dark water in the hope of spotting an eye or a flipper, and sometimes lying that we had. There were times when the boat wouldn't run at all because the sea was too rough. This could last hours, days or even weeks, and was common during the winter.

Looking back, this was a lifestyle that must have been unfathomably exhausting for a seven-year-old, but it was what we knew and it was our normal. In the early mornings, while it was still dark outside, we would sit next to each other on the boat and play card games, sometimes sharing stories of our favourite scenes from the latest episode of *Dragon Ball Z* on TV. And in the evenings, on our way back, we huddled at the same table on the boat and did our homework together, the older kids helping the younger ones, the whales swimming by. Life for us was simple and we were kids like any other, creating a childhood like any other … Except that, in reality, we weren't.

Sometimes I look back on my time on Robben Island and feel a deep sense of conflict in my heart. I look back, and my immediate association with the island is its warmth and innocence. I think of the afternoons I spent collecting seashells on the beach that I would later make into necklaces for my mother. Or when I rode my bike through the forest to chase springboks, or the first time I went fishing with Auntie Gaby and almost fell into the harbour because my small hands struggled to pull the rod back firmly enough. It is hard not to smile when I remember the names of all my friends and all the trouble we got up to, especially during the long, hot summer days when there was no one else around but us.

But how can it be that my immediate association with this place, this island, this prison, is not the hundreds and hundreds of men who were unjustly held away from their families, repeatedly broken and beaten by a regime that feared their hope more than anything else? How can it be that I was so oblivious to the pain and the weight of the island when the prisons were right there, and barricaded walls were right there, and the people from all over the world filling the tour buses would wave at us children, us 'children of the island', and I would put down my seashells and wave back, not understanding that their tour was my very own history?

I think what tinges my memories of Robben Island with pain is the acknowledgment that, as I said above, I met my grandfather only partially during this period of my lifetime when, physically, I was as close to him as I ever will be. To put it simply, and blatantly, I played where he wept. And, to be clear, the pain that I feel is not guilt, but is rather this surreal sense of being connected so uniquely, so unexpectedly, and, to some degree, so perversely, to a history that I might otherwise have never experienced with such intimacy.

Robben Island was my childhood home, and when I spoke to the butterflies and the whales, and even at times to the seashells, I still felt his presence watching me. I was a child who, 30 years after the death of her grandfather, would look up to the very same sky that he looked up at and count the very same stars he counted, but I was free and he was not. He was a prisoner, and I was not. We both lived on Robben Island but the reality is that we lived in two different islands, because nothing can be more separate than the worlds in which that space bore our existence. To me, the blueness of the sky never lost its colour, as candyfloss clouds morphed into grey patches; the singing tune of seagulls never mimicked a pained cry; the tranquil ebb and flow of the sea never became melancholic, yearning; and the mainland, the shimmering lights, their faintness, were always picturesque, always romantic, never a cold reminder of the separating distance and the harsh reality, the harsh juxtaposition, that you are indeed alone.

And this was the case for us 'children of the island'. We were bound to a history that shaped our childhood before we understood the depths of that history, and that our small hands, our small fingers, our small eyes could perceive only partially. We thought the unjust incarceration of the black body to be an issue of the past, an outdated horror of the 'dark times' – how lucky we were to not be behind those bars. But yet, our black and brown bodies that ran wildly around the island were still trapped in invisible shackles; we just could not perceive them. To this day, our childhood still baffles, confuses and perhaps even torments me. I wonder sometimes whether its complexity, in many ways, is in fact a microcosm of the lives of the born-free generation – affected but unaffected, aware but unaware. The post-1994 born-frees, whose lack of freedom renders this date indeed insignificant, who are still fighting the same fight, I wonder, how much do we really understand? How much of our ancestors' sacrifices do we really comprehend? And, if we comprehend, if anything at all, how much are we willing to give for those to come after us?

Teenage discovery

I met my grandfather again when I was 13 years old. This was by far our most significant encounter. My mother and I lived on the island for just over a year. After leaving, in the years that followed as I grew up, I developed a slow understanding of who he was. While he was no longer a part of the mystical creatures of my childhood, he was in this strange, undefined category of 'other' that felt important but lacked context that I knew existed. South Africa is a place where, as a child, you will grow up hearing the word 'apartheid' used almost daily. For a long time I heard this word and I understood most of its meaning, but it was only when I was 13 that I really started to make the deeper connection between 'apartheid' and 'my grandfather'.

It is hard to recall the exact moment at which everything clicked because for so long things were so disjointed. Perhaps if I had not been at a French school the discovery would have happened much sooner. But the school that I attended for almost nine years was in many ways insulated from South African culture, and this extended into its curriculum, which was heavily based on French/European history. And so, the dates and the names from apartheid that we had learnt vaguely in primary school never piqued my interest or deeper understanding because I struggled to perceive their relevance.

But, you might ask, what about at home? What about my family, did they not tell me about him? And here's the thing: they certainly did, but my mother spoke of him mostly as her father, not as an activist. She told me what he did, historically, but when she spoke from her heart and let her mind wander, she would tell me stories of her childhood and the memories that she painfully missed. She always told me how gentle and loving he was, how when they would walk down in the street together everyone greeted him with a smile. How in the evenings, he would teach her Xhosa riddles while she helped cook for the family, and when she spoke in English he would always correct her pronunciation with encouraging remarks: 'Keep trying, keep trying.' She told me how he loved to give her small treats, how he loved Gogo.

These were the stories that captivated and stuck with me most as a kid, and so, for the longest time, my grandfather was this man who, through my mother's words, I had already begun to love as just my grandfather and who I only really knew as my grandfather. But when I was 13, everything changed. Earlier that year, my mother and I went to have dinner with Uncle Benjamin and his wife, Anne, who were visiting from Israel. Uncle Benjamin is the author of my grandfather's biography and over dinner he asked me if I had read the book. I was stumped. The book was on our bookshelf and I had certainly seen it over the years, and perhaps even skimmed its pages a few times, but I remembered always feeling overwhelmed and discouraged by the complexity of its words. I told him no, sadly, I hadn't, and he encouraged me to try again.

A few weeks passed after that dinner but the conversation stuck with me, and the burning desire to understand, to truly understand, this story and what it meant eventually pushed me to pick the book off the shelf and try again. I thought, *Robert Sobukwe: How Can Man Die Better*, what does that even mean? But I read, and I read and read and read. I was completely engrossed and paused only occasionally to ask my mother clarifying questions. Once, when I saw her name in one of the chapters, I leapt from my chair and yelled, 'This part is about you, Mama!' When I read about my grandfather's early childhood education, I remember thinking how bizarre it was that he and I shared such an intense love for words and language.

When I read about the Sharpeville massacre, I remember being amazed and then bewildered by how this had never been taught to me, how it had never been part of the national discourse. I read and I got angry. I got angry, and then I read. I started highlighting and cross-referencing words and places and events, piecing together things that I had half-heard in the classroom, things that my mother had told me in memories, things that I had seen on my grandmother's bedroom wall. In a long sequence of late nights on my kitchen floor, reading, remembering and calculating, I began to fill in the gaps of a story that I felt had been stolen from me.

Reading that book for the first time was an experience I still struggle to explain, because how do you explain an experience that is both so uniquely exhilarating and devastating at the same time? How do you explain the discovery of a beautiful truth, only to realise that this truth has been systematically concealed from an entire nation? I met my grandfather as Sobukwe for the first time when I was 13, and to meet him as Sobukwe was, essentially, to re-meet him. While I might not have understood it then, 'Sobukwe' was to become a place of raw centring in my life, and, in many ways, a spiritual catalyst to a series of awakenings that continue to shape and challenge the authenticity and purpose of who I am to this day.

Sobukwe today

Dear Tata,

I am sitting in a room with my boyfriend, a boy whom I have been dating for a few months, a boy who on our first date identified himself as an anarchist, and I am here, in his room, meeting a friend of his for the first time. They are mid-conversation about campus politics and their student-organising group when he turns to me, noticing that I am silent and says, 'Otua, tell my friend about your grandfather.' I choke. Immediately I am small and speechless. My body not only feels paralysed but also invisible as I begin to scramble together words to describe you and your legacy, which is constantly being erased. In my poor attempt at an explanation – Where do I begin? How do I summarise? Who am I to discern what details are or aren't important? – I fail and stutter, and in this incoherency I feel as though I am erasing you again and again.

I am sitting across a dinner table with a group of elders when one of them turns to me and says, 'Otua, tell them your story.' And when I begin to tell 'my story' – my passion for writing, my studies, my dreams – their puzzled faces look back at me and I am instantly reminded that I misunderstood. I correct myself. To them, 'your story' is 'my story' and so I speak about you, Sobukwe, and I forget about Otua, and this is always really hard.

I am standing in a classroom of seniors in an Africana studies class at my American college, focusing on the South African liberation struggle. I was invited by the professor to speak about my heritage. I am defending you, I am telling your story, I am explaining to the class that history cannot be rewritten and all efforts of the struggle need to be acknowledged. I am faced with rebuttal comments from the professor and told that I am speaking from 'a position of bias'. I fight back the tears, and this is always really hard.

I am speaking with someone and they mistake our relation and confuse you with my father, and when this happens I always choke. When I correct them and say, 'You mean my grandfather?' I am betrayed by my own voice that shakes at the idea of having you so much closer to me. Imagine. Imagine if you were my own father. But instead I think of the father that I do have, that I don't have, and I am reminded of a juxtaposition between two men who could not be more opposite.

I am 21 years old now and I keep meeting you, Tata. The encounters happen more frequently now, almost on a daily basis, when small things that I would ordinarily not perceive to be significant remind me of you, and, inadvertently, remind me of why I am here. And by 'here' I mean in this world, in the spaces I occupy, in my relationships. I meet you when I look up in class and realise that I am the only black student in the classroom. I meet you when the white lady at the grocery store asks me where I am from and congratulates me on my 'perfect English'. I meet you when my white friends praise me for 'not acting that black' and when my black friends call me out for acting 'too white'.

I meet you when I open magazine covers, read a book, flick through the TV channels, go to the cinema to watch a movie – any form of entertainment in this world – and I am reminded that my black skin will never be the default. I meet you when the world feels like it was not designed for people like me and *when doors that do not open feel like they will always remain closed. When the news outlets tell me that my black skin is still a crime. When black men walk past me at parties to talk to lighter-skinned girls, white girls, because I am a representation of everything they were taught to hate. When professors discern my abilities before knowing what I am capable of.*

I meet you and the pain is so real, it feels like you are right here with me. And sometimes I want you with me, but at other times I feel like I am losing myself in this dual identity. Because the hardest thing about carrying your name is feeling as though, at times, mine is lost in the process. And so, it is especially hard to be so proud of someone, so thankful for someone, so inspired by someone that you are so closely related to while knowing that, in reality, your lives are greatly different. And so, it probes to my very existence and purpose on this earth every time I am reminded of you, because it forces me to remind myself of our separate realities. Was your sacrifice worth it? Would you be proud of the current state of the world? Am I continuing the fight? Who am I?

And so, I meet you mostly when I am afraid, and afraid of myself. But the fear helps me. Like all other things, I am forced to remember that my fear is not new, that my pain or discomfort is not new, there have been many before me who have feared and suffered far worse things, and together, these shared pains and shared hopes can only push us forward.

Notes

Benjamin Pogrund

1   Information for this chapter is drawn chiefly from my book *Sobukwe and Apartheid*, published in 1990 by Peter Halban Publishers, London; Rutgers University Press, New Brunswick, New Jersey; and Jonathan Ball Publishers, Johannesburg. It is now in its third edition, issued by Jonathan Ball Publishers as *Robert Sobukwe: How Can Man Die Better*.

2   'Inaugural Address', in Robert Mangaliso Sobukwe, *Speeches of Robert Mangaliso Sobukwe, 1949–1959* (PAC, 2010).

3   Ibid.

4   I was allowed six visits to Sobukwe during his first year on the island. He and I had no illusions about the reason for this. We believed the microphone was in the ceiling above us. My conclusion was that the government wanted to decide what to do with him and needed to know his thinking. He repeatedly made it abundantly clear: the moment he was free he would resume work to destroy white supremacy. He knew he was dooming himself to imprisonment.

5   Kwanele Sosibo, *Mail & Guardian*, 24–30 August 2018.

6   Benzi Ka-Soko, *City Press*, 15 July 2018.

7   Thando Sipuye, Robert Sobukwe Foundation, Graaff-Reinet, date uncertain, 2018.

8   Conversation, Johannesburg, 5 July 2018.

9   I donated my collection of documents to the library.

10 Jaki Seroke, *Sunday Independent*, 25 February 2018.

11 Kenneth Mokgatlhe, *The New Age*, 27 February 2018.

12 Tebogo Brown, letters to the editor, *The Star*, 2 March 2018.

13 Azande Ralephenya, *Sowetan*, 22 March 2018.

14 Baldwin Ndaba, Therese Owen, Masego Panyane, Rabbie Serumula and Janet Smith (eds), *The Black Consciousness Reader* (Jacana, 2018).

15 Xolisa Phillip, 'Forgotten heroes deliver a timely lesson on struggle', *Business Day*, 11 April 2018.

16 Panashe Chigumadzi, *Sunday Times*, 21 June 2018.

17 Lindani Ngcobo, letters to the editor, *Sunday Times*, 1 July 2018.

18 Thando Sipuye, *Sunday Independent*, 29 April 2018.

19 *The Star*, 4 July 2018.

20 Conversation, Johannesburg, 20 June 2018.

N Barney Pityana

1   Robert Mangaliso Sobukwe, *Speeches of Robert Mangaliso Sobukwe, 1949–1959* (PAC, 2010). All quotations from Sobukwe in this chapter are taken from this source.
2   Benjamin Pogrund, *Robert Sobukwe: How Can Man Die Better*, third edition (Jonathan Ball Publishers, 2015).
3   President Thabo Mbeki invited Dr Mangosuthu Buthelezi of the IFP to join government as deputy president in 1999. This did not materialise because there was no agreement about the role of the deputy president. Buthelezi wanted it to perform the same significant role that Thabo Mbeki performed under Mandela's presidency. Of course, during Mandela's government of national unity (GNU), Buthelezi occupied a senior ministerial post as minister of home affairs. The GNU was dissolved in 1996. Mbeki also invited Mosibudi Mangena of Azapo to join the cabinet.
4   Mgwebi Snail, 'The Black Consciousness Movement in South Africa: A Product of the Entire Black World', *Historia Actual Online*, no 15 (winter 2008), pp 51–68. Available at citeseerx.ist.psu.edu/viewdoc/download?doi=10.1.1.630.4779&rep=rep1&type=pdf, accessed on 20 June 2019.
5   Constitution of the Republic of South Africa, 1996, Preamble. Available at www.justice.gov.za/legislation/constitution/SAConstitution-web-eng.pdf, accessed on 20 June 2019.
6   Steve Biko, *I Write What I Like* (Picador Africa, 2004).

Claudelle von Eck

1   The Casspir is an armoured vehicle that was deployed in townships during the apartheid era. It was designed specifically for conditions encountered in the South African Border War (Wikipedia).
2   'Necklacing' is the practice of extrajudicial summary execution and torture carried out by forcing a rubber tyre, filled with petrol, around a victim's chest and arms, and setting it on fire. The victim may take up to 20 minutes to die, suffering severe burns in the process. (Wikipedia)
3   The World Bank, 'Overcoming Poverty and Inequality in South Africa: An Assessment of Drivers, Constraints and Opportunities', March 2018. Available at documents.worldbank.org/curated/en/530481521735906534/pdf/124521-REV-OUO-South-Africa-Poverty-and-Inequality-Assessment-Report-2018-FINAL-WEB.pdf, accessed on 30 July 2019.
4   M Gannon, 'Race is a social construct, scientists argue', LiveScience, 5 February 2016. Available at www.scientificamerican.com/article/race-is-a-social-construct-scientists-argue/, accessed on 20 June 2019.
5   When I was being groomed to take over as CEO of the IIA SA, my predecessor and I decided that I would benefit from coaching. We settled on one of the

lecturers at the Gordon Institute of Business Science (GIBS), a leading South African business school.

6 1 Peter 3:7.

7 In 2014, I found myself struggling to cope with a perfect storm of crises. My nutritionist referred me to a coach who takes an integrated approach, including working on the rewiring of one's neural pathways, to reverse the damages of the past.

8 Although apartheid existed before HF Verwoerd became prime minister, his efforts to place it on a firmer legal and theoretical footing, in particular his opposition to even the limited form of integration known as *baasskap* (literally, 'boss-ship'), have led him to be dubbed the 'architect of apartheid'.

9 Sean Cooper, 'Feel inferior to others? 8 Signs of an Inferiority Complex', no date. Available at shynesssocielanxiety.com/inferioritycomplex/, accessed on 20 June 2019.

10 See Clark McKown and Michael Strambler, 'Developmental antecedents and social and academic consequences of stereotype-consciousness in middle childhood', *Child Development*, vol 80, no 6 (November/December 2009), pp 1643–1659.

11 Alexandra Ossola, 'How discrimination changes your brain', *VICE* Health, 21 March 2017. Available at tonic.vice.com/en_us/article/qkmna7/how-discrimination-changes-your-brain, accessed on 20 June 2019.

12 EA Pascoe and LS Richman, 'Perceived discrimination and health: A meta-analytic review', *Psychological Bulletin*, vol 135, no 4 (2009), pp 531–554.

13 April D Thames, 'Toxic exposure: The impact of racial inequality on the brain', Psychology Benefits Society, 2 September 2014. Available at psychologybenefits. org/2014/09/02/toxic-exposure-the-impact-of-racial-inequality-on-the-brain/, accessed on 20 June 2019.

14 Ibid.

15 LL Barnes, TT Lewis, CT Begeny, L Yu, DA Bennett and RS Wilson, 'Perceived discrimination and cognition in older African Americans', *Journal of the International Neuropsychological Society*, vol 18, no 5 (2012), pp 856–865; see also AD Thames, CH Hinkin, DA Byrd, RM Bilder, KJ Duff, MR Mindt, A Arentoft and V Streiff, 'Effects of stereotype threat, perceived discrimination, and examiner race on neuropsychological performance: Simple as black and white?' *Journal of the International Neuropsychological Society*, vol 19, no 5 (2013), pp 583–593.

16 CV Nguyen-Robertson, 'The neuroscience of racism: science and stories', Inspiring Victoria, 6 October 2018. Available at inspiringvictoria.org.au/2018/10/06/the-neuroscience-of-racism-science-and-stories/, accessed on 20 June 2019.

17 Ibid.

18 B Major and JW Kunstman, 'Suspicion in interracial interactions: using measures of cardiovascular reactivity to index threat', in DS Belle Derks and Naomi Ellemers (eds), *Neuroscience of Prejudice and Intergroup Relations*, pp 321–322 (Psychology Press, 2013).

19 AJ Golby, JD Gabrieli, JY Chiao and JL Eberhardt, 'Differential responses in the fusiform region to same-race and other-race faces', *Nature Neuroscience*, vol 4 (2001), pp 845–850.
20 F Sheng and S Han, 'Manipulations of cognitive strategies and intergroup relationships reduce the racial bias in empathic neural responses', *NeuroImage*, vol 61, no 4 (2012), pp 786–797.
21 JW Findling and WF Young, Jr, 'Cushing's Syndrome', *The Journal of Clinical Endocrinology & Metabolism*, vol 90, no 2 (February 2005), E2.
22 Data from The Heart and Stroke Foundation South Africa website, www.heartfoundation.co.za/.

Adam Habib and Alexandra Leisegang

1 Benjamin Pogrund, *Robert Sobukwe: How Can Man Die Better*, third edition (Jonathan Ball Publishers, 2015).
2 Dikgang Moseneke, 'Address by Wits Chancellor, during the naming of the Robert Sobukwe Building, University of the Witwatersrand, Johannesburg, 2017'. Available at www.polity.org.za/print-version/sa-justice-dikgang-moseneke-address-by-wits-chancellor-during-the-naming-of-the-robert-sobukwe-building-university-of-witswatersrand-johannesburg-17092017-2017-09-18, accessed on 21 June 2019.
3 Derek Hook, 'A threatening personification of freedom or: Sobukwe and repression', *Safundi*, vol 17, no 2 (2016), p 205.
4 Ibid, p 206.

Thandeka Gqubule-Mbeki and Duma Gqubule

1 'Gail Gerhart interviews Robert Mangaliso Sobukwe (1970)', *Psychology in Society*, no 50 (2016). Available at www.scielo.org.za/scielo.php?script=sci_arttext&pid=S1015-60462016000100004, accessed on 9 July 2019.
2 Ibid.

Barney Mthombothi

1 *Hansard*, volume 6, column 4652, 24 April 1963, quoted in Neo Lekgotla laga Ramoupi, 'Sobukwe was no apartheid sellout, as Mapaila claims', *Mail & Guardian*, 20 February 2019. Available at mg.co.za/article/2019-02-20-sobukwe-was-no-apartheid-sellout-as-mapaila-claims, accessed on 30 July 2019.
2 'Address on Behalf of the Graduating Class at Fort Hare College, Delivered at the "Completers' Social," by R Sobukwe, October 21, 1949', in Robert Mangaliso Sobukwe, *Speeches of Robert Mangaliso Sobukwe, 1949–1959* (PAC, 2010). All other quotations from Sobukwe in this chapter are taken from this source.
3 *Citizen* Reporter, 'EFF remembers "revolutionary" PAC leader Robert Sobukwe', *The Citizen*, 28 February 2017. Available at citizen.co.za/news/south-

africa/1441939/eff-remembers-revolutionary-pac-leader-robert-sobukwe/, accessed on 30 July 2019.

Kwandiwe Kondlo

1   Hellicy Ngambi, 'RARE Leadership: An Alternative Leadership Approach for Africa', in Kwandiwe Kondlo (ed), *Perspectives on Thought Leadership for Africa's Renewal* (Africa Institute of South Africa, 2013), p 110.

2   A reference to WEB Du Bois' *The Souls of Black Folk* (1903).

3   Kwandiwe Kondlo, *In the Twilight of the Revolution: The Pan Africanist Congress of Azania in Exile, 1960–1990* (Basler Afrika Bibliographien, 2009), p 3.

4   Václav Havel, *Disturbing the Peace* (Vintage Books, 1991), p 9.

5   Cited in Paul Rabinow, 'Foucault's untimely struggle: Toward a form of spirituality', *Theory, Culture & Society*, vol 26, no 6 (November 2009), p 26.

6   Michel Foucault, *The Hermeneutics of the Subject: Lectures at the Collège de France, 1981–1982* (Picador, 2005).

7   Václav Havel, *Sunrise* magazine, April/May 1992, p 1.

8   Kondlo, *In the Twilight of the Revolution*, p 53.

9   Ibid.

10 'Gail Gerhart interviews Robert Mangaliso Sobukwe (1970)', *Psychology in Society*, no 50 (2016). Available at www.scielo.org.za/scielo.php?script=sci_arttext&pid=S1015-60462016000100004, accessed on 2 August 2019.

11 I interviewed the late Dr DD Mantshontsho when I was preparing for my PhD proposal and proceeded to interview other PAC founding members such as Elliot Mfaxa, Mfanasekhaya Gqobose and others during my tenure as a researcher with the Truth and Reconciliation Commission. But I tried as much as I could to cross-check some of the issues they raised against available archival sources. The passion and eloquence of Dr Mantshontsho was unforgettable.

12 Kondlo, *In the Twilight of the Revolution*, p 59.

13 Kwandiwe Kondlo, 'The Legacy and Relevance of Robert Mangaliso Sobukwe in the 21st Africa', Sixth Robert Sobukwe Memorial Lecture, University of Fort Hare, Alice, 17 March 2011.

14 'Pan Africanist Manifesto', in Robert Mangaliso Sobukwe, *Speeches of Robert Mangaliso Sobukwe, 1949–1959* (PAC, 2010), p 315.

15 'Gail Gerhart interviews Robert Mangaliso Sobukwe (1970)'.

16 Ibid.

17 Barry Streek, 'PAC Unbanned', Supplement, Cape Town, September 1990.

18 Ibid.

19 Ibid.

20 Ching Kwan Lee and Yelizavetta Kofman, 'The politics of precarity: Views beyond the United States', *Work and Occupations*, vol 39, no 4 (2012), pp 388–408.

21 Carl-Ulrik Schierup and Martin Bak Jørgensen, *Politics of Precarity: Migrant Conditions, Struggles and Experiences* (Brill, 2016).

22 'Gail Gerhart interviews Robert Mangaliso Sobukwe (1970)'.
23 Luther H Martin, Huck Gutman and Patrick H Hutton, *Technologies of the Self: A Seminar with Michel Foucault* (University of Massachusetts Press, 1988).
24 Benjamin Pogrund, *Robert Sobukwe: How Can Man Die Better*, third edition (Jonathan Ball Publishers, 2015).

Derek Hook

1   Derek Hook (ed), *Lie on Your Wounds: The Prison Correspondence of Robert Mangaliso Sobukwe* (Wits University Press, 2019).
2   Benjamin Pogrund, *Robert Sobukwe: How Can Man Die Better*, third edition (Jonathan Ball Publishers, 2015).
3   In isiXhosa, the phrase *'Ama-Afrika Poqo'* means 'The original owners of Africa'.
4   Nelson Mandela, *Long Walk to Freedom* (Macdonald Purnell, 1994), p 323.
5   This could also be expressed, in more idiomatic terms as: 'I'm reaching boiling point!', 'I am about to explode!'
6   'Gevreet' is crude slang for 'face'. In effect, 'afdrant gevreet' is something like 'downhill face' or 'sloping mug', but those phrases are without the insulting valence of the Afrikaans.
7   See Sobukwe's political speeches in TG Karis & GM Gerhart (eds), *From Protest to Challenge: A Documentary History of African Politics in South Africa, 1882–1990: Volume 3: Challenge and Violence, 1953–1964* (Jacana, 2013).
8   Cited in M Pheko, *The Land is Ours: The Political Legacy of Mangaliso Sobukwe* (Tokoloho, 1994), p 57.
9   Pogrund, *Robert Sobukwe*, p 204.
10 Tom Lodge, 'A liberal of a different colour', *Transformation*, 16 (1991), pp 76–88.
11 N Marquard, 'Robert Sobukwe: A personal note', *Reality*, vol 10, no 3 (1986), p 8.

Bobby Godsell

1   Later published as *The Eye of the Needle: Towards Participatory Democracy in South Africa* (Ravan Press, 1980).
2   Republic of South Africa, 'Report of the High Level Panel on the Assessment of Key Legislation and the Acceleration of Fundamental Change', November 2017. Available at www.parliament.gov.za/storage/app/media/Pages/2017/october/High_Level_Panel/HLP_Report/HLP_report.pdf, accessed on 1 July 2019.

Joel Mbhele

1   Michael Nowak and Luca Antonio Ricci (eds), *Post-Apartheid South Africa: The First Ten Years* (International Monetary Fund, 2005), p 1.
2   Moeletsi Mbeki, *Advocates for Change: How to Overcome Africa's Challenges* (Picador Africa, 2011).

3   Carolyn M Shields, Mark Edwards and Anish Sayani (eds), *Inspiring Practice: Spirituality & Educational Leadership* (ProActive, 2005).

4   Moeletsi Mbeki, *Architects of Poverty: Why African Capitalism Needs Changing* (Picador Africa, 2009).

5   Reuel J Khoza, *Attuned Leadership: African Humanism as Compass* (Penguin Random House, 2010).

6   Johann Broodryk, *Understanding South Africa: The Ubuntu Way of Living* (uBuntu School of Philosophy, 2002).

7   Mfuniselwa John Bhengu, *Ubuntu: The Essence of Democracy* (Rudolf Steiner Press, 1996).

8   Dirk Louw, 'Power sharing and the challenge of Ubuntu ethics', conference paper presented at the Forum for Religious Dialogue Symposium of the Research Institute for Theology and Religion, University of South Africa, Pretoria, 26–27 March 2009. Available at uir.unisa.ac.za/bitstream/handle/10500/4316/Louw.pdf?sequence=1, accessed on 1 July 2019.

9   Geoff Moore, 'Humanizing business: A modern virtue ethics approach', *Business Ethics Quarterly*, vol 15, no 2 (2005), pp 237–255.

10   'Address on Behalf of the Graduating Class at Fort Hare College Delivered at the "Completers' Social", by R Sobukwe, October 21, 1949', in Robert Mangaliso Sobukwe, *Speeches of Robert Mangaliso Sobukwe, 1949–1959* (PAC, 2010).

11   Proverbs 12:24.

12   Benjamin Pogrund, *Robert Sobukwe: How Can Man Die Better*, third edition (Jonathan Ball Publishers, 2015).

13   Ibid.

14   Ibid.

15   Viktor E Frankl, *Man's Search for Meaning* (Beacon Press, 1959), p 86.

Ishmael Mkhabela

1   Walter G Muelder, *Moral Law in Christian Social Ethics* (John Knox, 1966), p 119.

EF Daitz

1   Correspondence, Robert Sobukwe to Benjamin Pogrund, 3 January 1966, A2618. Ba4-1, Historical Papers Research Archive, University of the Witwatersrand, Johannesburg, South Africa (hereafter Robert Sobukwe Papers).

2   See the Robert Sobukwe Papers, 1954–2013, A2618.

3   Given the scope of this chapter, what follows is an impression of the letters that interested readers can pursue through the archive itself, which is digitised and available online at www.historicalpapers.wits.ac.za/index.php?inventory/U/collections&c=A2618/R/6325.

4   Correspondence, Robert Sobukwe to Benjamin Pogrund, 1 March 1967, A2618. Ba5-17, Robert Sobukwe Papers.

5   Correspondence, Benjamin Pogrund to Robert Sobukwe, 16 March 1967, A2618. Ba5-20, Robert Sobukwe Papers.
6   Correspondence, Veronica Sobukwe to Benjamin Pogrund, 1 February 1966, A2618. Ba4-6, Robert Sobukwe Papers.
7   Correspondence, Robert Sobukwe to Benjamin Pogrund, 30 March 1966, A2618. Ba4-21, Robert Sobukwe Papers.
8   Correspondence, Robert Sobukwe to Benjamin Pogrund, 5 October 1964, A2618. Ba2-38, Robert Sobukwe Papers.
9   Correspondence, Benjamin Pogrund to Robert Sobukwe, 12 October 1964, A2618. Ba2-52, Robert Sobukwe Papers.
10   Correspondence, Robert Sobukwe to Benjamin Pogrund, 1 June 1966, A2618. Ba4.34, Robert Sobukwe Papers.
11   Correspondence, Benjamin Pogrund to Sister-in-Charge, St Mary's Hostel, 20 July 1966, A2618. Ba4-47, Robert Sobukwe Papers.
12   Correspondence, Robert Sobukwe to Benjamin Pogrund, 21 July 1966, A2618. Ba4-52, Robert Sobukwe Papers. Author's emphasis.
13   Correspondence, Benjamin Pogrund to Robert Sobukwe, 28 July 1966, A2618. Ba4-55, Robert Sobukwe Papers.

Sources

Barnes, LL, TT Lewis, CT Begeny, L Yu, DA Bennett and RS Wilson. 'Perceived discrimination and cognition in older African Americans'. *Journal of the International Neuropsychological Society*, vol 18, no 5 (2012), pp 856–865.

Bhengu, Mfuniselwa John. *Ubuntu: The Essence of Democracy* (Rudolf Steiner Press, 1996).

Biko, Steve. *I Write What I Like* (Picador Africa, 2004).

Broodryk, Johann. *Understanding South Africa: The Ubuntu Way of Living* (uBuntu School of Philosophy, 2002).

Citizen Reporter. 'EFF remembers "revolutionary" PAC leader Robert Sobukwe'. *The Citizen*, 28 February 2017. Available at citizen.co.za/news/south-africa/1441939/eff-remembers-revolutionary-pac-leader-robert-sobukwe/. Accessed on 30 July 2019.

Cooper, Sean. 'Feel inferior to others? 8 signs of an inferiority complex', no date. Available at shynesssocialanxiety.com/inferioritycomplex/. Accessed on 20 June 2019.

Findling, JW and WF Young, Jr. 'Cushing's Syndrome'. *The Journal of Clinical Endocrinology & Metabolism*, vol 90, no 2 (February 2005), E2.

Foucault, Michel. *The Hermeneutics of the Subject: Lectures at the Collège de France, 1981–1982* (Picador, 2005).

Frankl, Viktor E. *Man's Search for Meaning* (Beacon Press, 1959).

'Gail Gerhart interviews Robert Mangaliso Sobukwe (1970)'. *Psychology in Society*, no 50 (2016). Available at www.scielo.org.za/scielo.php?script=sci_arttext&pid=S1015-60462016000100004. Accessed on 9 July 2019.

Gannon, Megan. 'Race is a social construct, scientists argue'. LiveScience, 5 February 2016. Available at www.scientificamerican.com/article/race-is-a-social-construct-scientists-argue/. Accessed on 20 June 2019.

Golby, AJ, JD Gabrieli, JY Chiao and JL Eberhardt. 'Differential responses in the fusiform region to same-race and other-race faces'. *Nature Neuroscience*, 4 (2001), pp 845–850.

Havel, Václav. *Disturbing the Peace* (Vintage Books, 1991).

Hook, Derek. 'A threatening personification of freedom or: Sobukwe and repression'. *Safundi*, vol 17, no 2 (2016), pp 189–212.

Hook, Derek (ed). *Lie on Your Wounds: The Prison Correspondence of Robert Mangaliso Sobukwe* (Wits University Press, 2019).

Karis, TG & GM Gerhart (eds). *From Protest to Challenge: A Documentary History of African Politics in South Africa, 1882–1990: Volume 3: Challenge and Violence, 1953–1964* (Jacana, 2013).

Khoza, Reuel J. *Attuned Leadership: African Humanism as Compass* (Penguin Random House, 2010).

Kondlo, Kwandiwe. *In the Twilight of the Revolution: The Pan Africanist Congress of Azania in Exile, 1960–1990* (Basler Afrika Bibliographien, 2009).

Kondlo, Kwandiwe. 'The Legacy and Relevance of Robert Mangaliso Sobukwe in the 21st Africa'. 6th Robert Sobukwe Memorial Lecture, University of Fort Hare, Alice, 17 March 2011.

Lee, Ching Kwan and Yelizavetta Kofman. 'The politics of precarity: Views beyond the United States'. *Work and Occupations*, vol 39, no 4 (2012), pp 388–408.

Lodge, Tom. 'A liberal of a different colour'. *Transformation*, 16 (1991), pp 76–88.

Louw, Dirk. 'Power sharing and the challenge of Ubuntu ethics'. Conference paper presented at the Forum for Religious Dialogue Symposium of the Research Institute for Theology and Religion, University of South Africa, Pretoria, 26–27 March 2009. Available at uir.unisa.ac.za/bitstream/handle/10500/4316/Louw.pdf?sequence=1. Accessed on 1 July 2019.

Major, B and JW Kunstman. 'Suspicion in interracial interactions: using measures of cardiovascular reactivity to index threat'. In DS Belle Derks and Naomi Ellemers (eds), *Neuroscience of Prejudice and Intergroup Relations*, pp 321–322 (Psychology Press, 2013).

Mandela, Nelson. *Long Walk to Freedom* (Macdonald Purnell, 1994).

Marquard, N. 'Robert Sobukwe: A personal note'. *Reality*, vol 10, no 3 (1986).

Mbeki, Moeletsi. *Architects of Poverty: Why African Capitalism Needs Changing* (Picador Africa, 2009).

Mbeki, Moeletsi. *Advocates for Change: How to Overcome Africa's Challenges* (Picador Africa, 2011).

McKown, Clark and Michael Strambler. 'Developmental antecedents and social and academic consequences of stereotype-consciousness in middle childhood'. *Child Development*, vol 80, no 6 (November/December 2009), pp 1643–1659.

Martin, Luther H, Huck Gutman and Patrick H Hutton. *Technologies of the Self: A Seminar with Michel Foucault* (University of Massachusetts Press, 1988).

Moore, Geoff. 'Humanizing business: A modern virtue ethics approach'. *Business Ethics Quarterly*, vol 15, no 2 (2005), pp 237–255.

Moseneke, Dikgang. 'Address by Wits Chancellor, during the naming of the Robert Sobukwe Building, University of the Witwatersrand, Johannesburg, 2017'. Available at www.polity.org.za/print-version/sa-justice-dikgang-moseneke-address-by-wits-chancellor-during-the-naming-of-the-robert-sobukwe-building-university-of-witswatersrand-johannesburg-17092017-2017-09-18. Accessed on 21 June 2019.

Muelder, Walter G. *Moral Law in Christian Social Ethics* (John Knox, 1966).

Ndaba, Baldwin, Therese Owen, Masego Panyane, Rabbie Serumula and Janet Smith (eds). *The Black Consciousness Reader* (Jacana, 2018).

Ngambi, Hellicy. 'RARE Leadership: An Alternative Leadership Approach for Africa'. In Kwandile Kondlo (ed), *Perspectives on Thought Leadership for Africa's Renewal* (Africa Institute of South Africa, 2013).

Nguyen-Robertson, CV. 'The neuroscience of racism: science and stories'. Inspiring Victoria, 6 October 2018. Available at inspiringvictoria.org.au/2018/10/06/ the-neuroscience-of-racism-science-and-stories/. Accessed on 20 June 2019.

Nowak, Michael Nowak and Luca Antonio Ricci. *Post-Apartheid South Africa: The First Ten Years* (International Monetary Fund, 2005).

Ossola, Alexandra. 'How discrimination changes your brain'. *VICE* Health, 21 March 2017. Available at tonic.vice.com/en_us/article/qkmna7/how-discrimination-changes-your-brain. Accessed on 20 June 2019.

Pascoe, EA and LS Richman. 'Perceived discrimination and health: A meta-analytic review'. *Psychological Bulletin*, vol 135, no 4 (2009), pp 531–554.

Pheko, M. *The Land is Ours: The Political Legacy of Mangaliso Sobukwe* (Tokoloho, 1994).

Pogrund, Benjamin. *Robert Sobukwe: How Can Man Die Better*, third edition (Jonathan Ball Publishers, 2015).

Rabinow, Paul. 'Foucault's untimely struggle: Toward a form of spirituality'. *Theory, Culture & Society*, vol 26, no 6 (November 2009), pp 25–44.

Ramoupi, Neo Lekgotla laga. 'Sobukwe was no apartheid sellout, as Mapaila claims'. *Mail & Guardian*, 20 February 2019. Available at mg.co.za/article/2019-02-20-sobukwe-was-no-apartheid-sellout-as-mapaila-claims. Accessed on 30 July 2019.

Republic of South Africa, The Constitution of the Republic of South Africa, Act 108 of 1996.

Republic of South Africa. The Constitution of the Republic of South Africa, 1996. Preamble. Available at www.justice.gov.za/legislation/constitution/SAConstitution-web-eng.pdf. Accessed on 20 June 2019.

Republic of South Africa. 'Report of the High Level Panel on the Assessment of Key Legislation and the Acceleration of Fundamental Change', November 2017. Available at www.parliament.gov.za/storage/app/media/Pages/2017/october/ High_Level_Panel/HLP_Report/HLP_report.pdf. Accessed on 1 July 2019.

Robert Sobukwe Papers, 1954–2013, A2618. Historical Papers Research Archive, University of the Witwatersrand, Johannesburg, South Africa. Available at www.historicalpapers.wits.ac.za/index.php?inventory/U/collections&c=A2618/ R/6325. Accessed on 3 July 2019.

Schierup, Carl-Ulrik and Martin Bak Jørgensen. *Politics of Precarity: Migrant Conditions, Struggles and Experiences* (Brill, 2016).

Sheng, F and S Han. 'Manipulations of cognitive strategies and intergroup relationships reduce the racial bias in empathic neural responses'. *NeuroImage*, vol 61, no 4 (2012), pp 786–797.

Shields, Carolyn M, Mark Edwards and Anish Sayani (eds). *Inspiring Practice: Spirituality & Educational Leadership* (ProActive, 2005).

Snail, Mgwebi. 'The Black Consciousness Movement in South Africa: A Product of the Entire Black World'. *Historia Actual Online*, no 15 (winter 2008), pp 51–68. Available at citeseerx.ist.psu.edu/viewdoc/download?doi=10.1.1.630.4779&rep=rep1&-type=pdf. Accessed on 20 June 2019.

Sobukwe, Robert Mangaliso. *Speeches of Robert Mangaliso Sobukwe, 1949–1959* (PAC, 2010).

Storey, Peter. *I Beg to Differ: Ministry Amid the Teargas* (Tafelberg, 2018).

Streek, Barry. 'PAC Unbanned'. Supplement, Cape Town, September 1990.

Thames, AD, CH Hinkin, DA Byrd, RM Bilder, KJ Duff, MR Mindt, A Arentoft and V Streiff. 'Effects of stereotype threat, perceived discrimination, and examiner race on neuropsychological performance: Simple as black and white?'. *Journal of the International Neuropsychological Society*, vol 19, no 5 (2013), pp 583–593.

Thames, April D. 'Toxic exposure: The impact of racial inequality on the brain'. Psychology Benefits Society, 2 September 2014. Available at psychologybenefits.org/2014/09/02/toxic-exposure-the-impact-of-racial-inequality-on-the-brain/. Accessed on 20 June 2019.

The World Bank. 'Overcoming Poverty and Inequality in South Africa: An Assessment of Drivers, Constraints and Opportunities', March 2018. Available at documents.worldbank.org/curated/en/530481521735906534/pdf/124521-REV-OUO-South-Africa-Poverty-and-Inequality-Assessment-Report-2018-FINAL-WEB.pdf. Accessed on 30 July 2019.

Turner, Rick. *The Eye of the Needle: Towards Participatory Democracy in South Africa* (Ravan Press, 1980).

Index

A

'abo-topi-royal' 75
accountability 65–69
Advocates for Change 181–182
Africa
    culture of 106–107, 146–147
    Human Development Index 225–227
    leadership in 182
    narrative of 121–123
    service to 29–31
    trade in 98
    United States of Africa 4, 96–98,
      110–112
    values of 146–147
'Africa for Africans' 4, 14, 31, 136, 217
African, definition of 30–31, 133, 235
'African Claims' document 166, 173
African Continental Free Trade Area 98
African Growth and Opportunity Act
  (Agoa) 199
African humanism 184
Africanist, The 81, 130–131
African National Congress (ANC)
    banning of 6
    Black Consciousness Movement and
      31–32
    civility 60–62, 69
    Defiance Campaign of 1952 3, 92–93
    Freedom Charter 19, 31, 33, 91,
      93–94, 159, 173, 192–193
    funeral of Veronica Sobukwe 16
    land restitution 35, 92, 94, 195, 202
    leadership of 61–63, 94
    PAC and 3, 5, 19–20, 31–32, 85–88,
      91–93, 126, 129–131, 159, 217
    Programme of Action of 1949 3, 92,
      129, 165, 173, 217
    race and racism 3, 33–34, 192
    support for 13, 87–89
    Umkhonto we Sizwe 13
    Youth League of 2–3, 58, 61–62, 65,
      92, 165–166, 224

African nationalism 2–5, 10, 14, 32, 34,
  91, 191–192
African Renaissance 32, 90, 97, 126
African Union (AU) 98, 224–225
Afrikaans language 153–156
Afrikaners 75, 106, 114, 168, 193
agency 169, 171
Agoa *see* African Growth and
  Opportunity Act
agricultural sector 175–176, 192, 195–201
Agri Gauteng 195–197
amnesty 67–68
ANC *see* African National Congress
anger 47–48, 114
Anglican Church 2, 27, 88
anti-Enlightenment 82
anti-whiteism 4, 86, 168–169, 210,
  218–219
apartheid
    born-free generation 249
    economic development and 75
    equality under 113
    Graaff-Reinet 155–157
    international resistance against 1, 205,
      210, 236
    legacy of 181–182
    legitimacy of 152
    Methodist Church 83, 108
    psychological effects of 48
    resistance against 1–5, 23, 60, 75–76,
      205–213
Apla *see* Azanian People's Liberation Army
Architects of Poverty 182
armed struggle 19, 76, 87, 168
assertiveness 100–101
AU *see* African Union
audio recordings of Robert Sobukwe
  11–12, 85, 127
Azanian People's Liberation Army (Apla)
  13, 19–20, 21, 88
Azanian People's Organisation (Azapo)
  218

B
banks 198–199
Bantustan system 23, 87
Barkly, Henry 149
Barnard, Chris 11
BCM *see* Black Consciousness Movement
beauty 47
Bhengu, Mfuniselwa John 184
Biko, Steve
    Africanist social democracy 35
    Black Consciousness Movement 32, 87, 166–167
    civility 56–57
    death of 167, 170, 205
    employment and 177–180
    just societies 167–170
    land restitution 174–176
    leadership of 205, 206
    race relations 171–172
    shared prosperity 173–174
    youth of 166–167
Bill of Rights 36, 173, 174–175
Black Consciousness Movement (BCM)
    ANC and 31–33, 38, 193, 217
    culture and 105–107
    land restitution 193
    PAC and 23, 31–33, 37–38, 87
    race relations 103–104, 169, 171–172, 192–193, 207–208
    Saso and 166–167
    Sobukwe and 11, 25
    theology and 220
'Black Consciousness Movement in South Africa, The' (essay) 32–33
Black Consciousness Reader 15
Black First Land First (BLF) 65
Black People's Convention 218
BLF *see* Black First Land First
Blyden, Edward 184
Bokwe, Rev John Knox 39
Bonhoeffer, Dietrich 28
born-free generation 248
Boshoff, Judge 170
Britain 75, 158–159
Broodryk, Johann 184–185
Bureau of African Nationalism 131

Buthelezi, Mangosuthu 23, 32, 223
C
Cape Town anti-pass campaign of 1960 5–6, 77
capitalism 177–178, 194
CAR *see* Central African Republic
cattle 79–80, 193
censorship of prison correspondence 231–233
Central African Republic (CAR) 226
Césaire, Aimé 184
Chad 226
Chigumadzi, Panashe 15
children *see* youth
churches 115, 219
Churchill, Winston 88
civility
    accountability and 65–69
    EFF and 63–65
    impact of 68–69
    radical politics and 56–69
    Zuma and 61–62
civil wars in Africa 97, 99
'Cloud in Trousers, A' (poem) 137
Codesa negotiations 21, 88, 93
collective imagination 43–55
colonialism 43, 74–75, 140, 174
communalism 31
communism 3, 31, 92, 169, 210, 218–219
Communist Party *see* South African Communist Party
commute from and to Robben Island 245–246
confrontation 216
Congress Alliance 3, 93, 192, 215
Congress of Democrats 91
Congress of South African Trade Unions (Cosatu) 61–62
Constitution of the Republic of South Africa 22, 33, 35–36, 117, 123, 173–174, 195, 198–200, 202
consumerism 123, 194
Contact 91
correspondence between Nell Marquard and Sobukwe
    African culture 146–147

childhood of Sobukwe 144, 148,
152–158
formality of 147–148
friendship 144–148
humour 144, 150–151, 154
languages 153–157
liberalism 158–160
pain 161–164
political views 148–152, 153, 158–160
correspondence between Benjamin
Pogrund and Sobukwe
background to 228–229
censorship of 231–233
domestic issues 233–235
friendship 230–235
political views 229–230, 231–233
register of 231–235
corruption 62, 69, 89, 93, 99, 140–141,
182, 187
cortisol levels 50–51, 53–54
Cosatu *see* Congress of South African
Trade Unions
crime 89
critical reflection 136–137
Cry, the Beloved Country 237
culture, African 106–107, 146–147

D
DA *see* Democratic Alliance
Daitz, EF, chapter by 228–235
decolonisation 74–75, 127
Defiance Campaign of 1952 3, 92–93
De Lille, Patricia 126
democracy 119–120, 167–169
Democratic Alliance (DA) 60, 64
Democratic Republic of Congo 97, 226
dependency 207–208
deportation 104–105
deprivation theory 188–189
differences 112
digital revolution 178–180, 199
dignity 183, 185, 223
diligence 186–187
discipline 57–58
discrimination 50–55
Dlamini-Zuma, Nkosazana, chapter by
17, 223–227

Duncan, Patrick 136
Dyani, Malcom 126

E
Ebrahim, Gora 126
Economic Community of West African
States (Ecowas) 98
economic development 34–35, 41–42,
75, 95, 98–99, 118–119, 123, 177–180,
225–227
Economic Freedom Fighters (EFF) 36,
58, 62–65, 93–95
Ecowas *see* Economic Community of
West African States
education 29–31, 44–45, 54, 80–82, 83,
111, 120–121, 211
EFF *see* Economic Freedom Fighters
elections 21–22, 41, 129
emigration *see* migration
empathy 52–53
employment 177–180
see also unemployment
English language 75, 155
equality of all people 100–101, 104–105,
107, 113–116
see also inequality
Equatorial Guinea 226
ethics 219–222
Ethiopia 97, 226
ethnicity 111–112, 219
evictions 108–109
expropriation of land without
compensation *see* land expropriation
without compensation
extravagance 58, 79–80, 211
'Eye of the Needle, The' (essay) 167–168,
173

F
Facebook 16, 239–240
factions 208
faith 8–9, 29, 107–108, 134, 219–222
Fanon, Frantz 56, 206
farming *see* agricultural sector
fascism 59, 65, 69, 103, 107, 114
fear 52, 212–213, 253
#FeesMustFall protests 67–68, 127

fight-or-flight response 52–54
flag of South Africa 20, 22
food on Robben Island, rumours about 11
food production 175–176, 195, 200–201
forced removals 109
Fort Hare *see* University College of Fort Hare; University of Fort Hare
Foucault, Michel 128, 137
fourth industrial revolution *see* digital revolution
Frankl, Viktor 189
freedom 42–55
Freedom Charter 19, 31, 33, 91, 93–94, 159, 173, 192–193
Frost, Robert 148
frugality 79–80
fund manager capitalism 177–178

G
Gaddafi, Muammar 225
Galeshewe location *see* Kimberley
Gandhi, Mahatma 215
gardening 145
GDP growth 225–227
General Law Amendment Act, Sobukwe Clause 7, 18, 118, 166, 224, 228–229
Gen-Xers 40–41
Gerhart, Gail, interview with Robert Sobukwe 79, 80–81, 130–131, 133, 136
glass in prison food, rumours about 11
global financial crisis of 2008/2009 179, 226
God as white and male 45–46
Godsell, Bobby, chapter by 165–180
golden generation 71–72, 75
Gordhan, Pravin 62, 64
government failure 14, 62, 110, 135–136, 182
Gqubule, Duma, chapter by 70–83
Gqubule, Rev Dr Simon 72–78, 80
Gqubule-Mbeki, Thandeka, chapter by 70–83
Graaff-Reinet 2, 10, 20, 72, 74, 148, 152–158
grants 180
Groote Schuur Hospital 11

gross domestic product (GDP) growth 225–227
Gukurahundi genocide 112
Gupta family 63

H
Habib, Adam, chapter by 56–69
Haq, Mahbub ul 225
hard work 186–187
hatred 114
Havel, Václav 128
HDI *see* Human Development Index
Healdtown school 8, 70–74, 78–81, 83
healing 48, 54–55, 201–202
health and racism 49–55
Heart and Stroke Foundation 53
Hermeneutics of the Subject, The 128
hero-worshipping 134
High Level Report of 2017 175, 176, 196
history, importance of 77–78
'homelands' *see* Bantustan system
Honest to God 28
Hook, Derek
   chapter by 143–164
   on EFF 58
   Lie on Your Wounds 15, 235
How Can Man Die Better 129, 144, 182, 229, 238–242, 250–251
Human Development Index (HDI) 225–226
'human race' 3, 44, 82, 192
Human Rights Day 2
Human Sciences Research Council 168
humility 26, 100–101
humour 144, 150–151, 154

I
'I am an African' speech 32, 90, 126
I Beg to Differ 7–9
identity politics 62, 81–82
ideology 229–230
IFP *see* Inkatha Freedom Party
imagination 43–55
IMF *see* International Monetary Fund
immigration *see* migration
imperialism 26, 43, 92, 140
independence 141, 208–209

Indian congresses 169
Indian Kenyans 158–159
'indigenous Africans' 34, 36
inequality 41–42, 62, 66–67, 74–75, 224, 226
    see also equality of all people
inferiority complex 42–55, 100–101
Inkatha Freedom Party (IFP) 23, 32
Inspiring Practice 182
Institute for Justice and Reconciliation 224
integrity 141–142, 182–190, 211
intellectuals 80–82
International Day for the Elimination of Racial Discrimination 2
International Monetary Fund (IMF) 225–226
investment 68, 199
isiXhosa language 28, 153, 156–157, 162, 163
    see also Xhosa people
J
jobs see employment
Johnson, Lyndon 177
journalists 63–64
just societies 167–170
K
Ka Plaatjie, Thami 126
Kenya 158–159
Kgosana, Philip 6
Khoisan 26, 157–158
Khoza, Reuel 184
Khwezi 61
Kimberley 10–11, 18, 84–85, 166
King, Martin Luther, Jr 215
Kofman, Yelizavetta 135
Kondlo, Kwandiwe, chapter by 124–138
L
land expropriation without compensation 35–36, 94–95, 192, 195–196, 198–199, 202
land restitution 22, 35–37, 84, 90–95, 108–110, 174–176, 193–203, 224
languages 153–157
Laurence, Patrick 29
leadership

oppression and 204–205
political leaders of today 89, 125, 135–136, 141–142, 182, 211
Sobukwe's leadership style 25–29, 37, 57, 74, 76–83, 86, 100–101, 119, 124–127, 135–138, 205–216
spirituality and 128–129, 219–222
Leballo, Potlako 12–13, 81, 91, 150
Lee, Ching Kwan 135
Leisegang, Alexandra, chapter by 56–69
Leon, Tony 60
letters see correspondence
Letters and Papers from Prison 28
Lewis, Anthony 135
liberalism 158–160, 168, 218–219, 229–230
Libya 225
Lie on Your Wounds 15, 235
'Lie on your wound(s)' (isiXhosa words of condolence) 163
Life Esidimeni patients 121
life insurance 177–178
literature 143–145
Long Walk to Freedom 152
'lost generation' 40–41
Louw, Dirk 184
M
Madzunya, Josias 132
magnanimity 241–242
magnetic resonance imaging (MRI) scans 52
Malema, Julius 58, 62, 64, 93–94
Mandela, Nelson
    armed struggle 76
    on bitterness 122
    civility 60
    EFF and 93–94
    Healdtown school 72–73
    leadership of 205
    on RDP of the soul 201
    release of 237
    on Robben Island 26, 87
    Sobukwe and 13–14, 152
    US support for 236
Mangani, N Chabani 15
Mantshontsho, DD 131

Marievale 108
market capitalisation 178
Marquard, Leo 162
Marquard, Nell *see* correspondence
  between Nell Marquard and Sobukwe
Masekela, Hugh 120, 196
Masters, The 161
Mayakovsky, Vladimir 137
Mbeki, Govan 72–73
Mbeki, Moeletsi 181–182
Mbeki, Thabo 32, 37, 38, 60–62, 90, 94,
  97, 126
Mbhele, Joel, chapter by 181–190
Mda, AP 79, 133
'Mending Wall' (poem) 148
mental clarity 79
mental health 38, 50–53
Methodist Church 8, 27–28, 73–75, 83,
  107–108, 155–157, 219
Mfaxa, Elliot 132–133
migration 89, 97, 99, 104–105, 110–111,
  158–159
minorities 3, 31, 34
missionary churches 219
Mkhabela, Ishmael, chapter by 204–222
Mlambo, Johnson 17
mob justice 65–66
Mohale, Bonang, chapter by 117–123
Moiloanyane, Modise 16
Mokitimi, Rev Seth 8, 76
Moloto, Narius 13
Molteno, John 72
Moore, Geoff 184–185
Moral Law in Christian Social Ethics
  220–221
moral standards 128–129, 219–222
Moseneke, Dikgang 57
Motlanthe, Kgalema 175, 196
Motlhabi, Mokgethi 220
Mqhayi, SEK 73
Mthombothi, Barney, chapter by 84–99
Muelder, Walter G 220–221
Mugabe, Robert 93
multiracialism 3, 192, 210–211
N
national anthem 22

National Development Plan (NDP) 120,
  173, 176, 192–193, 195
National Foundations Dialogue Initiative
  (NFDI) 20–21
National Party 85, 129
National Student Financial Aid Scheme
  (NSFAS) 120
National Treasury 62
National Union of South African
  Students (Nusas) 166
Natives Land Act of 1913 75, 92, 174
Native Trust and Land Act of 1936 174
nativism 74
NDP *see* National Development Plan
Ndungane, Njongo 26–27
necklacing 41
négritude 184
Nelson Mandela Bay 64
neoliberal economic policies 179–180
neuroscience 46, 50–55
New York Times, The 135
NFDI *see* National Foundations Dialogue
  Initiative
Ngambi, Hellicy 125
Ngendane, Selby 131
Niger 226
Nigeria 97, 140–141
Nkadimeng, Julia 101
Nongqawuse cattle-killing episode 79–80
non-racialism 33–34, 211, 217, 222
NSFAS *see* National Student Financial Aid
  Scheme
Nusas *see* National Union of South
  African Students
Nyerere, Mwalimu Julius 31
Nzimande, Anele, chapter by 139–142
O
OAU *see* Organization of African Unity
Obioma, Chigozie 140–141
Okri, Ben 135
O'Neill, Tip 98
Operation Fiela 105
Organization of African Unity (OAU)
  98, 224–225
Orwell, George 122
othering 43, 52

P

PAC *see* Pan Africanist Congress of Azania
Padmore, George 92
pain 46–49, 52, 142, 161–164
  see also trauma
Palmerston, Lord 97–98
pan-Africanism
  ANC and 3, 90, 126
  history of 3–6, 207–208, 215
  race relations 169, 171–172
  Sobukwe on 3–4, 29–35, 38,
    90–92, 96–98, 110–113, 124–125,
    224–226
Pan Africanist Congress of Azania (PAC)
  ANC and 3, 5, 19–20, 31–32, 85–88,
    91–93, 126, 129–131, 159, 217
  Apla 13, 19–20, 21, 88
  banning of 6, 19
  Black Consciousness Movement and
    23, 31–33, 37–38, 87
  Cape Town anti-pass campaign of
    1960 5–6, 77
  Codesa negotiations 21, 88
  elections 13, 21, 24
  founding of 3–4, 18–19, 32, 131–132,
    166, 215
  funeral of Robert Sobukwe 22–23
  funeral of Veronica Sobukwe 20–24
  land restitution 35–36, 91–93
  leadership of 5–6, 12–13, 19–20, 37,
    86, 116, 131–132
  liberalism and 159–160
  manifesto of 1959 32–34, 133
  Poqo 12–13, 17, 86, 150
  race relations 34–35, 133, 136,
    168–169
  Sharpeville massacre 1–2, 4–5, 13, 19,
    76–77, 86, 102–104, 166, 205–206,
    215, 250
  symbols of state 21–22
Parker, Aida 134–135
pass laws 1–2, 4–6, 18, 77, 101–102, 166
Paton, Alan 160, 237
pension funds 177–178, 179
Pilgrimage of Hope to Robben Island
  26–27

Pitts, Rev Stanley 81
Pityana, N Barney, chapter by 18–39
'Plea for Africa, A' 39
poetry 28, 137, 148
Pogrund, Benjamin
  on 'Africa for Africans' slogan 136
  on Black Consciousness 87
  chapter by 1–17
  How Can Man Die Better 129, 144,
    182, 229, 238–242, 250–251
  on legacy of Sobukwe 57
  on liberalism 160
  on Poqo 150
  on speech at Fort Hare 188
  see also correspondence between
    Benjamin Pogrund and Sobukwe
Pogrund, Jennie 239–240
poisoning, rumours of 11
Pokela, Nyathi John 132
police
  of apartheid era 4–6, 162–163, 224,
    232
  of today 105, 110
'political spirituality' 124–138
'politics of precarity' 124, 135–136
population growth 200
populism 58, 81
Poqo 12–13, 17, 86, 150
Port Elizabeth railway station 72
positive consciousness 171
poverty 14, 42, 62, 139–142, 178, 182
prayer 134
prejudice 43–44
Pretoria Prison 13
Pretorius, Willem, chapter by 191–203
productivity 194, 199
Programme of Action of 1949 3, 92, 129,
  166, 173, 217
property rights 93, 94, 199
protests 41, 67–68, 110, 127, 236
  see also Cape Town anti-pass campaign
    of 1960; Sharpeville massacre
proto-fascism 65, 69
public holidays 88

Q

Qunta, Christine 209

R

race relations
  Black Consciousness Movement and
    103–104, 171–172
  in churches 219
  EFF and 64
  equality and 100–101, 104–105, 107,
    113–116
  health and 49–55
  identity politics and 82
  multiracialism 3, 192, 210–211
  non-racialism 33–34, 211, 217, 222
  prejudice and 43
  racism 30–31, 33–34, 43–44, 49–55,
    74, 103, 219, 252–253
  radical politics and 56–58
radical politics
  accountability and 65–69
  civility and 56–69
  EFF and 63–65
  impact of 68–69
  Zuma and 61–62
Ramaphosa, Cyril 14, 16, 20, 67–68, 94,
  119–120, 196, 201
rape trial of Jacob Zuma 61
'RDP of the soul' 201–202
Reagan, Ronald 177
reconciliation 114, 201–202
Rhodes University 4
right-wing politics 59
Rivonia trial 73
Robben Island 7–11, 26–27, 77–78, 166,
  237–240, 244–248
Robert Mangaliso Sobukwe Trust 21,
  240
Robert Sobukwe Papers 14, 229, 235
Robinson, Bishop JAT 28
Roosevelt, Franklin 177
Royal Reader 75
rumours about Robert Sobukwe 11–12
Russell, Bertrand 28
S
SACP *see* South African Communist
  Party
SADC *see* Southern African Development
  Community

Saftu *see* South African Federation of
  Trade Unions
SANDF *see* South African National
  Defence Force
Saso *see* South African Students'
  Organisation
schools *see* education
Second World War 74, 103
'see – judge – act' model 220
'self-fashioning' 137
selflessness 141–142, 183
Sen, Amartya 122
'Send Me (*Thuma Mina*)' (song) 120, 196
servanthood 107, 183
shared prosperity 173–174
Sharpeville massacre 1–2, 4–5, 13, 19,
  76–77, 86, 102–104, 166, 205–206, 215,
  250
Shivambu, Floyd 62, 64
slogans 13, 16, 91, 136
Snail, Mgwebi 32–33
Sobukwe, Angelina (mother) 2
Sobukwe, Dini (son) 134, 240, 242, 244
Sobukwe, Ernest (brother) 2
Sobukwe, Hubert (father) 2
Sobukwe, Miliswa (daughter) 234,
  243–244, 246–250
Sobukwe, Otua (granddaughter)
  Andrew Walker and 240–241
  chapter by 243–253
Sobukwe, Robert Mangaliso
  apartheid government's fear of 2, 9,
    10
  career of 4, 10, 14, 26, 28–29, 81,
    143–144, 211, 229
  childhood of 2, 74, 144, 148, 152–158
  children of 28–29, 146, 231–235
  death of 10–11, 18, 166, 223–224, 229
  funeral of 22–23, 223, 242
  at Healdtown school 8, 70–74, 78–81,
    187–188
  health of 10–11, 27, 38
  imprisonment of 2, 6–11, 18, 26–27,
    38, 77–78, 84, 107–108, 118, 166,
    169–170, 188–190, 192, 228–229,
    238

interview with Gail Gerhart 79, 80–81, 130–131, 133, 136
in Kimberley 10–11, 18, 25–26, 84–85, 166, 229
leadership style of 25–29, 37, 57, 74, 76–83, 86, 100–101, 119, 124–127, 135–138, 205–216
on legitimacy of apartheid government 152
misconceptions about 210–211
nickname 'Prof' 2, 18, 29, 84
popularity of 24–33, 89–90, 126–127, 134, 204–205
recognition of 2, 13–17, 38–39, 57, 84–86, 125–127, 189–190, 207, 213–215, 239–242, 251–253
rumours about 11–12
speeches of 29, 33, 34, 90–91, 133, 185, 188, 224–225
at University College of Fort Hare 2, 28, 29, 149, 165, 185, 188, 211, 224
at Wits University 4, 14, 26, 81, 229
see also correspondence between Benjamin Pogrund and Sobukwe; correspondence between Nell Marquard and Sobukwe
Sobukwe, Veronica Zodwa Zondeni (wife) 7, 10, 15–16, 20–24, 27–28, 132, 189, 223, 232, 234–235
Sobukwe Clause 7, 18, 118, 166, 224, 228–229
social media 16, 64, 65, 239–240
SOEs see state-owned enterprises
Somalia 97, 112
South African Communist Party (SACP) 3, 13, 61–62
'South African exceptionalism' 90, 96, 97
South African Federation of Trade Unions (Saftu) 64
South African National Defence Force (SANDF) 20, 22
South African Reconciliation Barometer 224
South African Students' Organisation (Saso) 166–170, 218
Southern African Development

Community (SADC) 98
speeches 29, 32–34, 90–91, 126, 133, 185, 188, 224–225
Speeches of Robert Mangaliso Sobukwe, 1949–1959 24, 29
spirituality 8–9, 128, 193
see also 'political spirituality'
Stanford University 52
Star, The 15, 17
state capture 14, 63, 120
see also government failure
State of the Nation Address, February 2018 119–120, 196
state-owned enterprises (SOEs) 121
state symbols 21–22
stereotypes, racial 49–55
St James Anglican Church, attack on 88
stock market 178
Storey, Bishop Peter 7–9
storytelling 143–144
Streek, Barry 135
stress 50–51, 53–54
Study Project on Christianity in an Apartheid Society 168
suffering 161–164, 201–202, 216–217
suicides 109
Summer Meditations 128
Sunday Times 15
superiority complex 42–55
Swart, CR 151
symbols of state 21–22
T
Tambo, Oliver R 38, 73
Tanzania 97
teamwork 119–120
television footage of Robert Sobukwe 11–12, 127
test performances and racism 51
Thatcher, Margaret 177
theology 220–221
thrift 79–80
Tlhagale, Father Buti 212–213
tombstone of Sobukwe, words inscribed on 134, 137–138
trade in Africa 98
train journey to Healdtown school 70–72

trauma 47–48, 105
  see also pain
TRC see Truth and Reconciliation
  Commission
Treason Trial 93
tribalism 111–112, 219
Truth and Reconciliation Commission
  (TRC) 102, 114, 223
Tsedu, Mathatha 209
Turner, Rick
  death of 167
  employment and 177–180
  'Eye of the Needle, The' 167–168
  just societies 167–170
  land restitution 174–176
  race relations 171–172
  shared prosperity 173–174
  youth of 167
Tutu, Desmond 183, 185
Twitter 65
U
Ubuntu 183–186, 187
UDM see United Democratic Movement
Uitenhage 72, 74, 75
Umkhonto we Sizwe 13
UN see United Nations
unemployment 74, 89, 177–180
UNESCO see United Nations
  Educational, Scientific and Cultural
  Organization
Union of South Africa 92
United Democratic Front 75
United Democratic Movement (UDM)
  64
United Nations 76
United Nations Educational, Scientific
  and Cultural Organization (UNESCO)
  2
United Nations Human Development
  Index (HDI) 225–226
United States of Africa 4, 96–98,
  110–112
United States of America 177, 199, 236,
  241

University Christian Movement 218
University College of Fort Hare 2, 29,
  73, 149, 165, 185, 211, 224
University of Fort Hare 120
University of Natal 166, 167
University of the Witwatersrand (Wits
  University) 4, 14, 26, 57, 81, 229
US see United States of America
V
Vaal University of Technology 15
validation 48
Verryn, Paul, chapter by 100–116
Verwoerd, HF 6
vigilantes see mob justice
violence 56–58, 60, 66–68, 104
Von Eck, Claudelle, chapter by 40–55
Vorster, John 85, 91, 212–213
W
Walker, Alan 9
Walker, Andrew, chapter by 236–242
wealth, distaste for 58, 79–80
Wellesley College 241
whales 246
white supremacy 3, 72, 91–92, 129–130,
  191, 219, 222
Why I Am Not a Christian 28
'willing buyer, willing seller' principle 35,
  93, 174, 198
Wits University see University of the
  Witwatersrand
World Bank 41–42
World Economic Outlook 226
World War II 74, 103
X
xenophobia 97, 105, 110–111
Xhosa people 26, 79–80, 149, 157–158
  see also isiXhosa language
Y
youth 41, 49–54, 62–63, 65, 89–90
Z
Zimbabwe 93, 108, 112
Zuma, Jacob 14, 33, 60–62, 66, 69, 89, 94,
  126
Zwelithini, King Goodwill 94